Mirabile Dictu

STYLUS
Studies in Medieval Culture

Series Editors:
Eugene Vance, University of Washington, Principal Editor
R. Howard Bloch, Columbia University
Caroline Walker Bynum, Columbia University
Mary Carruthers, New York University
Herbert Kessler, The Johns Hopkins University
Seth Lerer, Stanford University
Gabrielle Spiegel, The Johns Hopkins University
Brian Stock, University of Toronto

Mirabile Dictu: Representations of the Marvelous in Medieval and
Renaissance Epic, *by Douglas Biow*

This interdisciplinary series is devoted to that millennium of Western culture extending from the fall of Rome to the rise of Humanism that we call the Middle Ages. The series promotes scholarship based on the study of primary sources and artifacts within their social and discursive contexts. With its emphasis on cultural studies, the series favors research that considers how the psychological, ideological, and spiritual dimensions of the medieval world converge in expressions of individual experience and in perceptions of material events.

Mirabile Dictu

Representations of the Marvelous in Medieval and Renaissance Epic

Douglas Biow

Ann Arbor

THE UNIVERSITY OF MICHIGAN PRESS

Copyright © by the University of Michigan 1996
All rights reserved
Published in the United States of America by
The University of Michigan Press
Manufactured in the United States of America
♾ Printed on acid-free paper

1999   1998   1997   1996   4   3   2   1

A CIP catalog record for this book is available from the British Library.

Library of Congress Cataloging-in-Publication Data

Biow, Douglas.
    Mirabile dictu : representations of the marvelous in medieval and
Renaissance epic / Douglas Biow.
        p.   cm. — (Stylus)
    Includes bibliographical references and index.
    ISBN 0-472-10691-0 (alk. paper)
    1. Marvelous, The, in literature. 2. Epic literature—History and
criticism. 3. Literature, Medieval—History and criticism.
4. European literature—Renaissance, 1450–1600—History and
criticism.   I. Title.   II. Series.
PN56.M3B56   1996
809.1'32091—dc20   96-3475
                                                                    CIP

To Maura

Preface

The richness of the marvelous as an object of poetic, epistemological, and cultural concern has generally been lost on literary theory in the latter half of this century, which puts greater emphasis on the fantastic and its importance in the literatures of the nineteenth and twentieth centuries. It was, however, arguably in the classical and early modern period (roughly from Homer to Vico, or from ancient Greece to the neoromantic period that marks the advent of interest in the sublime) when the marvelous found varied expression in truly complex discursive form, though it has never entirely disappeared from literature or critical inquiry. In focusing on the marvelous in epic, I therefore hope I have served not only classical, medieval, and Renaissance scholars but those who wish to explore how the marvelous in early modern literature is related to, and differs from, important issues in their own disciplines (e.g., the Romantic sublime, the fantastic, and magic realism), as well as issues in the works of the authors that they treat from later periods (the surrealists among others).

As befitting a comparative study that draws on different disciplines and scholars, this book, which has traveled with me from Baltimore to Florence to New York City to Syracuse to Austin, has benefited from the advice and help of many. In particular I would like to thank Eduardo Saccone and Diskin Clay, who guided me through the initial phases while I was at Johns Hopkins University, as well as Nancy Struever and Pier Massimo Forni for their additional insights. While in Florence, I benefited from conversations with John Kleiner and the various scholars attending and associated with the symposiums held at the Villa Spelman (John Pocock, Richard Goldthwaite, Jane Tylus, and Nancy Struever, among many). At Syracuse University I profited from the observations of Paul Archambault, Beverly Allen, and Dennis Romano, and at the University of Texas at Austin I have gained much from my colleagues in Italian—

Penny Marcus, Daniela Bini, and Guy Raffa—all of whom have been so supportive of my work and a pleasure to work with.

I would like to thank Albert Ascoli and the additional reviewer for the University of Michigan Press for their perceptive, helpful, and detailed readings, as well as Jeffrey Schnapp and Rachel Jacoff for their comments on an earlier version of chapter 2; some material was previously published in the article "From Ignorance to Knowledge," by Douglas Biow, in *The Poetry of Allusion: Virgil and Ovid in Dante's "Commedia,"* edited by Rachel Jacoff and Jeffrey T. Schnapp, and is used with the permission of the publishers, Stanford University Press, © 1991 by the Board of Trustees of the Leland Stanford Junior University. I am especially grateful to Eugene Vance for his early interest in this project and to Ellen Bauerle, the kindest editor I have ever had the privilege of working with, as well as a wonderfully witty and engaging correspondent. I also thank Christina Milton for seeing this book through the press and for a careful reading of the text. My greatest debt lies with my friend and colleague Wayne Rebhorn, who not only read through the manuscript once but reread parts of it twice and three times, in each instance offering invaluable comments; I am sure that this study would be a much poorer one without his fine editorial and scholarly suggestions.

For financial assistance I thank Ben Ware of Syracuse University for a summer research grant; the United States Department of Education for a Fulbright grant and a Javits Fellowship (the latter not directly awarded for but so much applied to this project that it here merits recognition and warm thanks); Elizabeth Cropper of Johns Hopkins University for a fellowship at the Charles S. Singleton Center for Italian Studies, Villa Spelman, Florence, Italy; and—last but not least—my parents. I thank the libraries in Florence and Siena (Biblioteca Nazionale, Biblioteca Riccardiana, Biblioteca Laurenziana, and Biblioteca Comunale di Siena) and the Villa I Tatti for their assistance and permission to consult their works, and I thank the Biblioteca Laurenziana for permission to cite from their manuscript collection.

I dedicate this study to my wife with gratitude and affection, and I add the following note to my three daughters, who may find themselves disappointed not to see their names here in print, and who may be equally disappointed to find that this book, with the term *marvelous* on the cover, does not contain fairy tales: Though this study is not dedicated to you, you may rest assured that the next one—God forbid I should have to write one for each!—will be.

Contents

Introduction

In this book, I examine the marvelous as an object of representation within epic and of larger cultural concern both before and during the European Renaissance, when the notion gradually developed into an aesthetic.[1] In the process, I also investigate the ways in which a given period's conception as to what constitutes history in turn underpins the representation of the marvelous. For history has everything to do with the making of epic since Homer's *Iliad* and Ennius's *Annales,* and the marvelous has much to do with exposing history as a distinct social practice concerned with writing and viewing the past. In working with these concerns, I do not seek to reconstruct an overarching historical vision of how the marvelous was transformed from the golden age of Augustan Rome to the Renaissance of Ferrarese Italy and Elizabethan England. I concentrate instead on the marvelous as one aspect of epic, traditionally the locus of what is left over and left out. To study the marvelous in epic, I shall claim, is to study that which epic would exclude but cannot somehow do without. At the same time, to study the marvelous itself is to study something so entrenched in humankind, as David Hume laments in his skeptical yet progressive vision of history, that it "can never be thoroughly extirpated from human nature."[2]

To clarify the nature of the marvelous in the six epics examined in this book, as well as the relationships among these epics, I follow in separate

---

1. On the marvelous in the Renaissance see Baxter Hathaway, *Marvels and Commonplaces: Renaissance Literary Theory* (New York: Random House, 1968); James V. Cunningham, *Woe and Wonder* (Denver: Denver University Press, 1951); and James Mirollo, "The Aesthetics of the Marvelous," in *The Age of the Marvelous,* ed. J. Kenseth (Chicago: University of Chicago Press, 1991).

2. David Hume, *An Inquiry concerning Human Understanding,* ed. Charles W. Hendel (Indianapolis: Bobbs-Merrill, 1955), 127.

chapters a single dramatic episode from Virgil to Spenser, the episode of the bleeding branch, which also supplies me with my title.[3] In doing so, my aim has been to provide a controlled yet flexible framework in which to develop readings that engage a multiplicity of theories and approaches, while remaining sensitive to issues of historical change and cultural specificity. At the same time, my treatment of the Virgilian topos is not uniform throughout. In some instances I provide an extended analysis (chaps. 1, 5, and 6); in others, I glance only fleetingly at the episode of the bleeding branch before turning to broader considerations of the marvelous in the work concerned (chaps. 2, 3, and 4). Moreover, my definition of epic ranges in this study to encompass poems written in the idiom of epic (*Orlando furioso, Commedia*), as well as works in prose (*Filocolo*). Finally, if I include a few pages on the *Decameron,* it is not to claim the text as an epic but to anticipate ways in which the marvelous will be handled in the realistic discourse of the novel, the form often conceived as the ironic bearer of the epic tradition in the modern world.

Mirabile dictu—these words are spoken by Aeneas as he describes the marvel of a man transformed into a bush on the shores of Thrace. Repeated throughout the *Aeneid,* Aeneas's phrase has the unmistakable quality of being Virgil's imitation of the Homeric oral formula "marvelous to behold" (*thauma idesthai*). But whereas Homer minimizes authorial presence by stressing the actual witnessing of marvels in the *Iliad* and the *Odyssey,* Virgil's written formula shifts the emphasis away from an objec-

---

3. I am indebted to the prior models of Thomas Greene, *Descent from Heaven: A Study in Epic Continuity* (New Haven: Yale University Press, 1963); A. Bartlett Giamatti, *The Earthly Paradise and the Renaissance Epic* (Princeton: Princeton University Press, 1966); and David Quint, *Origin and Originality in Renaissance Literature: Versions of the Source* (New Haven: Yale University Press, 1983). For other readings of this episode, see William Kennedy, "Modes of Allegory in Ariosto, Tasso, and Spenser" (Ph.D. diss., Yale University, 1969), portions of which have been separately published as "Irony, Allegoresis, and Allegory in Virgil, Ovid, and Dante," *Arcadia: Zeitschrift für vergleichnende Literaturwissenschaft* 7 (1972): 115–34; "Ariosto's Ironic Allegory," *Modern Language Notes* 88 (1973): 44–67; "The Problem of Allegory in Tasso's *Gerusalemme liberata,*" *Italian Quarterly* 15–16 (1972): 27–51; and "Rhetoric, Allegory, and Dramatic Modality in Spenser's Fradubio Episode," *English Literary Renaissance* 3 (1973): 351–68. The topos of the bleeding branch has been traced by Charles Speroni, "The Motif of the Bleeding and Speaking Trees of Dante's Suicides," *Italian Quarterly* 9 (1965): 44–55; it is studied as a problem of "heuristic" imitation by Shirley Clay Scott, "From Polydorus to Fradubio: The History of a *Topos,*" *Spenser Studies* 7 (1986): 27–57. For a recent psychoanalytic study, see Elizabeth J. Bellamy, "From Virgil to Tasso: The Epic Topos as an Uncanny Return," in *Desire in the Renaissance: Psychoanalysis and Literature,* ed. Valeria Finucci and Regina Schwartz (Princeton: Princeton University Press, 1994).

tive representation of the marvelous to the poet's subjective response to what is represented. From Homer to Virgil, then, we move from the oral poet's characteristic emphasis on the vision shown (*idesthai*) to the writerly poet's concern for the reflexive act of telling (*et dictu*).[4] Virgil's formula in this way raises a question, as challenging now as it was for Virgil when he articulated it in the Polydorus episode: what exactly does it mean to represent in epic, and hence in a culture's imaginative writing of its own history, something that is "wondrous to tell"?[5]

In responding to this question, Aristotle, generally considered the first literary theorist of the marvelous, stood squarely on the side of realism in his *Poetics*. Aristotle preferred the limited usage of marvels in epic, because, in the final analysis, they defied all probability. It was best to keep such "irrational" elements outside the main story, if indeed they must

---

4. In Virgil, the phrase occurs in *Aen.* 1.439 (Aeneas in cloud), 2.174 (Palladium in Achaean camp), 2.680 (portent of flame around Iulius's temples), 3.26 (the bleeding branch of Polydorus's tomb), 4.182 (description of Fama), 7.64 (bees gathered on laurel), and 8.252 (Cacus belching flames). The phrase almost always appears parenthetically at the end of the verse (1.439, 2.174, 4.182, 7.64, 8.252). In the *Georgics, mirabile dictu* appears at 2.30 (resprouting of olive root after trunk is cleft), 3.275 (horses spurred by Love), and 4.554 (the miracle of bugonia). In Homer, the formula appears in *Od.* 6.306, 8.366, 7.45, and 13.108; *Il.* 6.725, 10.439, 18.83, and 18.377. On Homer's objective mimetic style, the classic study is the first chapter of Erich Auerbach's *Mimesis: The Representation of Reality in Western Literature*, trans. Willard R. Trask (Princeton: Princeton University Press, 1968); on the differences between the mimetic practices of Homer and Virgil, see W. R. Johnson's *Darkness Visible: A Study of Vergil's "Aeneid"* (Berkeley: University of California Press, 1976); on Virgil's "subjective" style and authorial intrusions, see Brooks Otis, *Virgil: A Study in Civilized Poetry* (Oxford: Clarendon, 1964). For a reappraisal, see Gian Biagio Conte, *The Rhetoric of Imitation: Genre and Poetic Memory in Virgil and Other Latin Poets,* trans. C. Segal (Ithaca: Cornell University Press, 1986). For the marvelous in Homer, see Giuseppe Nenci, "A concezione del miracoloso nei poemi omerici," *Atto della Accademia delle Scienze di Torino* 92 (1957–58): 275–311, θαῦμα 286–88; and Raymond Adolph Prier, *Thauma Idesthai: The Phenomenology of Sight and Appearance in Archaic Greek* (Tallahassee: Florida State University Press, 1989).

5. Theorists and commentators, both before and during the revival of Aristotelian poetics in the Renaissance, followed Servius, Virgil's first commentator, in viewing the Polydorus episode as both exemplary and problematic in their discussions of the marvelous. See, for instance, Giovanni Pontano *Actius Dialogus,* in *Girolamo Fracastoro "Naugerius, sive de Poetica Dialogus,"* trans. Ruth Kelso, with an introduction by M. Bundy (Urbana: University of Illinois Press, 1924), 9:84; Francesco Robortello, *Francisci Robortelli Utinensis in librum Aristotelis De Arte Poetica Explicationes* (Florence: Laurentii Torrentini, 1548), 88; Iacopo Mazzoni, *Discorso di Giacopo Mazzoni in difesa della "Commedia" del divino poeta Dante,* ed. Mario Rossi, vols. 51–52 of *Collezione di opuscoli danteschi inediti o rari,* ed. G. L. Passerini (Città di Castello: Lapi, 1898), 34–35; and Francesco Patrizi da Cherso, *Della poetica,* ed. Danilo Aguzzi Barbagli (Florence: Istituto di Studi Rinascimentali, 1970), 3:356, 358.

remain in the poem at all (1460a).[6] Consequently, though the marvelous was pleasurable and could be handled better in epic poetry than in tragedy, the marvelous was still barely "tolerable" material that could be cut from the poem with no real structural loss to the whole (1460a). The marvelous, in being "irrational," could be both alluring and exciting for Aristotle. But it nevertheless remained—even in the *Odyssey,* where "Homer uses his other virtues to disguise the absurdity and to make it enjoyable" (1460a)—superfluous. Yet this very superfluousness represents the proper function of the marvelous. For *superfluous* here indicates not only what is extraneous or frivolous but also what transgresses—what "overflows" (*superfluit*)—the conventional boundaries of epic form and a culture's sense of itself as a systemic whole. This transgression is apparent when the marvelous is seen to foreground the uses and abuses of the poetic imagination, when it stimulates wonder about the causes of things, and when it calls attention to the transgression of boundaries defining a cultural system—three cases that should be understood as often overlapping rather than rigidly distinct.

First, as a problem of narrative self-reflexivity, the marvelous discloses the poet's awareness of his or her imagination as an act unto itself. Marvels, as Aristotle claimed, reveal how an author can tell a lie and get away with it in a manner that is pleasurable but superfluous to the tale and in no way apparently edifying.[7] Through the use of marvels, epic poets expose themselves to be masterful manipulators of signs that signify nothing referentially real yet deceptively enchant an audience. At the same time, as epic poets reveal themselves through their talk of marvels to be highly skilled makers entertaining a public with captivating lies, they also begin to resemble the confidence person who likewise makes a practice of telling mesmerizing, fabulous tales. The two roles, however, are fundamentally

---

6. I cite from Aristotle, *The "Poetics" of Aristotle: Translation and Commentary,* trans. Stephen Halliwell (Chapel Hill: University of North Carolina Press, 1987), from which I have benefited greatly, as I have from Halliwell, *Aristotle's "Poetics"* (Chapel Hill: University of North Carolina Press, 1986); and Aristotle, *Aristotle's "Poetics": The Argument,* ed. Gerald F. Else (Cambridge: Harvard University Press, 1957).

7. It is important to remember, in this context, Aristotle's resistance to allegory as a means for explaining the presence of marvels in texts, a tradition that was already well developed with respect to the Homeric epics and that survived through the centuries. See, for example, D. C. Allen, *Mysteriously Meant: The Rediscovery of Pagan Symbolism and Allegorical Interpretation in the Renaissance* (Baltimore: Johns Hopkins University Press, 1970). For a distinction between "allegoresis" and allegory in terms of contemporary and "ancient" theory and approaches, see Maureen Quilligan, *The Language of Allegory: Defining the Genre* (Ithaca: Cornell University Press, 1979).

distinct. The epic poet ideally sings of marvels before a presumed aristocratic audience to inspire them with a sense of awe for both the poet's art and their heroic past. The trickster characteristically speaks of marvels in the open market to cast a spell over his or her audience and rhetorically move them to act according to his or her own will. Nevertheless, out of this comparison, which is often blurred in narrators of realistic prose, a number of related questions arise. To begin with, for what or for whom are the marvels being exchanged, both inside the text and in the actual production of the text? Moreover, who "buys" these marvels, either in the sense of accepting them at face value as "true" or in the sense of choosing them for the pleasure they afford within an overall network of representational and social exchanges? What, in short, is the social and cultural value of the marvels produced in epic, both as objects of exchange and even, to be sure, as agents of exchange?[8] In studying what is "wondrous to tell," we are often then studying in epic the performative and social function of representing marvels themselves.

In addition to foregrounding the cultural uses and abuses of the poetic imagination, marvels function in epic to trigger speculative inquiry when one is invited to witness, and by extension contemplate, something "wondrous to behold." This conception of the marvelous, indebted to both Platonic philosophy and Aristotle's *Metaphysics* and encapsulated in the Homeric formula *thauma idesthai,* envisions the marvelous as contributing to a cognitive act that in turn consumes the inquirer as he or she quests after knowledge. Marvels in this respect do not become the site of a specific, hidden knowledge made accessible to the initiated few through allegory. They instead produce a desire for knowledge through the wonder they evoke. This desire for knowledge, which leads in metaphysical thought to a comprehensive vision of the universe, is problematic in epic, because in epic—traditionally the genre above all concerned with providing a complete view of the order of things—the totality desired may be understood as objective, knowable, and verifiable or as a reflection of the subject's desire for totality itself. On the one hand, the wonder evoked by the marvelous may lead one to conclude that there is an objective universal order, one that the mind can grasp in thought but cannot always ade-

---

8. For the notion of the marvelous as an "agent of exchange" I am indebted to Stephen Greenblatt's *Marvelous Possessions: The Wonder of the New World* (Chicago: University of Chicago Press, 1991). The relation of money to the marvelous in epic-romance is discussed by Eugene Vance in chapter 5 of *Mervelous Signals: Poetics and Sign Theory in the Middle Ages* (Lincoln: University of Nebraska Press, 1986).

quately represent in language. On the other hand, the wonder evoked by the marvelous may lead one to conclude that the subject's desire for a total vision alone structures, and therefore unreliably represents, the universe as a reassuring whole. Viewed as an issue of epistemological concern, then, the desire for the marvelous strives to embrace, often in the form of an impassioned quest in epic, a totality grounded either in the subject's desire for cognitive wholeness or in a universe taken to be objectively whole all along.

Finally, marvels are typically conceived by epic within the ethnographic context of the humanly strange and monstrous. They thus symbolically define the normative boundaries of a cultural system, either by being excluded from that very system or by existing on, or just within, its margins. This is certainly the case with monsters who are represented from time to time in histories, natural histories, encyclopedias, cosmographies, and travelogues from antiquity through the Renaissance.[9] Like the *mirabilia* depicted in the marginalia of gothic manuscripts, such marvels tend to be placed in lands just on or beyond the edge of the world. Nature, in other words, deviates from the norm where it is given freer reign beyond the dominant point of view and power structures of a given culture. At the same time, this freedom ensures the production of creatures whose bodies are marvelous and who reflect a seemingly anarchic breakdown of familiar categories in alien, though not necessarily hostile, body politics. A man with eight fingers and eight toes has, from a certain point of view, a superfluous number, three toes and three fingers too many. And he is "strange," etymologically speaking, because he is extraneous, a product of the superfluous, of what is left over and left out from a given cultural system. In this context, the marvelous is, to borrow and adapt from the work of the social anthropologist Mary Douglas, symbolically impure. It is a

---

9. See John Block Friedman, *The Monstrous Races in Medieval Art and Thought* (Cambridge: Harvard University Press, 1981); Jean Céard, *La nature et les prodiges: L'insolite au 16e siècle en France* (Geneva: Droz, 1971); Rudolf Wittkower, "Marvels of the East: A Study in the History of Monsters," *Journal of the Warburg and Courtauld Institutes* 5 (1942): 159–97; Jacques Le Goff, *L'imaginaire médiéval* (Paris: Gallimard, 1985); Paula Findlen, "Jokes of Nature and Jokes of Knowledge," *Renaissance Quarterly* 43 (1990): 292–331; and William B. Ashworth, Jr., "Remarkable Humans and Singular Beasts," in *The Age of the Marvelous,* ed. J. Kenseth (Chicago: University of Chicago Press, 1991). For the marvelous in medieval and Renaissance travelogues and histories, see Greenblatt, *Marvelous Possessions;* Mary B. Campbell, *The Witness and the Other World* (Ithaca: Cornell University Press, 1988); Leonardo Olschki, *Storia della letteratura delle scoperte geografiche* (Florence: Olschki, 1937); and Rosario Romero, *Le scoperte americane nella coscienza italiana del cinquecento* (Bari: Laterza, 1989).

sign of something out of place within a cultural system, "the by-product of a systematic ordering and classification of matter, in so far as ordering involves rejecting inappropriate elements."[10] Where there are marvels, there is, in short, system—a set of discernible normative cultural constraints.

Epic is a system, a representational system of extraordinary social power and scope. In its totalizing effort to offer a complete view of a culture and its past, epic has often stood out as seeking to contain within itself even that which it must ideologically suppress, so that it may present itself as the most inclusive of all genres and reconstitute itself, in the words of Lukács, as "a world rounded from within."[11] In the six epics treated in this study, each writer seeks in some way to systematize the superfluousness of the marvelous according to the readerly conventions and expectations encoded into his text. Yet something is also inevitably left out and left over for subsequent writers to consider in the context of their own quite different cultures. In this respect, the marvelous, in its nature and its function, heightens and challenges the totalizing drive behind epic as the comprehensive bearer of a culture's present and past. It does so in the six epics examined in this study, beginning with Virgil's *Aeneid*, where the marvels are few and far between, and ending with Spenser's *Faerie Queene*, where the marvelous has positively swallowed up the whole.

Focusing on the *Aeneid* in chapter 1, I examine how Virgil discloses through the marvelous his awareness of, yet inability to envisage a solution to, history's endless processes of mimetic violence. The chapter's initial and primary focus is the transformation of Polydorus into a bush, a *monstrum* indeed representative of the marvelous in its obvious transgression of the normal boundaries separating humans and nature. In coming into contact with the blood emerging from the broken branch, Aeneas has in truth come into contact with the cyclical violence of a heroic past that

---

10. Mary Douglas, *Purity and Danger: An Analysis of the Concepts of Pollution and Taboo* (New York: Praeger, 1966), 35. In this way the marvelous may operate, though not exclusively, within the context of the grotesque and a poetics of transgression, on which see Mikhail Bakhtin, *Rabelais and His World,* trans. Hélène Iswolsky (Cambridge: MIT Press, 1968); and, in particular, Peter Stallybrass and Alon White, *The Politics and Poetics of Transgression* (Ithaca: Cornell University Press, 1986).

11. Georg Lukács, *The Theory of the Novel,* trans. Anna Bostock (Cambridge: MIT Press, 1971), 60. On the totalizing force of epic, see David Quint, *Epic and Empire: Politics and Generic Form from Virgil to Milton* (Princeton: Princeton University Press, 1993), chap. 1; A. Bartlett Giamatti, "The Forms of Epic," in *Play of Double Senses: Spenser's "Faerie Queene"* (Englewood Cliffs: Prentice Hall, 1975); and Thomas Greene, *Descent from Heaven,* especially 10.

he cannot escape and that he now bears into the Roman world. Aeneas never realizes this, however. The marvel provokes wonder. But as Aeneas probes for hidden causes and repeatedly transgresses boundaries by staining his hands with impure blood, he is denied knowledge of both his and Rome's future conflicts. In much the same way, Virgil uses the marvelous throughout the *Aeneid* to reveal Aeneas's ignorance of the role he must play in a history that knows no end to violence.

Virgil's representation of the marvelous always exists in relation to, but never as, history. The poetic imagination, foregrounded through the marvelous as a "wonder to tell," may periodically represent realms or events with no claim to verisimilitude or historicity in the *Aeneid,* but it can never represent an end to the violence of history about which the epic poet sings. In contrast, Dante insists in the *Commedia* that he can represent as historically true everything revealed to him in his voyage, no matter how incredible the otherworld may appear. Moreover, the world Dante offers is meant as an alternative to human history; for the wayfarer, who has sinned, it is truly the only history that counts. I thus begin chapter 2 by arguing that Virgil's marvels, once appropriated by Dante, become historical yet signifying realities in a Christian poem. They are things and signs, both objects of wonder and signs of God's presence and power. And as the wayfarer comes upon these and other signifying marvels fulfilled in a Christian universe, he is gradually guided toward a vision of the deeper mysteries of the cosmos in a voyage often understood as the principal marvel of the poem. In the *Commedia,* the marvelous functions primarily at the service of a cognitive act, though the poet often obliquely reveals in his poem that marvels are not just things once witnessed but also representations self-consciously created by him alone. The poet has indeed invented these marvels for the wayfarer, who may stand in awe of the poet's own transgressive imagination.

By sometimes using the marvelous to call attention to superfluous elements in the poem, elements that are "irrational" in Aristotelian terms, Dante not only works with but simultaneously challenges the image he consciously creates of himself throughout the *Commedia* as the poet who has solved and experienced it all. The chapter on Dante thus finally reveals through the marvelous a self-conscious playfulness on the part of the poet with regard to his own desire for a total synthesizing view of the cosmos. Unlike Dante, however, Boccaccio, who is equally playful and inventive as a poet, does not aim to shape or understand the universe through his use of marvels. His distinctive aim is to investigate the social value of marvels in a world where processes of exchange (both linguistic and financial) are constantly taking place. This aim is particularly apparent in the *Decameron.* I argue in chapter 3 that it is also evidenced in Boccaccio's early epic romance, the *Filocolo.* In the *Filocolo,* Boccaccio experiments, for the first time, with the frame-setting of having a group of noblemen and noblewomen gather together to tell stories in a garden during the hottest hours of the day. There, in a novella later incorporated with substantial revisions into the *Decameron,* Boccaccio describes how a poor wizard receives from a knight both land and treasures in exchange for making a springtime garden flourish in the middle of winter. In this novella, marvels, as products of labor, have value, and their value lies not in themselves but in the object or objects for which they may be exchanged. Wealth permits a person to buy whatever he or she wants, and it is the great mechanism for social advancement and mobility in protocapitalist Italy. Through wealth a rich man actually brings the realm of imagination into sensuous existence, and a poor wizard rises up to become the social equal of a nobleman who possesses vast landed estates. Through wealth—in particular money, which is ironically viewed as a marvel itself in the *Decameron*—people acquire fabulous lands of wish fulfillment and make themselves over into images that they desire.

Like Boccaccio, Ariosto is concerned with the marvelous as an object and instrument of desire. In the *Furioso,* however, the desire for the marvelous is fundamentally an expression of a desire for an absolute, for a total vision of things. The hippogriff in particular exemplifies this desire insofar as it twice gives rise in the poem to the yearning to circumnavigate the globe. Through the voyaging of the hippogriff, the poet further draws a conceptual circle about the confines of the Ptolemaic map, which all along anachronistically defines the closed worldview of Ariosto's poem. Yet along with inspiring totalizing quests, marvels function in the *Furioso* as instruments of power. Like explosive Renaissance artillery, to which marvels are both implicitly and explicitly likened in the *Furioso,* they serve to protect and preserve boundaries, providing a precarious sense of order and security in a warring, fractured world. Marvels in the *Furioso* do not therefore lead, as they did in Dante's poem, to an objective eternal vision of all things. They lead instead to an awareness that totalities are temporal constructs of desire and that the only way to achieve a semblance of totality in this world, both now as in the past, is through the constant exercising of power.

Marvels in the *Furioso* permit Ariosto to reflect on the power and totalizing desires that make the world appear as a coherent, though still vulnerable, whole. For Tasso, marvels are also central to his poem and his conception of the world, but for different reasons and in different ways. Marvels are central because they stimulate wonder about the order of things, inform us of a community's beliefs, and help define a culture's relation to its history. But marvels are also central because they elicit the response of admiration—*meraviglia*—which for Tasso is the passion proper to epic. Admiration, Tasso believed, best moves men and women to action. Hence marvels, by evoking admiration, have a rhetorical function. They persuade. And in the *Liberata* they persuade in essentially one of two ways. Either they move men and women to work for the construction of a united Christian community in a colonizing crusade, or they stimulate individuals to seek out private domains far from the more pressing corporate demands of the community. Yet even when marvels induce individuals to wander in solitude, the private spaces they locate, and indeed long for, are envisioned as places of public performances subject to the communal gaze. In this way, Tasso discloses through his use of marvels in the *Liberata* an overriding concern with the blurring of the boundaries that constitute individuals and communities.

For Tasso, the individual is always an agent of the community; every private moment is somehow a public one. As a result, Tasso's treatment of the marvelous exposes a sense of the loss of privacy in the world, though that loss is always seen as a necessary part of the civilizing process if a unified community's goals are ever to be achieved. Spenser is likewise concerned with issues of loss in his treatment of the marvelous in *The Faerie Queene*. He is further concerned with loss as an essential element in the construction of communities, both religious and political. But Spenser's distinctive focus, as he goes about rhetorically fashioning for the Elizabethan community the perfect "gentleman or noble person," is on loss in the construction of individual identities. In chapter 6 I explore this specific type of loss by focusing primarily on the character of the Redcrosse Knight. The knight, as he confronts the Virgilian marvel of the bleeding branch, reveals a deep-rooted fear of losing his identity by blending into what is strange. The marvel pollutes, transgressing boundaries and indicating not just the possibility of loss but the inevitability of loss for the Redcrosse Knight, who has set out to prove himself in a largely impure, foreign world. In much the same way, marvels in *The Faerie Queene* blur the fundamental boundaries separating the inside from the outside, estranging men and women through processes of contamination. Yet in doing so, marvels make possible self-discovery, for the self is defined, and indeed continually redefined in Spenser's *Faerie Queene*, through the alienating precondition of loss.

Although all six writers treated in this study attend to the superfluousness of the marvelous, they do so in different ways. Virgil, Dante, and Ariosto use the marvelous to foreground the power of the poetic imagination, while Boccaccio, Tasso, and Spenser locate that power within a poetics that is primarily concerned with rhetoric and processes of worldly exchange. Dante and Ariosto characteristically view the marvelous as a vehicle to explore a culture's determined conceptions about where boundaries of knowledge lie, and may be represented, within the context of quests for an absolute. Virgil, Boccaccio, Tasso, and Spenser frequently indicate how the marvelous serves to transgress and define boundaries in the construction of both personal and communal identities. But all the writers examined in this study treat the marvelous as an indispensable element in epic, as one by one they return to the topos of the bleeding branch to investigate what it means to talk in their own time about something that is "wondrous to tell."

Chapter 1

Virgil's *Aeneid:* Marvels, Violence, and Narrative Self-Consciousness

felix qui potuit rerum cognoscere causas
atque metus omnis et inexorabile fatum
subiecit pedibus strepitumque Acherontis auari.
—Georgics 2.490–92

In the beginning of the third book of the *Aeneid,* Aeneas, seated in Dido's palace, recalls how he first traveled to the land of Thrace after the fall of Troy.[1] At the outset of his seven-year voyage through strange and unfamiliar realms, he approached a mound topped with cornel bushes, myrtles, and javelins. When he tore up some branches to cover the altars with boughs—a further mark of the hero's devotion to the gods—he witnessed an extraordinary sight "wondrous to tell" [*dictu . . . mirabile*] (3.26). From the roots of the uptorn branch oozed drops of blood. Filled with fear, Aeneas nevertheless gripped two more branches, but then a voice emerged from the bush. The voice belonged to Polydorus, Priam's youngest son, who then explained to Aeneas what happened to him after he had died:

nam Polydorus ego. hic confixum ferrea texit
telorum seges et iaculis increuit acutis.

(3.45–46)

[For I am Polydorus. Here an iron harvest of spears covered my pierced body, and grew up into sharp javelins.]

---

1. Selective commentaries referred to in my text are in Virgil, *Liber tertius,* ed. R. D. Williams (Oxford: Clarendon, 1962). Citations from the *Aeneid* and *Georgics* are from Virgil, *Opera,* ed. R. A. B. Mynors (Oxford: Clarendon, 1985); all translations are from Virgil, *Eclogues, Georgics, Aeneid,* ed. and trans. H. Rushton Fairclough, 2 vols. (Cambridge: Harvard University Press, 1986).

Servius, Virgil's first commentator, was troubled by the Polydorus episode. For the first time in his commentary he voices concern over the element of the marvelous in the *Aeneid* when he notes that "surely it is thought not verisimilar [*non verisimile*] that the boy was killed by hurled javelins crowding together, for it goes against what is said [in verse 55]: *Polydorum obtruncat.* For it is a marvel [*mirum*] that javelins put forth roots, except if it is monstrous [*monstruosum*]."[2] In an attempt to defend the scene, Servius then asserts that Virgil here "drew this from Roman history [*de historia Romana*]. For Romulus, on receiving an omen, threw a spear from the Aventine mountain onto the Palatine: which spear, fixed into the ground, grew leaves and became a tree."[3] Finally, Servius compares this scene with other episodes, no doubt both equally *mirum* and *monstruosum,* and concludes by registering the following complaint: "Indeed it is blameworthy [*vituperabile*] that a poet invents [*fingere*] something because he may depart too deeply from the truth [*veritate*]. Precisely this is charged against Virgil concerning the changing of the ships into nymphs, and insofar as he says that he descended to the infernal regions by means of a golden bough, and thirdly when Iris cuts the lock of Dido. But this last is excused by the example of Euripides, who says this about Alcestes when she undergoes the fate of her husband."[4]

2. Servius (46): "sane putatur non verisimile iaculis coniectis puerum occisum, nam repugnat cum illo <55> Polydorum obtruncat: nam et misisse radices iacula mirum est, nisi monstruosum sit." All citations of Servius are from Servius, *Commentarii in Vergilii Carmina,* ed. G. Thilo and H. Hagen, 2 vols. (Hildesheim: Georg Olms, 1961); all translations are mine.

3. Servius (46): "INCREVIT reviruit. traxit autem hoc de historia Romana. nam Romulus, captato augurio, hastam de Aventino monte in Palatinum iecit: quae fixa fronduit et arborem fecit." See Ovid *Met.* 15.560–64 and Plutarch *Rom.* 20.5.

4. Servius (46): "vituperabile enim est, poetam aliquid fingere, quod penitus a veritate discedat. denique obicitur Vergilio de mutatione navium in nymphas; et quod dicit per aureum ramum ad inferos esse descensum; tertium, cur Iris Didoni comam secuerit. sed hoc purgatur Euripidis exemplo, qui de Alcesti hoc dixit, cum subiret fatum mariti." The marvel of the golden bough has, of course, been the subject of extensive learned studies. From those consulted, I single out above all Robert Brooks, "*Discolor Aura:* Reflections of a Golden Bough," *American Journal of Philology* 74 (1953): 260–80; and C. P. Segal, "*Aeternum per saecula nomen:* The Golden Bough and the Tragedy of History," parts 1 and 2, *Arion* 4 (1965): 617–57; 5 (1966): 34–72. Both essays were of immense value to this study and remain excellent guides into the subject of the marvelous. I also single out Elaine Fantham, "*Nymphas . . . e Navibus Esse:* Decorum and Poetic Fiction in *Aeneid* 9.77–122 and 10.215–59," *Classical Philology* 85 (1990): 102–19. The two scholars who have most directly and extensively addressed the problem of the marvelous in the *Aeneid* are R. D. Williams, in two studies— *Virgil: Greece and Rome* (Oxford: Clarendon, 1967) and "The Purpose of the *Aeneid,*" *Antichthon* 1 (1967): 29–41—and, in disagreement with R. D. Williams's interpretation, Gordon Williams, in *Technique and Ideas in the "Aeneid"* (New Haven: Yale University Press,

Servius has set up two oppositions to validate inventions that would otherwise appear incredible by virtue of their radical departure from the truth, with *truth* here understood to mean literary convention or a probable, rather than transcendent, cause. Servius's two oppositions may briefly be defined as that between history and fantasy and that between literary precedent and literary invention. In the first case, a fantastic invention is permissible when underpinned by a presumed historical event (i.e., Romulus's sprouting spear). In the second case, a fantastic invention is permissible when traceable to a literary model (i.e., Euripides). Both these oppositions are familiar enough to readers of Servius, whose commentary begins by assuming that Virgil's sole intention in writing the *Aeneid* was to praise Augustus and imitate Homer. Yet Servius's oppositions are also familiar enough to Virgilian criticism as a whole. The degree to which recognizable historical fact, or at least recognizable Augustan ideology, grounds the fiction of the *Aeneid* has been considered one of the hallmarks of the Virgilian epic. Both history and ideology are at work in major extensive allusions, such as Aeneas operating as a prototype of Augustus, or in minor local parallels, such as the widow in the simile of book 10, who stokes the hearth and works through the night to raise her children according to the Roman ideal of the *univira*, the woman devoted to a single man.[5] By the same token, Virgil scholars commonly reveal how literary precedent formally and thematically structures the *Aeneid*, beginning with the epic's two opening words, which forecast the assimilation of Homer's *Odyssey* and *Iliad*, and extending to Catullan echoes and Virgilian autocitations from the *Eclogues* and *Georgics*.[6] Either way, by challenging literary and histor-

---

1983). Though the title seemingly points the way, J. R. Bacon, "Aeneas in Wonderland," *Classical Review* 53 (1939): 97–104, does not really touch on the subject of the marvelous. Cecil Bowra paid lip service to Virgil's treatment of the marvels in his *From Virgil to Milton* (London: Macmillan, 1945). Greene, who studied the descent of Mercury in book 4 in *Descent from Heaven*, notes the element of the marvel in the ice-bearded Atlas holding up the globe at the edge of the world, but his attention to the problem is more of a passing glance. K. W. Gransden, *Virgil's "Iliad": An Essay on Epic Narrative* (Cambridge: Cambridge University Press, 1984), only marginally deals with the issue of the marvels though some of what Gordon Williams labels as "rococo" occur in the second half of the poem. Philippe Heuzé, *L'image du corps dans l'oeuvre de Virgile* (Rome: École Française de Rome, Palais Farnèse, 1985), has some discussion of the *merveilleux* at 48 and 482. Renaissance critics, following and exaggerating Servius's tempered objections, repeatedly criticized the transformation of ships into nymphs as the most glaringly incongruous of the marvels and for this reason invariably considered it superfluous. Hathaway, *Marvels and Commonplaces*, discusses the problem in a subchapter aptly entitled "Ships Turned into Nymphs," 109–32.

5. See for the latter example the discussion of Gordon Williams, *Technique*, 126–27.

6. See, for example, the dense allusions investigated in Conte, *Rhetoric of Imitation*.

ical precedent, the marvels in the *Aeneid* raise issues conventionally considered to be at the core of the poem. Simply put, these issues involve the poet's role and stance with respect to history and literature.

Over time the judgments that go into evaluating these issues have ranged drastically. Virgil has been the dull copier of Homer and an Augustan propagandist. He has also emerged as the dark and somber poet whose epic undercuts the mimetic style of Homer with "blurred uncertainties" and pessimistically places in question the role of Augustus's Rome and its history as stable sources of external meaning.[7] Yet whatever the final judgments, Virgilian critics continue to ask two pertinent questions: Is the historical allusion or the literary precedent contextually relevant? And, if so, what sort of tension, if any, is produced in the act of making those historical allusions or literary conventions relevant? Both these questions guide my discussion of the Polydorus episode in the first half of this chapter, after which I turn to discuss those marvels singled out by Servius, focusing particularly on the transformation of the ships into nymphs and on Iris's cutting of a lock of Dido's hair.

When commenting on the *mirabile monstrum* of the Polydorus episode, Servius was troubled not so much by the omen of the bleeding branch as by the javelins sprouting from the wounds. Dryads and hamadryads living in trees, though not a common feature in life, were by no means an uncommon feature in literature.[8] In the second book of Apollonius of Rhodes's *Argonautica*—a work whose presence in the first six books of the *Aeneid* is matched and surpassed only by Homer's *Odyssey*—Phineus the seer tells how the father of Peraebius cut down a tree despite a hamadryad's pleas from within (2.448–90). Not surprisingly, as Aeneas is about to grasp a

7. Overviews of these changing attitudes include the first chapter of Johnson, *Darkness Visible*, 1–22, and the extensive bibliography in Johnson's notes; and R. D. Williams, "Changing Attitudes to Virgil: A Study in the History of Taste from Dryden to Tennyson," in *Virgil*, ed. D. R. Dudley (London: Routledge and Kegan Paul, 1969). Much can be gleaned from Frank Kermode, *The Classic* (Cambridge: Harvard University Press, 1983). The phrase "blurred uncertainties" comes from Johnson, *Darkness Visible*, 40. In general, my own reading of the poem has been strongly shaped by this study by Johnson; by the studies of Michael C. J. Putnam collected in *Essays on Latin Lyric, Elegy, and Epic* (Princeton: Princeton University Press, 1982) and *The Poetry of the "Aeneid"* (Cambridge: Harvard University Press, 1965); by Eugene Vance, "Warfare and the Structure of Thought in Virgil's *Aeneid*," *Quaderni urbinati di cultura classica* 15 (1973): 111–62; and by Adam Parry, "The Two Voices of Virgil's *Aeneid*," *Arion* 2 (1963): 66–80.

8. See Speroni, "The Motif of the Bleeding and Speaking Trees"; and R. D. Williams, in Virgil, *Liber tertius*, 59.

branch of the bush for the third and last time, he prays to woodland nymphs. But therein lies the problem. Within the bush is not a nymph but a man, and the voice that emerges from within belongs to Polydorus, a compatriot from fallen Troy. Moreover, it is not the bush that is animated but a man who has in part become a bush.[9] Even if Polydorus denies that the blood comes from a mere branch ("[non] cruor hic de stipite manat," 3.43), his language demonstrates the opposite. Rather than simply talking of spears, Polydorus speaks of an "iron harvest" [ferrea seges] (3.45–46), a metaphor that can only strike a discordant note when originating from someone who has just denied that he is a bush. Along the same lines, the spears have become vegetation that both covers ("texit," 3.45) and penetrates ("confixum," 3.45). Further blurring the boundaries between animate and inanimate objects, Polydorus describes how the spears took root and grew out of his body as though that body were a seed: "iaculis increuit acutis" [it grew up into sharp javelins] (3.46). Virgil may therefore initially evoke the literary precedent of spirits dwelling in trees when he has Aeneas pray to the local deities, but he then radically alters that precedent by having Aeneas break a branch that has grown not from the body of a nymph but from the body of a man pierced by what are sprouting javelins too.

This is not the only literary precedent that Virgil at once recalls and overturns in this episode.[10] After recounting the breaking of the branch, Aeneas interrupts his narrative and addresses his audience to explain who Polydorus is and how he came to die on the shore (3.49–56). In doing so, Aeneas's account of the events prior to Polydorus's death largely conforms to those outlined in Euripides' *Hecuba*. In that tragedy, Priam, in fear of Troy's imminent doom, is said to have sent Polydorus to Thrace, Polydorus is sent with gold, Polymestor slaughters Polydorus for the gold, and the slaughter is interpreted as the breaking of the sacred bond of hospitality made under Jove's auspices and blessing. According to Euripides, who in turn deviated from Homer (*Iliad* 20.407–18), Polydorus is then thrown onto the shore, brought to Hecuba, and later buried (*Hec.* 1287–88). In the *Aeneid*, by contrast, Virgil adds the transformation of

---

9. Sir James George Frazer, *The Golden Bough* (London: Macmillan, 1920), 2:7–58, especially 33 with regard to Polydorus, discusses the concept of tree spirits, along with bleeding trees and trees inhabited by dead spirits.

10. As suggested, the most likely precedent is Apollonius. The transformation, as so many scholars have observed, is more typically Ovidian. For metamorphoses from antiquity to the Renaissance, see Leonard Barkan, *The Gods Made Flesh: Metamorphosis and the Pursuit of Paganism* (New Haven: Yale University Press, 1986).

Polydorus into a bleeding bush. Aeneas's summary does not in any way clarify why Virgil includes this metamorphosis, nor does it begin to clarify why the broken branches bleed.[11] In short, Aeneas's summary does not explain the "marvel." By having Aeneas summarize the events prior to Polydorus's death, Virgil instead indicates that he knew Euripides' version, used it as a model, and then deviated from it. From the perspective of a reader even vaguely familiar with Polydorus's death in the *Hecuba,* Virgil has foregrounded a context that could easily be left submerged or altogether unreported. The question, then, is why does he foreground this context.

We may begin to answer this question by examining why Virgil chose Polydorus in the first place, for Aeneas's encounter with Polydorus does not figure into the legend of the wanderings, though the visit to Thrace belongs to the "normal tradition."[12] In this regard, R. B. Lloyd offers a plausible explanation of Virgil's choice by recalling how Polydorus's ghost, "prophetic in the prologue of the *Hecuba,* was admirably suited to give the Aeneadae their first supernatural direction."[13] Through his adaptation of Polydorus's prophetic role, Virgil fit the traditional stop at Thrace into the larger scheme of progressive revelations in book 3, each of which leads Aeneas to an awareness of his mission. Accordingly, Polydorus's prophetic cry at the beginning of the book, when Aeneas is ignorant of his mission ("heu fuge crudelis terras, fuge litus auarum," 3.44), is echoed in the final episode of book 3, when Aeneas, now cognizant of what he must do, receives Achaemenides' warning to flee from the Cyclops: "sed fugite, o miseri, fugite atque ab litore funem / rumpite" [But flee, ye hapless ones, flee and cut your cables from the shore!] (3.639–40).[14] This ring-composition provides formal closure to the book and reinforces the overall narrative movement from fortune to fate, ignorance to knowledge, Aeneas the Trojan to Aeneas the proto-Roman.[15] Yet Virgil had another

---

11. As, for example, Ettore Paratore assumes in Virgil, *L'"Eneide": Libri III–IV,* ed. Paratore, trans. L. Canali (Verona: Mondadori, 1978), 2: ad locum.

12. See R. D. Williams, in Virgil, *Liber tertius,* 57.

13. R. B. Lloyd, *"Aeneid* III and the Aeneas Legend," *American Journal of Philology* 78 (1957): 393.

14. As Lloyd points out in *"Aeneid* III and the Aeneas Legend," 397, and again in *"Aeneid* III: A New Approach," *American Journal of Philology* 78 (1957): 137.

15. See Lloyd, *"Aeneid* III and the Aeneas Legend" and *"Aeneid* III: A New Approach"; Michael C. J. Putnam, "The Third Book of the Aeneid: From Homer to Rome," in *Essays on Latin Lyric, Elegy, and Epic;* Mario Di Cesare, "The Wanderer," in *The Altar and the City: A Reading of Vergil's "Aeneid"* (New York: Columbia University Press, 1974); A. W. Allen, "The Dullest Book of the *Aeneid,*" *Classical Journal* 47 (1952): 119–23; Otis, *Virgil,* 251–64; R. D. Williams's introduction to his commentary in Virgil, *Liber tertius;* and Quint, "The Return of the Past in *Aeneid* 3," in *Epic and Empire.*

reason for choosing and including Polydorus at this point in his narrative. That reason lies in Polydorus's role in Euripides' tragedy as the youthful avenger of the fallen Troy.

At the end of the *Hecuba,* Polymestor, bereft of his children and blinded by Hecuba, seeks to justify his slaughtering of Polydorus. He claims before Agamemnon that he killed Priam's son, not out of lust for gold, but because Polydorus, if left alive, would have remustered the scattered Trojan forces and rebuilt the fallen rival city of Troy. Agamemnon would then have returned with the Achaean forces. There would have been a new war—yet another *Iliad*—and the Thracian lands would have been ravaged once again. As long as Polydorus remained alive, there was hope for Troy. Once Polydorus died, Troy too was forever gone. Polymestor therefore claims that he slaughtered Polydorus in self-protective concern for his own people and that he did it, as a true and faithful ally, for the Achaeans as well:

> Then listen, Agamemnon.
>   Hecuba had a son
> called Polydorus, her youngest. His father Priam,
> apprehensive that Troy would shortly be taken,
> sent the boy to me to be raised in my own house.
> I killed him, and I admit it.
>   My action, however,
> was dictated, as you see, by a policy
> of wise precaution.
>   My primary motive was fear,
> fear that if this boy, your enemy, survived,
> he might someday found a second and resurgent Troy.
> Further, when the Greeks heard that Priam's son
> was still alive, I feared that they would raise
> a second expedition against this new Troy,
> in which case these fertile plains of Thrace
> would once again be ravaged by war; once again
> Troy and her troubles would work her neighbor's harm—
> those same hardships, my lord, which we in Thrace
> have suffered in this war.
>
> .   .   .   .
>
>   This is my reward, Agamemnon,
> for my efforts in disposing of your enemies.

What I suffer now I suffer for you.

$(1132-44, 1177-79)^{16}$

There are reasons for taking Polymestor's defense of his actions seriously, though not quite literally. In terms of the underlying threat of cyclical and reciprocal violence explored by René Girard in *Violence and the Sacred,* underpinning Polymestor's excuse is ostensibly the mythic archetype of the hidden child who later grows to revive his nation and become the conscience and vengeance of his race.[17] In *The Trojan Women,* Euripides makes this myth the powerful substance of Hecuba's last flicker of hope; it is also the substance of the fear that drives the Achaeans to hurl Astyanax from the citadel of Troy. By the same token, in the *Hecuba,* a drama that repeatedly draws on the use and abuse of the power to persuade,[18] Euripides has Polymestor rhetorically exploit the threat of cyclical violence to defend his actions. A faint echo still lingers in Hecuba's prior longing for the renewal of Troy, as she cries out early on in the drama, unaware that her son has already been slain:

O gods who protect this land,
preserve my son, save him,
the last surviving anchor of my house,
still holding in the snows of Thrace,
still warded by his father's friend.

(78–82)

Liminally present in Hecuba's lament is the notion that Polydorus, as the last "anchor" of Troy, is also the last hope for its rebirth and revenge.

A reconsideration of the relationship between Priam and his son, along with a retrospective reading of *Georgics* 4, further suggests that Polydorus in the *Aeneid* represents Troy's last hope for renewal and revenge. In book 2, Troy dies when Priam dies:

---

16. All citations of Euripides' *Hecuba* in my text are from the translation by William Arrowsmith in *Euripides,* vol. 3, ed. David Greene and Richard Lattimore (Chicago: University of Chicago Press, 1958).

17. René Girard, *Violence and the Sacred,* trans. Patrick Gregory (Baltimore: Johns Hopkins University Press, 1977).

18. See the discussion, for example, of D. J. Conacher, *Euripidean Drama: Myth, Theme, and Structure* (Toronto: University of Toronto Press, 1967).

haec finis Priami fatorum, hic exitus illum
sorte tulit Troiam incensam et prolapsa uidentem
Pergama, tot quondam populis terrisque superbum
regnatorem Asiae.

(2.554–57)

[Such was the close of Priam's fortunes; such the doom that by fate
befell him—to see Troy in flames and Pergamus laid low, he once lord
of so many tribes and lands, the monarch of Asia.]

Virgil's verses here duplicate the metaphoric relationship between the king
and his empire.[19] "Death" [exitus] (2.554), the subject of the sentence, first
invades Priam. But then, in the very moment that Death overwhelms him,
Priam becomes the subject who watches ("uidentem," 2.555) Death
destroy Troy, the citadel, and his kingdom, all of which are syntactically
dependent on Priam ("illum," "uidentem," "superbum regnatorem,"
2.554–57). Priam is not just a part of his kingdom but its organic essence;
his death is synonymous with the death of Troy. The adjective *superbum,*
used here to characterize Priam (2.556), is later used to describe Troy (3.2).

Priam is the center and turning point. His palace, from which all the
surrounding kingdom can be seen, rises in the center of the city, where the
fighting is louder than anywhere else (2.438–39). Deep in this central building, Priam dies in the center as well, in the inner sanctuary, beneath the
open sky (2.512). Not until Priam dies does Aeneas then realize that all is
over for Troy. He alone remains. All about lie bodies that have fallen from
the ramparts onto the ground or into the flames. In the deserted burning
city, the former heroic value of a glorious death in battle gives way to the
burgeoning Roman value of *pietas* as the image of Anchises enters
Aeneas's mind: "subiit cari genitoris imago" (2.560). Now that Priam is
dead, Rome can emerge. And so, with Priam's death, Venus can reveal to
her son what was known all along: the gods were against Troy from the
beginning. Soon after Priam's death, Venus draws away the veil before
Aeneas's eyes to reveal the gods reveling in the destruction of the city
(2.622–23). Only after Priam has died can Venus remove the mist that
clouds mortal eyes and hence the illusion that Troy may be restored. The
king's death signifies the death of the entire community, much as the
queen's does for the bees who destroy their own hive in the *Georgics*

19. See, for the classic work on these issues, Ernst H. Kantorowicz, *The King's Two Bodies: A Study in Mediaeval Political Theology* (Princeton: Princeton University Press, 1957).

(4.210–18), the gods instead having accomplished this task for the Trojans in the *Aeneid.* Despite all the differences between the *Aeneid* and the fourth *Georgics,* both works nevertheless portray the same heroic impulse to seek a glorious death in battle, defending the king or queen who stands at the center of the community that he or she physically and spiritually embodies.

An underlying problem in both the fourth *Georgics* and the *Aeneid* is how to renew and regenerate the society once the king or queen has died. In the *Aeneid,* Polydorus, as the last remaining vestige of Priam, represents this possibility of renewal. If Priam's body is a metaphor of Troy—its essence, center, and identity—Polydorus, as Priam's last surviving son, is by extension a synecdoche for Priam and in turn a synecdoche for Troy. In this respect, it is no accident that for all the differences in the ways the son and father die—Polydorus pierced by javelins, Priam by a sword into his side (2.553)—they also paradoxically die in the same manner. From the time of Servius critics have been troubled by Virgil's use of the word *obtruncat* as a description of Polydorus's death. *Obtruncat,* which means "literally to cut off the head" ("nam obtruncare proprie est capite caedere"), contradicts the previous description of Polydorus transfixed by spears. Hence, Servius reasonably understood the verb to mean "kills" ("occidit intellege").[20] Recent critics have noted the same inconsistency, with R. D. Williams attempting to explain the discrepancy by suggesting that "Virgil is combining two different sources for the story."[21] But what Servius and Williams failed to observe is that the word *obtruncat* recalls the description of Priam beheaded along the shore in the previous book: "iacet ingens litore truncus, / auulsumque umeris caput et sine nomine corpus" [He lies a huge trunk upon the shore, a head severed from the shoulders, a nameless corpse] (2.557–58). Moreover, the only prior use of the word *obtruncat* occurs in Aeneas's recollection of Priam's death at the altars: "patrem qui obtruncat ad aras" (2.663).[22] Polydorus, though laid low by spears, is described as beheaded because that was the way his father died. The youngest son must participate, if only through language, in the death of his father. The word *obtruncat* is a diacritical sign pointing to the body of Polydorus as the last remaining link with the larger unburied body of the father, stranded, just as Polydorus was, by the shore.

---

20. Servius, ad locum (55).

21. In Virgil, *Liber tertius,* 65.

22. And here the verb, once more, is used in an entirely incongruous way since Priam is not beheaded at the altar but stabbed in the side (2.550–53).

What Aeneas does not realize, then, is that he is pulling up, and pulling at, the last hope for Troy's renewal. Aeneas's act thus describes, as perhaps no other in the entire poem, what David Quint has identified in Freudian terms as the compulsion to repeat in the third book, as "an obsessive return to—and of—the past."[23] Indeed, Aeneas's desire to reach the hidden causes—the sheer force by which he returns three times, despite the omen and his fear—symbolizes at one level his desire to return and rebuild Troy. The scattered forces Polymestor threatened that Polydorus would have led back, both to rebuild Troy and to exact vengeance on the Achaeans in a renewed cycle of reciprocal violence, have now been gathered together by Aeneas instead. Unaware of his fate or of who lies beneath the mound, Aeneas has become Polydorus's double and has taken on the burden of being Priam's last son. In this way, the Polydorus episode is proleptic of a desire that runs throughout the third book and the Odyssean half of the *Aeneid:* the desire to rebuild or resurrect Troy (1.206; 3.132–34, 349–52; 4.340–44; 5.631–34, 756–57).

Yet for all their longing to return home, there is no hope in regenerating Troy. What Aeneas finds beneath the mound is Polydorus. Yet what he does not realize is that in finding Polydorus he finds that Troy is dead. So long as Polydorus remained alive, there was hope for the Trojans. Now that Polydorus is dead, Troy too is irrevocably gone. As the last hope for Troy's renewal, Polydorus not only participates in the death of Troy through the beheading of his father. His body, as the synecdoche of Priam's body and Troy, is polluted. The drops of blood that come from the tomb of Polydorus and cover the ground with gore are "taboo" ("et terram tabo maculant," 3.29), a contaminating substance. The polluting presence of Polydorus's blood thus once more indicates, as in the Euripidean subtext to this episode, the eventual return to, and threat of, reciprocal violence amid untimely death. As Girard writes:

Spilt blood of any origin, unless it has been associated with a sacrificial act, is considered impure. This universal attribution of impurity to spilt blood springs directly from the definition we have just proposed: wherever violence threatens, ritual impurity is present. When men are enjoying peace and security, blood is a rare sight. When violence is unloosed,

---

23. Quint, *Epic and Empire,* 56. Quint does not discuss this episode in his reading of the *Aeneid,* despite the fact that Freud refers to it indirectly through Tasso in *Beyond the Pleasure Principle,* on which see chap. 5. Quint as well develops his reading in light of Girardian doubling and mimetic vengeance.

however, blood appears everywhere—on the ground, underfoot, form-ing great pools. Its very fluidity gives form to the contagious nature of violence. Its presence proclaims murder and announces new upheavals to come. Blood stains everything it touches the color of violence and death. Its very appearance seems, as the saying goes, to "cry out for vengeance."[24]

The voyage hardly begun, the marvel of the blood from the broken branch makes plain from the outset that Aeneas and his weary band cannot go back any more than they can settle in the place to which they have come.[25]

Polydorus's death at the beginning of book 3 thus stands at the edge of two distinctly separate, yet closely connected, worlds. It is a sign of the death of Troy and the mimetic violence unleashed in such tragedies as Euripides' *Hecuba.* At the same time, it is a sign of the birth of Rome and the desired, though finally questioned, ethics of restraint in Virgil's own imperial epic.[26] This renewal and transformation, as Servius noted, is implicit, if only ironically, in the marvel of the javelins growing from Poly-dorus's body. Behind the marvel of Polydorus's death lies the *historia* of Romulus's fertile and bewitched spear: "Romulus, having received a sign, hurled his spear from the Aventine mountain onto the Palatine: where-upon, fixed into the ground, the spear grew leaves and became a tree." Through the marvel of the bleeding branch and the sign of the regenerat-ing leaves, Virgil has linked the last possible founder and avenger of the dead Troy with the first violent, vengeful founder of Rome. Polydorus, the first victim on the way to Rome, has become the first link in a long chain of victims leading to the first true father of Rome. Polydorus, who violently died for Rome and did not know it, died for Romulus and the power of the Palatine.

At the outset of book 3, Aeneas does not know that Latium, and hence Rome, is his goal. The passive tenses of the opening of the third book reveal a hero who leads reluctantly, almost by chance—a man who has a profound sense of his destiny but does not know what that destiny is.

---

24. Girard, *Violence and the Sacred,* 33–34.

25. On this, see A. W. Allen, "The Dullest Book," 122. Putnam explores ways in which vengeance operates in book 3 in *Essays on Latin Lyric, Elegy, and Epic,* 278–79.

26. The scholar who has consistently illumined Virgil's questioning of Roman restraint is Michael C. J. Putnam in his various studies. See as well A. W. Allen, "The Dullest Book," 121; Allen anticipates some of this discussion, though in a far more optimistic light.

Aeneas's *pietas,* his famed duty to his gods, fatherland, and family, leads him on. And it is while being pious, while performing his duties to the gods so that he may establish his first colony, that Aeneas comes upon the omen. Blood flows as soon as the first branch is ripped ("uellitur," 28). Again ("rursus," 31) Aeneas tries to uproot another of the branches ("alterius . . . conuellere," 31) until, frustrated, with many things going through his mind ("multa mouens animo," 34), he returns for a third time ("tertia," 37). This time Aeneas kneels down and braces himself against the sand to employ a greater effort ("maiore . . . nisu," 37). Contrasting sharply with the opening passivity of the book ("agimur," 5; "detur," 7; "feror," 11), the progression from the first to the second to the third breaking of the branch is marked by ever increasing violence. First Aeneas approaches and tries ("accessi," 24; "conatus," 25); then he follows through and probes deeper ("insequor," "temptare," 32); lastly he assails and struggles ("adgredior," "obluctor," 38).

In essence, Aeneas's threefold rending of the branch may be understood as an interpretive act. Before him stands an "omen" (36). Because of its opacity as a sign Aeneas demands an explanation from the resistant root ("lentum . . . uimen," 31). Though frightened, Aeneas must test the "deep hidden causes" [causas penitus . . . latentis] (32). He confronts a "monstrum" (26), and so he must understand what this warning means if he is to lead his people and understand their combined destiny. Aeneas's pious sense of duty is perhaps the most ready response to Polydorus's plaintive question "quid miserum, Aenea, laceras?" [why, Aeneas, dost thou tear me?] (41): his duty obliged him to uproot the branches. In this way, Virgil may have framed Aeneas's actions as part of the wider stoic test Cecil Bowra asserts Aeneas undergoes as preparation for the second half of the *Aeneid.*[27]

But if that is the case, Aeneas has failed miserably. The repeated uprooting of the branches describes not stalwart control but irrational behavior. Aeneas's puzzled movement of the mind ("multa mouens animo," 34) anticipates not Anchises' serene knowledge of the *animus mundi* but a desire to achieve through force a knowledge that is thwarted. Proverbially, in both Greek and Latin, the third event in a sequence carried a sense of completeness and perfection, but there is no completeness or perfection in the threes of the Polydorus episode.[28] By the time Aeneas

---

27. Bowra, *From Virgil to Milton.*
28. I owe this observation to Diskin Clay.

uproots the branch the third time, his piety is marred with violence, his innocence stained with blood, his passivity transmuted into aggression. Moreover, Aeneas has all along been grasping at spears—the fecund spears in Polydorus's body, the fertile spear proleptic of Rome's fratricidal founder—spears that are reminders of Troy's warrior past and, more importantly, signs of the martial violence yet to come in the poem and in Roman history, a violence to which even love, in the form of Venus's myrtle bush, has symbolically given a hand. Needless to say, Aeneas does not know of this symbolic significance any more than he is aware that Polydorus's death represents the death of Troy and the birth of Rome. Though Aeneas returns time and again to understand the meaning of the bleeding branch, he remains in the end frustratingly ignorant of the deep hidden causes he so passionately yearns to grasp.

Frustratingly *nescius* is how Virgil characterizes Aeneas throughout the *Aeneid*—as forever incapable of comprehending the meaning of the drama he must enact. That, I maintain, is how the marvels at one level operate in the *Aeneid.* Aeneas descends to the depths of Hades and beholds all his race, yet he departs through a gleaming ivory portal of false dreams (6.893–98). He holds up a shield that boasts Rome's future, yet he never has an inkling about what those images on an "ineffable fabric" [non enarrabile textum] (8.625) really represent, even after his descent (8.729–31). So too, as Robert Brooks argues, "the deeper stranger antithesis of success in actions/frustration is the central and fundamental significance of the golden bough."[29] "It is far stranger, and more moving," Brooks says, "that [Aeneas] never fully possesses that divine order of which he is the literal and symbolic carrier. . . . The causes of things are never to be known with the same ecstatic certainty as Lucretius."[30]

The marvel of Iris, which Servius singles out along with the Polydorus episode as problematic, underscores Aeneas's profound ignorance of the causes of things. At the end of book 4, as Iris descends, "drawing against the sun a thousand shifting tints" [mille trahens uarios aduerso sole colores] (701), Virgil reveals through his imagery why the rainbow should have been associated with the marvelous in classical thought, given its obvious striking beauty as a "wonder to behold." As Plato wrote, philosophy "has no other origin [than wonder], and he was a good genealogist who made Iris the daughter of Thaumas."[31] So Iris, later described as

---

29. Brooks, "*Discolor Aura,*" 286.
30. Brooks, "*Discolor Aura,*" 280.
31. *Theaetetus* 155d, from Plato, *The Collected Dialogues,* ed. Edith Hamilton and Huntington Cairns (Princeton: Princeton University Press, 1961).

"Thaumantias" (9.5), is recorded as born from wonder in the *Aeneid* too. But behind the image of Iris as a privileged object of beauty in Platonic contemplation lies the compacted violence of a single word. The verb *secat* ("she shears," 704), the last word associated with Iris at the end of book 4, undercuts the contemplative serenity of Iris's beauty and reminds the reader that Iris's action derives from Juno's wrath. As she descends, Iris all along mediates between the "struggling" [luctantem] (695) Dido, whose tragedy anticipates the Punic Wars, and Juno, "omnipotent" [omnipotens] (693), a principal cause of that tragedy, which produces countless deaths in the course of history. The violence and tragedy of the episode have not so much disappeared but been absorbed into the marvel itself. *Soluo,* Iris's final word, indeed indicates that she comes as a solution to Dido's pain, though little has been resolved in terms of the larger consequences of Dido's tragedy in history.

So why has Dido died? Is it sufficient to say that Dido's tragedy was her ignorance of history, that she must be the harbinger of doom because Carthage would one day wage war on Rome, or that she should have behaved in a manner proleptically Roman by remaining a *univira,* a woman forever faithful to her first husband, Sychaeus? The personal sacrifice that must be paid to found Rome is never quite explained. With Dido released from the prison of her body, her personal tragedy, along with the future conflicts in Roman and Carthaginian history, fade away: "dilapsus calor atque in uentos uita recessit" [the life passed away into the winds] (4.705). Dido is cut loose, and so too is Aeneas and the *Aeneid* from tragedy in literature and in history. Even Juno, by sending Iris down at the end of book 4, momentarily appears as the pitying savior rather than the angry goddess who helped bring about Dido's death. Thus, book 5 begins almost as though nothing had ever happened in the "meanwhile" [interea] (5.1). Juno has disappeared. Aeneas, glancing back at the walls of Carthage, has no idea what "cause" [causa] feeds the burning flames seen from afar (5.4–5). Later, Aeneas will wonder whether he is the cause of Dido's death, "funeris heu tibi causa fui?" [Was I, alas! the cause of death to thee?] (6.458). Yet even in this self-reflexive moment in the *Lugentes campi,* Aeneas lacks the historical hindsight to understand the true causes of Dido's tragedy, causes that the marvel of Iris would momentarily seem to question as well as mask.

The transformation of the ships into nymphs, perhaps the most memorable marvel singled out by Servius in his commentary,[32] reflects once

---

32. Memorable because it would have such a lasting impression on the Renaissance, as outlined in Hathaway, *Marvels and Commonplaces.*

again Aeneas's inability to understand the causes of the drama he must enact. "The loss of the ships, regarded simply as a loss," Gordon Williams observes, "symbolizes the severance of the last tie with the life in Troy; not only can there be no going back, but the Trojans are now decisively located on Italian soil."[33] History thus appears to have favored Aeneas, though Aeneas could never have known that when he first set out. Jove's refusal to guarantee the immortality of the ships when Cybele first makes the request underscores this point. As Gordon Williams writes:

> A retrospective survey of the *Aeneid* is enforced by these words so that the Trojan ships are seen metaphorically as human beings subject to the lottery of chance: some will survive, some will not. What was the unknown future in Juppiter's words is now history, and the reader knows what has happened to various ships and can sense the pathos of the few survivors now made immortal. More important is the retrospective judgment enforced by Juppiter's words about Aeneas. He has got safely to the shores of Italy and, consequently, it can now be seen to have been his destiny to do so; but divine protection did not bring him through. A re-reading of the earlier books is compelled by those words: each human being has only himself to rely on.[34]

In making this claim, Gordon Williams has nevertheless neglected to take into consideration the reappearance of the nymphs in book 10, where they do not have such a benevolent role to play.[35] Indeed, rather than severing Aeneas from Troy, the nymphs in book 10 lead him back into the heroic "furor" of the second book.

Aeneas loses his ships in book 9. He has, however, gathered forces in the meantime, and the ships he brings back in book 10 are no ordinary ones.[36] By virtue of their figureheads, they appear as "great beasts," Philip Hardie comments, because of "their snouts or beaks, *rostra*."[37] Aeneas

---

33. Gordon Williams, *Technique,* 130.

34. Gordon Williams, *Technique,* 131.

35. It is instead discussed in Fantham, "*Nymphas . . . e Navibus Esse.*" See as well Philip Hardie, "Ships and Ship-names in the *Aeneid,*" in *Homo Viator: Classical Essays for John Bramble,* ed. Michael Whitby, Mary Whitby, and P. Hardie (Bristol: Bristol Classical Press, 1987).

36. On this see in particular Hardie, "Ships and Ship-names"; and Fantham, "*Nymphas . . . e Navibus Esse.*" They note the literary precedents in Catullus and Apollonius.

37. Hardie, "Ships and Ship-names," 165; he also notes that "it is often unclear whether a ship-name is to be referred to the figurehead or to the whole ship."

commands a ship with lions beneath the figurehead and with the mountain of Ida imaged overhead (10.157–58). Massicus navigates on a bronze-plated Tiger (10.166), Cupauo on a Centaur (10.195–98), and Aulestes on a Triton (10.209–12). The nymphs then reappear and swim around this parade of human-crafted marvels. It is the middle of the night, and as they arrive, one of them, Cymodocea, hoists herself up above the water by grasping the stern with her right hand and treading water with the left. She then tells how and why Aeneas's ships were transformed into nymphs, along with what has happened to his camp while he has been away:

> nos sumus, Idaeae sacro de uertice pinus,
> nunc pelagi nymphae, classis tua. perfidus ut nos
> praecipitis ferro Rutulus flammaque premebat,
> rupimus inuitae tua uincula teque per aequor
> quaerimus. hanc genetrix faciem miserata refecit
> et dedit esse deas aeuumque agitare sub undis.
> at puer Ascanius muro fossisque tenetur
> tela inter media atque horrentis Marte Latinos.
> iam loca iussa tenent forti permixtus Etrusco
> Arcas eques; medias illis opponere turmas,
> ne castris iungant, certa est sententia Turno.
>
> (10.230–40)

[We—pines of Ida, from her sacred crest, now nymphs of the sea—are thy fleet! When the traitorous Rutulian was driving us headlong with fire and sword, reluctant we broke thy bonds, and are seeking thee over the main. This new shape the Great Mother gave us in pity, and granted us to be goddesses and spend our life beneath the waves. But thy boy Ascanius is hemmed in by wall and trench, in the midst of arms and of Latins, bristling with war. Already the Arcadian horse, joined with brave Etruscans, hold the appointed place; to bar their way with interposing squadrons, lest they approach the camp, is Turnus's fixed resolve.]

Cymodocea's tale enforces a retrospective reading of Aeneas's prior thoughts and actions when he was back at camp. At the beginning of book 8, Aeneas, troubled by the impending war, tosses awake on an anxious "sea of troubles" ("magno curarum fluctuat aestu") "seeing all" [cuncta uidens] (8.19). But the total picture still wavers, divides, reseparates

(8.20–21). Amid his cares, Aeneas's vision of the war becomes as fragmented as the sun's or moon's light flung from a bronze bowl onto roof
beams:

> sicut aquae tremulum labris ubi lumen aënis
> sole repercussum aut radiantis imagine lunae
> omnia peruolitat late loca, iamque sub auras
> erigitur summique ferit laquearia tecti.

(8.22–25)

[as when in brazen bowls a flickering light from water, flung back by the
sun or the moon's glittering form, flits far and wide o'er all things, and
now mounts high and smites the fretted ceiling of the roof aloft.]

Reflections upon reflections mount in Aeneas's mind as in the room. But
then the river god Tiberinus appears and bids Aeneas to seek Evander.
Soon after, Aeneas is moving down the Tiber toward Evander's Arcadia,
and as he sails, the shields of war become reflections of a marveling gaze,
the ships themselves insubstantial painted images on the waves: "mirantur
et undae, / miratur nemus insuetum fulgentia longe / scuta uirum fluuio
pictasque innare carinas" [in wonder the waves, in wonder the unwonted
woods view the far gleaming shields of warriors and the painted hulls
floating on the stream] (8.91–93).[38] Aeneas has moved into, not away
from, the wavering fragmentation of the simile in book 8. Like the light
from the bowl flickering about the room, Aeneas merges into a highly aestheticized landscape of reflection upon reflection.

Later, when Aeneas returns from Evander's Arcadia, he once again
moves through a world of superimposed images and contemplative wonder. Now, as at the beginning of book 8, he is considering the various
issues of war, turning them over in his mind (10.159–60). Pallas, beside
him, inquires about the stars that guide their way through the night
(10.161–62). The stars, whose *causas* the bard Iopas and the Lucretian
philosopher of the *Georgics* understood (*Aen.* 1.742–76, *G.* 2.475–82), nevertheless move through a night that is opaque ("opacae / noctis,"

---

38. See David S. Wiesen, "The Pessimism of the Eighth *Aeneid,*" *Latomus: Revue d'Études
Latines* 32 (1973): 737–65; the implications of this magical moment in terms of Augustus's
future Rome are discussed at 748 and passim. See as well Bacon, "Aeneas in Wonderland."
Fantham, "*Nymphas . . . e Navibus Esse,*" notes the Catullan underpinnings from 64.12–16.

10.161–62). Pallas then asks about Aeneas's "trials by land and sea" [quae passus terraque marique] (162), precisely the tales Dido longed to hear over and over again in her passion. Yet whether Aeneas answers Pallas is never known. The poet suddenly intrudes with an invocation. He bids the muses to open Helicon and move his song. Cymodocea then arrives and tells Aeneas that he is in truth not quite awake: "uigila" [Wake up!] (229); "surge age!" [Up, then!] (241).

Cymodocea's warning finally awakens Aeneas from Evander's aestheticized realm. The ships, as Cymodocea makes plain, were transformed into nymphs not just to escape Turnus but to seek Aeneas: "teque per aequor / quaerimus" [we are seeking thee over the main] (10.233–34). They have come to propel him back to war. And as they do so, Aeneas's boat, now no longer a marvel traveling through a world of contemplative wonder, is likened to weapons of war; it moves over the waves "fleeter than a javelin and wind-swift arrow" [ocior et iaculo et uentos aequante sagitta] (10.247–48). A few verses later, as his boat is propelled forward, Aeneas takes his stance at the head of the ship just as Augustus did in Virgil's version of the battle of Actium ("stans celsa in puppi," 10.261; cf. 8.680). Moments later, Aeneas uplifts his shield as Achilles did before reentering battle to avenge Patroclus's death. It took the transformation of ships to transform Aeneas into a heroic avenging warrior. For the Rutulians on the shore, Aeneas, standing on the ship as Augustus stood, his shield blazing as Achilles's did, seems a terrible sight. The entire sea appears to move toward them as the forest moved toward Macbeth. And Aeneas has become a plague that wastes the land.[39]

Aeneas is ignorant ("nescius," 249) of this transformation. When the nymphs first approach, they "recognize" Aeneas ("adgnoscunt," 224). He, "all unaware" [ignarum] (228), does not recognize them. He remains ignorant even after Cymodocea tells him how Cybele saved his ships by turning them into nymphs. He has heard the causes but does not fully understand their meaning. He "marvels" [stupet] (10.249). He has no more understanding of the meaning of the ships turned into nymphs than he does of the stars that move through the night. The marvels guide, as the stars guide, but their deeper causes remain occult. Aeneas instead is only cheered by a sign ("omine," 250) without ever understanding what it means. And he is cheered, no doubt, by Cymodocea's last words that por-

---

39. Discussed by Michael C. J. Putnam in "The Virgilian Achievement," in *Essays on Latin Lyric, Elegy, and Epic*, 341–42.

tend victory: "crastina lux, mea si non inrita dicta putaris, / ingentis Rutulae spectabit caedis aceruos" [Tomorrow's light, if thou deem not my words idle, shall look on mighty heaps of Rutulian carnage] (10.244–45). Once again, while signaling Aeneas's complete acceptance of his duty, Virgil's marvel reveals Aeneas's deeper ignorance of the role he is compelled to play.

So, too, through the marvel of the bleeding branch in the Polydorus episode, Virgil dramatizes Aeneas's inability to understand the causes of things. In plucking the branch, Aeneas seeks "deep hidden causes" [causas penitus . . . latentis] (3.32). He does eventually learn who lies beneath the mound, after rending the bleeding branch three times. But the true meaning of the event—that Troy is dead, that Rome is being born in all her violence and vengeful glory—escapes Aeneas, just as the true meaning of the ineffable narrative of the shield later evades him. And he never understands the true meaning of his descent into the underworld, Dido's death, the golden bough, or the ships turned into nymphs. The frustration with which Aeneas wrenches the branch is a frustration he must bear throughout the *Aeneid*. It is a frustration borne, gladly or grimly, from an ignorance of his role in history.

At one level, then, the marvels singled out by Servius repeatedly reveal Aeneas's inability to comprehend the full significance of the drama he must enact amid history's endless cycles of mimetic violence. At another level, however, these same marvels allow the poet of the *Aeneid* to allude to his own artistry as the deep hidden cause underlying the events about which he sings. For even after the marvels have been examined and explained in the light of historical events, they continue to operate as "irrational" elements—in Aristotle's terms—that create a tension in the poem. Indeed, as R. D. Williams points out, and as early commentators often observed, Virgil's marvels simply do not belong in the *Aeneid*. They may stand in Odysseus's world with perfect aplomb. They make absolute sense in Apollonius's scheme of things. And they are completely at one with Ovid's *Metamorphoses,* which unravels Virgil's marvels and entwines them together in an abbreviated and parodic revision of the *Aeneid.* But what, R. D. Williams wonders, are they doing in Virgil's poem?[40] Critics contend

40. R. D. Williams, "The Purpose of the Aeneid," 38 and 39, writes: "In *Aeneid* iii, the book of Aeneas' voyages, the Trojans come into contact with the Harpies and with the Cyclops, and nearly into contact with Scylla and Charybdis; in Book v they pass the islands of the Sirens; at the beginning of Book vii they sail past the land of Circe. What, we may ask, are these Homeric fantasies doing in the well-charted Mediterranean with which the Romans were very familiar?" [. . .] "We are not surprised when we find that [the transformation of the ships into nymphs] figures largely in Ovid's *Metamorphoses* (xiv 530f.), where it very properly

from the time of Servius to the present day that Virgil's marvels do not belong in Aeneas's proto-Roman world any more than we can imagine Aeneas clinging like Odysseus to the underside of a sheep to escape the Cyclops, or Euryalus sliding into manure rather than a slippery puddle of spilt blood.[41] Virgil's introduction of marvels into his poem has, for this reason, consistently been seen as a frivolous departure from the serious main substance of the poem. Castelvetro, for instance, thought one could actually exclude the most glaring example of the marvelous discussed in the Renaissance: the transformation of the ships into nymphs. Yet precisely because Virgil's marvels are so often perceived as superfluous to the poem, they inevitably call attention to the fact that the *Aeneid* is indeed a poem. Setting themselves off as separate, though not necessarily complete, elements, they periodically foreground poetic discourse as an act unto itself.

In this light, the marvels singled out by Servius continually vacillate between two sources of meaning, one externally grounded in history, the other in the reflexivity of the poet's art. Polydorus's spears recall Romulus's spear; the ships transformed into nymphs propel Aeneas into assuming Augustus's heroic stance; the shield tells the story of Rome's future race; Iris glosses over the Punic Wars; the golden bough and the portal of false dreams bracket the Elysian fields where Aeneas beholds the heroic future of Rome. History is always present within the marvel being represented. But history is also always submerged by and/or bracketed by the marvels. In this way, Virgil's marvels remind us that this is *Virgil*'s version of history. And the vision is not a happy one. Polydorus grasps at bleeding spears to which Venus's love, symbolically present in the myrtle bush, has even given a hand. The golden bough and ivory portal embrace a vision of Rome's heroes that ends with a dirge for promising youth cut short. The

---

belongs: but how does it fit in the hard world of Turnus going into battle against the proto-Romans? Servius (on ix 82) reports uneasiness: he says that, although the passage may be partly excused as a *figmentum poeticum,* it nevertheless is blamed by the critics (*notatur a criticis*) because it lacks precedents—*quia exemplo caret.* The Renaissance commentators, Germanus and La Cerda, defend the passage by producing precedents for such a supernatural event; in Apollonius (iv 580f.) the good ship Argo can talk, and in Homer (*Od.* viii 557f.) the Phaeacian ships steer themselves. True, we may say, but the Argo and the Phaeacians belong wholly to a heroic and Odyssean world, in contrast with Aeneas' fleet which is entering a proto-Roman world. Page regards the subject itself as 'somewhat ludicrous,' but considers that Virgil's 'handling of it is marked by admirable tact.' Conington cryptically says that 'modern criticism will be more disposed to account for it than to justify it.'"

41. In Virgil, *Liber tertius,* 17, R. D. Williams briefly and effectively compares the Virgilian reworking of these Homeric episodes.

nymphs cheer Aeneas with the assurance that he will see Rutulian carnage the next day. The golden shield joyfully envisions Augustus "stans celsa in puppi" (8.680); but in book 10, when Aeneas adopts it, he becomes a death-bringing star who, at the end of the book, will slaughter Lausus and see his own piety ebb away with a groan (10.823–24). The wonder of Iris brings death to Dido, whose demise foreshadows the fall of Carthage in the Punic Wars. Behind each and every marvel singled out by Servius, Virgil's version of history is one of love transformed into war, of senseless death, and of hopes crushed.[42] And there seems to be no end to the violence in history. For no matter how much Virgil seeks to incorporate history and give it meaning through his art, Virgil's vision of history reminds us that his art, even where it is most "wondrous to tell," is never sufficient to provide closure to history's violence.

Lucretius, for the poet of the *Georgics,* could confidently, happily, know the causes of things ("felix qui potuit rerum cognoscere causas," 2.490). Virgil's marvels, however, reflect a refusal to take a stance with respect to the poet's conception of history or his own art as the final stable source of meaning. History remains an outside source of meaning that circumscribes the text and becomes the realm to which Virgil's own text owes its meaning. Yet the aesthetic experience of Virgil's poetic language and imagination repeatedly reasserts itself with his marvels as *the* determining feature over and above the historical allusion or summary. This is not a final, felicitous synthesis but instead an indication of the inability to define precisely where one may find "truth," the deep hidden causes of things. Both history and poetry seek to explain where truth lies, but neither is sufficient, alone or together. Truth constantly shifts between Virgil's art and Virgil's vision of history, between poetry as a source of truth that can absorb history, on the one hand, and history as a source of truth that gives meaning to art and absorbs art, on the other. And it is impossible to say which truth triumphs as the ultimate touchstone. Truth is repeatedly deferred, rendered always a signifier, not a cause but an event.

From a perspective willing to conflate Aristotle's *Poetics* with his *Metaphysics,* however, this instability may nevertheless be viewed as an indication that Virgil's marvels are still signs pointing toward truth even if they

---

42. With the prosect of an empire *sine fine,* this vision of history may represent, as many critics suggest, a growing sense of anxiety about the outcome of the Augustan reforms. See, for example, the last chapter of Johnson, *Darkness Visible;* the studies of Putnam; and Wiesen, "The Pessimism of the Eighth *Aeneid,*" 761. Quint provides a strong counterresponse in *Epic and Empire.*

do not reveal the deep hidden causes themselves. For Aristotle, so long as marvels do not become so disruptive as to completely challenge a coherent explanation of their role in the text, they add to the enjoyment of the tale (*Poetics* 1460a); in fact, according to the *Metaphysics,* they may stimulate "wonder," which is the act that lies at the basis of philosophical inquiry. "It is through wonder," Aristotle writes, "that men now begin and originally began to philosophize; wondering in the first place at obvious perplexities, and then by gradual progression raising questions about the greater matters too, e.g. about the changes of the moon and of the sun, about the stars and about the origin of the universe. Now he who wonders and is perplexed feels that he is ignorant (thus the myth-lover is in a sense a philosopher, since myths are composed of wonders)" (*Metaphysics* 982b 9–10).[43] In this context, Virgil, as both a mythmaker and myth-lover, moves his poetry toward philosophy through his marvels, toward the stars and the moon and the origin of the universe. These marvels are all the wonders that Lucretius understood in his happy vision of the cosmos, though Aeneas was never able to comprehend them; and Virgil was not able, or at least refused, to sing directly about them too.

Such a reflexive insight into the power of the marvelous to stimulate people to engage in philosophical inquiry was familiar to the Middle Ages, which relied on Aristotle's *Metaphysics* rather than on his *Poetics.* Nevertheless, this insight represented for Dante a profound historical blindness that prevented a *vates* from doing precisely what a *vates* was expected to do: foresee the future and, beyond all the epic representations of the marvelous, catch sight of the miracle of the Word made flesh. The poet of the *Aeneid* may therefore recognize his own marvels in the *Commedia* as real historical facts prefiguring God's justice in a Christian universe. He may further wonder occasionally about the causes of the cosmos in another *vates'* poem. But he can never understand, both in or beyond the suspended confines of limbo where so many pagan thinkers dwell, "l'amor che move il sole e l'altre stelle" [the Love which moves the sun and the other stars] (*Par.* 33.145). For Virgil, even where wonder gives way to insight, there can be no underlying awareness of the love of Him who saved us, not only from our sins, but from the vengeance and violence of human history itself.

---

43. Translation from Aristotle, *Metaphysics,* trans. Hugh Tredennich (London: Putnam's Sons, 1933), 1:13.

Chapter 2

Dante: From Ignorance to Knowledge

Historia dicitur a verbo graeco, ιστορέω, historeo, quod est video et narro. Propterea quod apud veteres nulli licebat scribere res gestas, nisi a se visas, ne falsitas admisceretur veritati peccato scriptoris, plus, aut minus, aut aliter dicentis.

—Hugh of St. Victor

Dante comincia con la meraviglia, et maraviglia grande
è che e' la continua, l'augmenta et la termina nella
meraviglia d'ogni maraviglia.

—Alessandro Rinuccini

In the thirteenth canto of the *Inferno,* in the zone of the suicides and in the middle of the circle of the violent, the wayfarer learns from Virgil that he will see things that would take faith away from Virgil's own speech were he himself to tell them: "sì vederai / cose che torrien fede al mio sermone" [you shall see things that would make my words incredible] (13.20–21).[1] In the meantime, the wayfarer has been borne beyond the river of blood into a pathless woods, and when Virgil tells him to look carefully about him, he hears laments from all sides. Yet seeing no one in the forest, he stops dead in his tracks, bewildered ("smarrito," 13.24). In this moment of apparent uncertainty and tension, the *smarrimento* of the wayfarer in this dense dark woods verbally and thematically recalls his *smarrimento* in the "selva oscura" [dark wood] (1.2) of the opening canto. But rather than con-

---

1. The epigraph from Hugh of St. Victor is from *De Scripturis,* vol 175 of *Patrologiae Cursus Completus: Series Latina,* ed. J. P. Migne (Paris: Garnier Fratres, 1879), 12; the epigraph from Alessandro Rinuccini—which Bernard Weinberg, *A History of Literary Criticism in the Italian Renaissance* (Chicago: University of Chicago Press, 1961), 2:884–89, dates at approximately 1587—appears on fol. 50 in MS Ashburnham 562, Biblioteca Laurenziana, Florence. Citations from, and translations of, the *Commedia* are from Dante Alighieri, *The Divine Comedy,* ed. and trans. Charles S. Singleton, 6 vols. (Princeton: Princeton University Press, 1970–75).

fronting beasts that loom with a ferocious, though essentially allegorical, force, and rather than being aided by the guiding Virgilian voice of "chi per lungo silenzio parea fioco" [one who seemed faint through long silence] (1.63), the wayfarer now stands suspended between Virgil's silent knowledge of what he will soon witness and his own bewildering ignorance of the causes of the disorienting laments emerging from the dark woods.

Whereas the highly symbolic forest of *Inferno* 1 represented the way-farer's, as well as our own, allegorical *selva* of sin, this forest seems to belong primarily to Virgil. He knows the causes of things here, and, as he soon makes clear, this forest has much to do with his poem. "Però riguarda ben" [Look well, therefore] (13.20), the poet of the *Aeneid* fore-warns. After seeing the wayfarer bewildered, Virgil then urges him to break a branch, for by doing so the wayfarer will cut short all his concerns and come to know the causes of things, causes that the poet of the *Aeneid* expects to reveal as verifiably Virgilian. Somewhat hesitantly, the wayfarer reaches out as bidden and plucks a twig from a great thornbush (13.31–32). The stub instantly cries out and bleeds. The "selva selvaggia" of *Inferno* 1, a very abstract forest, is here transformed and materialized into a talking thicket whose voices fuse with blood to form what Leo Spitzer describes as "bleeding screams."[2] Terrified, the wayfarer lets fall the tip of the broken branch, whereupon Virgil responds to the wounded spirit with the following words:

> "S'elli avesse potuto creder prima,"
>   rispuose 'l savio mio, "anima lesa,
>   ciò c'ha veduto pur con la mia rima,
> non averebbe in te la man distesa;
>   ma la cosa incredibile mi fece
>   indurlo ad ovra ch'a me stesso pesa."

(13.46–51)

["If he, O wounded spirit, had been able to believe before," replied my sage, "what he had never seen save in my verses, he would not have stretched forth his hand against you; but the incredible thing made me prompt him to a deed that grieves me."]

Here, for the first time in the *Commedia*, Virgil openly calls attention to his own text. In *Inferno* 1, in the midst of an unreal woods in an unreal

---

2. Leo Spitzer, "Speech and Language in *Inferno* XIII," *Italica* 19 (1942): 88.

place, a pattern of events from the *Aeneid* underlies the more evident design of theological allusions. As Robert Hollander has shown, multiple features of the *Aeneid* are programmatically inscribed there, just as they are throughout the *Commedia*.[3] But the Virgilian reference in *Inferno* 13 differs radically from such oblique subtextual patterning. The context here is not submerged in the least. The reader is not obliged to recover the *Aeneid* through a more or less visible tissue of allusions. Rather, Virgil has the wayfarer duplicate Aeneas's breaking of the branch explicitly according to "ciò c'ha veduto pur con la mia rima" [what he had never seen save in my verses] (13.48), where the *pur* makes plain—so far as Virgil is concerned—that the model derives uniquely from the *Aeneid*.[4] Far from a veiled allusion that enriches a reading of the text, the opening of canto 13 stages a comparison between Dante's and Virgil's art. Like the pointing hands that appear from time to time in the margins of medieval and Renaissance manuscripts, Virgil acts as a finger boldly indicating and glossing his own text within Dante's.

Despite scholarly concern over "the overly discussed differences between the Polydorus episode and Dante's creation," very little has actually been said regarding Virgil's staging of his own text within Dante's *Commedia*.[5] Among the scholars who have treated this issue, Étienne Gilson considers Dante's poetic strategy to be primarily mimetic. "The poet," he writes, "wants Virgil to show him the horrible spectacle, because he wants to force us to see too, in our minds, what words do not suffice to express. . . . The unhappy Pier della Vigna is victim of a vivisection, but this is required for the effective poetics of demonstration [poétique de la

---

3. Robert Hollander, *Allegory in Dante's "Commedia"* (Princeton: Princeton University Press, 1969), 76–93.

4. Many scholars of this canto have detected the presence of Ovid's *Metamorphoses* as an additional subtext, but Ettore Paratore, "Analisi 'retorica' del canto di Pier della Vigna," in *Tradizione e struttura in Dante* (Florence: Sansoni, 1968), argues well that the opening of the canto is "evidentemente ricalcato sull'episodio di Enea e Polidoro, come lo stesso poeta sottolinea al v. 48: 'ciò c'ha veduto *pur* con la mia rima': sì ch'è da prendere con cautela l'opinione di quei critici che basandosi sulla profonda conoscenza delle *Metamorfosi* da parte di Dante, hanno postulato l'influsso anche dell'episodio di Driope nel L. IX del poema ovidiano" (187, Paratore's emphasis).

5. The quoted observation belongs to Anthony K. Cassell, "Pier della Vigna's Metamorphosis: Iconography and History," in *Dante, Petrarch, Boccaccio: Studies in the Italian Trecento in Honor of Charles S. Singleton,* ed. Aldo S. Bernardo and Anthony L. Pellegrini (Binghamton: Medieval and Renaissance Texts and Studies, 1983), 46; Cassell in fact has absolutely nothing to say about the comparison between Dante and Virgil.

démonstration]."[6] Gilson's explanation tacitly accords with Charles Singleton's emphasis on the "substance of things seen" or Erich Auerbach's stress on Dante's extraordinary "representation of reality."[7] But Gilson's explanation also tends to reduce Virgil's demonstration to an almost gratuitous technical expedient employed by the poet to make his vision as vivid as possible. Viewing Virgil's demonstration strictly as a problem of representation, Gilson's analysis fails to indicate how the demonstration adds to the "vision" and why the poet simply does not have Virgil bid Dante break the branch without calling attention to his *Aeneid.* If the poet makes the wayfarer see so that the reader in turn can see, Gilson does not indicate why the poet does not have the wayfarer experience the reality directly, without the mediation of a "poétique de la démonstration." If the poet aims to render the wayfarer a participant in the reality, it is not clear from Gilson's discussion why Dante does not have the wayfarer accidentally break the twig, just as he has him "accidentally" thrust his boot into the gelid face of an outraged sinner in the lowest pit of hell (32.73–78).

This becomes a doubly problematic issue given Gilson's assertion that Dante has here suggested through Virgil's demonstration that words do not suffice to represent reality adequately. The wayfarer must experience reality directly because Virgil's "speech" [sermone] (21) and "poem" [rima] (48) cannot presumably do so. Yet by virtue of the same "poétique de la démonstration," the reader is then expected to see through the mediation of Dante's language exactly what the wayfarer sees. Language is thus both adequate and inadequate in its representation of reality. A solution to such an apparent contradiction, however, might be that for Dante the language of the *Commedia* represents reality adequately while the language of Virgil's *Aeneid* somehow fails—or more precisely, as W. R. Johnson has shown, refuses—to accomplish the same mimetic task.[8] Throughout the *Commedia,* Dante sets up contrasts that serve to measure the ontological gulf between his and Virgil's modes of representation. *Inferno* 3, for instance, opens with the reader confronting a reproduction, on the page, of precisely the same words the wayfarer sees engraved above the portal in

6. Étienne Gilson, "Poésie et théologie dans la *Divine Comédie,*" in *Atti del congresso internazionale di studi danteschi* (Florence: Sansoni, 1965), 214–15, my translation.

7. See the fourth chapter of Charles S. Singleton, *Dante's "Commedia": Elements of Structure* (Baltimore: Johns Hopkins University Press, 1954), 61–83; and Erich Auerbach, "Farinata and Cavalcante," in *Mimesis,* 174–202, as well as "Figura," in *Scenes from the Drama of European Literature: Six Essays,* trans. Ralph Manheim (New York: Meridian Books, 1959), 11–76.

8. Johnson, *Darkness Visible,* 40.

his initial descent. Aeneas, by contrast, begins his descent in book 6 by gazing on an unfinished human artifact. Where Virgil intervenes to provide the reader with an explanation of what might have been represented, Dante realizes the supplement of language into an actual re-representation of things seen and thereby opens the *Inferno* proper by seeming to assert the capacity of language to represent—a language that feigns to belong not to an intruding poet but to God.[9]

The differences in these respective positions regarding representation— a mortal art, on the one hand, in which mortal things touch the heart, and, on the other hand, an art that feigns divinity—should be understood in the *Commedia* as an issue of both moral and epistemological concern. The "blurred uncertainties" of Virgil's representation of reality, while accomplished in defiance of the Homeric mimetic tradition, stand in Dante's *Commedia* as an index of Virgil's inability to see adequately on account of a profound historical and epistemological blindness.[10] As Erich Auerbach, Charles Singleton, and others have demonstrated to varying degrees, Dante owes his realism not so much to Virgil but to the "allegory of theologians" and, ultimately, to the Incarnation, which provides the transcendent controlling model of the Word made flesh.[11] Since the pagan Virgil lacks this transcendent source of meaning, how could he have ever

---

9. Hollander treats this issue in his *Allegory;* John Freccero treats the problem in terms of Romantic irony in an effort to define the poetics of the *Inferno,* in "Infernal Irony: The Gates of Hell," in *Dante: The Poetics of Conversion,* ed. Rachel Jacoff (Cambridge: Harvard University Press, 1986), 93–109. To cite another example where Dante implicitly compares his mode of representation with Virgil's, one might here recall, to remain within the bounds of comparative treatments of ecphrasis, Aeneas reading the pictures on Juno's temple and the wayfarer's experience of the images on the first terrace of Mount Purgatory. Whereas Aeneas's viewing is a highly subjective reading of a mortal art that tells the story about mortal things that touch the heart, Dante insists that the art the wayfarer views is God's art and as such is more real than reality, producing an experience that invades his senses from without. Virgil instructs the wayfarer how to look at the images he sees; the poet of the *Commedia* can be said to have revealed to Virgil how those images should be represented. For a detailed treatment of the ecphrasis in canto 10, see chapter 6 of Teodolinda Barolini, *The Undivine "Comedy": Detheologizing Dante* (Princeton: Princeton University Press, 1992).

10. On Virgil's antimimetic style, compared to Homer, see above all the study of Johnson, *Darkness Visible.*

11. Auerbach, *Scenes from the Drama of European Literature,* 11–76; Singleton's important study on the allegory of theologians appears in "Appendix: Two Kinds of Allegory," in his *Dante's "Commedia",* 84–98; Hollander develops the observations of Auerbach and Singleton throughout his *Allegory.* For the centrality of the Incarnation in Dante's mode of representation, see Singleton, "The Irreducible Dove," *Comparative Literature* 9 (1957): 129–35; and, above all, Marcia L. Colish, *The Mirror of Language: A Study in the Medieval Theory of Knowledge* (New Haven: Yale University Press, 1968), who traces the centrality of the Incarnation in Augustinian semiotics to Dante.

represented reality accurately or adequately? The first part of canto 13 addresses just this question. It places Virgil as a reader of his own poem and reveals his inadequacy in foreseeing and speaking about his marvel that he is now revisiting in Dante's *Inferno.* By contrast, the Christian wayfarer, though accused of lacking faith in Virgil's speech and poem, dimly anticipates the fulfillment of Virgil's marvel as a reality in a Christian universe. The wayfarer's faith in the *Aeneid* and Virgil's speech, as it turns out, exceeds Virgil's faith in his own poem and its rhetoric in canto 13. Though the wayfarer is an actor in a drama staged by Virgil, this drama is in turn staged by the poet.

For a long time the thirteenth canto was considered Pier della Vigna's canto; his name headed it in most editions of the *Commedia.* But in many ways this canto is Virgil's, and in the opening section much takes place for his benefit and at his expense. Virgil urges the wayfarer to break the branch. Virgil, not the wayfarer, converses with Pier della Vigna. Indeed, the poet strategically silences the wayfarer: the one time Dante speaks in the entire canto, he begs Virgil to speak in his stead (13.82–84). Throughout the first part of the canto, Virgil thus mediates the wayfarer's thoughts. We hear what the poet believes Virgil believed the wayfarer believed (13.25); we hear Virgil declare how he believes the wayfarer read his *Aeneid* (13.46); we hear Virgil frame the thoughts of the wayfarer because the latter is too moved to speak after hearing Pier della Vigna tell the story of his political downfall and suicide (13.82–83). In each of these instances the word employed is *credere.* We never actually hear the wayfarer articulate his own thoughts. We only hear what Virgil believes.

As Francesco D'Ovidio long ago observed, Virgil urges the wayfarer to break the branch largely because Virgil believes he has read the Polydorus episode as incredible fiction: "Here Virgil has his mind on his Polydorus; he reflects with a certain satisfaction that Dante, if he believed that the story of the *Aeneid* was poetic falsehood [fandonia poetica], a pure, impossible fable [mera favola], must think again and touch the real truth, at least down there."[12] By prompting the wayfarer to break the branch, Virgil proves his poem is not "fandonia poetica" or "mera favola," but—as Gian Roberto Sarolli observed—*historia,* much as the *Aeneid* is ironically con-

12. Francesco D'Ovidio, "Il canto di Pier della Vigna," in *Nuovi studii danteschi* (Milan: Hoepli, 1907), 215, my translation; see also 217.

ceived in the second book of the *De monarchia.* There Dante posits Virgil, along with Livy and Lucan, as a faithful witness to historical events.[13]

Yet inasmuch as Virgil's demonstration in canto 13 defines his own poem as *historia,* it raises a problem by classifying the *Aeneid* by negation. Virgil has presumably acted on the assumption that the wayfarer would never have considered the events of the Polydorus episode to be anything other than "fandonia poetica." The obvious question is why, at this juncture in the *Inferno,* does Virgil believe the wayfarer would have doubted the legitimacy of the *Aeneid* as a faithful description of real events? I suggest that Virgil's doubt in the wayfarer's faith reflects instead his own doubt about his poem's capacity to persuade and represent the incredible. The opening of canto 13, I argue, makes Virgil a reader of his own poem and reveals his inadequacy in foreseeing and speaking about the fulfillment of his marvel as revisited in Dante's *Inferno.* But to see how this is so, one must first explain why Dante chose the Polydorus episode, not so much as the model for his realm of the suicides, but as the model—to borrow Gilson's felicitous phrase—for Virgil's *and Dante's* "poétique de la démonstration."[14]

---

13. *Mon.* 2.3.6: nam divinus poeta noster Virgilius per totam *Eneydem* gloriosissimum regem Eneam patrem romani populi fuisse testatur in memoriam sempiternam; quod Titus Livius, gestorum romanorum scriba egregius, in prima parte sui voluminis, que a capta Troya summit exordium, contestatur (see also 2.3.11). Citations of the *De monarchia* are from Dante Alighieri, *De monarchia,* ed. Pier Giorgio Ricci, vol. 5 of *Le opere di Dante Alighieri* (Verona: Mondadori, 1965). For the comments of Gian Roberto Sarolli, see his *Prolegomena alla "Divina Commedia"* (Florence: Olschki, 1971), 140.

14. D'Ovidio, "Il canto di Pier della Vigna," in *Nuovi studii danteschi,* answered this question by declaring that Dante's choice was inevitable. The Polydorus episode was so dramatic that when Dante came to write the thirteenth canto he simply found the correct moment when he could put the episode to use, the breaking of the branch offering the perfect *contrapasso* for the sin of the suicides: those who separated themselves from their bodies are now eternally severed. Along these lines, some have maintained that the connection between the two episodes is that there simply is no connection: the innocent Polydorus is killed, whereas Pier della Vigna kills himself. Antithesis thus structures the relationship between Virgil's episode and Dante's version. Though this may be the case, critics have since failed to investigate the irony inherent in such an antithesis.

In an effort to seize on a thematic thread between Dante's and Virgil's version, both Cassell, "Pier della Vigna's Metamorphosis," and William Kennedy, "Irony, Allegoresis, and Allegory," have brought into play the allegorical reading of the Polydorus episode in Bernardus Silvestris's commentary of the *Aeneid.* By doing so they offer plausible, though contradictory, explanations as to why Dante associated the woods of the suicides with Virgil's Polydorus episode. Many scholars, however, have also demonstrated in recent years the self-conscious directness of Dante's readings of pagan literature, thereby placing him in a literary agon with his classical heritage in a way that is familiarly Bloomian, though not always characterized by scholars as such. See, for example, Hollander's *Allegory,* the last chapter of his *Stud-*

In the Polydorus episode in the *Aeneid,* Aeneas risks pollution three times by returning to tear a bleeding branch from the ground. After the third rending of the branch, a voice emerges from within the tomb. At this, Aeneas may be said to have come to understand the deep hidden causes. But his knowledge remains only partial. He knows the circumstances— Polydorus was struck down because of Polymestor's greed, and the spears that pierced him grew into branches—but he never understands the meaning of the bleeding branch. He does not attempt to probe further either, because, as Polydorus makes clear, to continue would pollute his pious hands: "Parce pias scelerare manus" [Spare the pollution of thy pure hands] (3.42). Aeneas's purity, though threatened, must remain intact, and though it may be argued that his hands have already been stained by the threefold rending of the branches, for him to seek the causes of things any further would surely make contamination inescapable. The realm of the impure is a realm that Aeneas must always avoid.

In Dante's poem, one must pass through the impure to arrive at knowledge of the self and of the higher truths that move the universe and govern its laws. As the wayfarer travels through the infernal realm to where the light of the stars issues in from the portal of Mount Purgatory, he is made to confront every crime, no matter how heinous and impure it may seem. Aeneas makes a similar descent in Virgil's poem. But when he arrives at the crossroads of hell, the sibyl can only relate hearsay information about the punishments suffered beyond the iron towers of Dis, for "nulli fas casto sceleratum insistere limen" [no pure soul may tread the accursed threshold] (6.563).[15] The word *sceleratum* in book 6, as in the Polydorus episode, where both *scelerare* (42) and *scelerata* (60) are used, connotes the realm of impurity. Aeneas descends, but his knowledge of the impure remains limited because he must maintain his purity. As a sign of his purity, he is cleansed and leaves the golden bough before entering the Elysian fields. In Dante's poem, however, by stopping at the edge and hearing only what lies beyond through hearsay, one would miss the deeper mysteries.

---

ies in Dante (Ravenna: Longo, 1980), and his *Il Virgilio Dantesco: Tragedia nella "Commedia"* (Florence: Olschki, 1983), chaps. 2 and 3; Teodolinda Barolini, *Dante's Poets: Textuality and Truth in the "Comedy"* (Princeton: Princeton University Press, 1984); Jeffrey T. Schnapp, *The Transfiguration of History at the Center of Paradise* (Princeton: Princeton University Press, 1986), which analyzes Dante's revision in *Paradise* of Aeneas's encounter with Anchises in the sixth book of the *Aeneid;* and now the collection of essays in Rachel Jacoff and Jeffrey T. Schnapp, eds., *The Poetry of Allusion: Virgil and Ovid in Dante's "Commedia"* (Stanford: Stanford University Press, 1991), in which a shorter version of this chapter was published.

15. I owe this observation to Diskin Clay.

The Polydorus episode still stands apart in the *Aeneid* as the one moment when Aeneas is willing to risk impurity for knowledge, the one moment when he comes, by his own force, closest to penetrating mysteries, the "deep hidden causes" [causas penitus . . . latentis] (3.32). For the poet of the *Commedia,* Aeneas's frustrated desire to know could only have represented Virgil's desire, and refusal, to know those same mysteries. Through Aeneas's actions in the Polydorus episode, Virgil approached, yet finally shied away from, envisioning the realm of the impure. Virgil's knowledge, like Aeneas's, must therefore remain partial in the *Commedia.* He may understand the bleeding branch as a pagan reality, but the fulfillment of his marvel as an objective reality in God's Christian universe will have to remain for Virgil an experience about which he can at first hardly speak.

In the *Aeneid,* the mystery of the bleeding branch resides at least as much in language as in the concrete reality of the marvel, which Aeneas has experienced and remembers vividly. At the outset of the episode, Aeneas utters the emblematic phrase "dictu uideo mirabile monstrum" [I see an awful portent, wondrous to tell] (3.26), and in his editorializing comments to Dido he frames the question: "eloquar an sileam?" [Should I speak or be silent?] (3.39). The marvel in the first phrase occupies the status of an object seen by the subject in his memory ("monstrum uideo"). But the Virgilian formula *dictu mirabile* shifts the emphasis away from the marvel as an objective reality, previously witnessed firsthand, to focus on the narrator's subjective reality, which lies in the act of representing as marvelous. The narrator sees ("uideo") and his vision is transformed into gazing, a concept evoked by the word *mirabile,* from *miror.* But insofar as the reality envisioned is wondrous to gaze at ("mirabile"), the recollected vision of the *monstrum* is then rendered opaque by the mediation of language ("dictu") and incorporated back into the distanced speaking subject who retrospectively recounts it. This passage away from the envisioned object as a marvelous reality to the reality of telling as a marvel, *mirabile dictu,* does not deny, though it nevertheless places in question, the overall adequacy of language to represent. This becomes particularly evident when the narrator wonders whether language could ever accomplish the task of describing the fabulous event: "eloquar an sileam?" The marvel is wondrous to tell, perhaps "too wondrous to tell," and it is also something about which it is perhaps better to remain cautiously silent.

In the thirteenth canto, Dante registers Aeneas's apprehension about language's adequacy to represent the incredible, and he does so through

Virgil. Soon after entering the woods, Virgil refrains from telling what the wayfarer is about to see because he attributes to the wayfarer a lack of faith in his "sermone," even though the wayfarer has heretofore never questioned the reliability of Virgil's speech. This apprehension on Virgil's part recalls Aeneas's doubts about whether he should speak. For Virgil to remain silent at the moment when he anticipates the fulfillment of his marvel in the otherworld is telling. He has come upon his own marvel, not in memory but in experience, and he now finds his rhetoric wanting. More important, once the wayfarer breaks the branch, Virgil, who refused to describe the event, is pained, as though in Dante's poem the language of the *Aeneid* had achieved through experience a validity he never quite imagined: "ma la cosa incredibile mi fece / indurlo ad ovra ch'a me stesso pesa" [But the incredible thing made me prompt him to a deed that grieves me] (13.50–51).[16] Apparently, one effect of fulfilling Virgil's marvel through a "poétique de la démonstration" is to turn Polydorus's speeches into things. In contrast to Virgil's episode, in which the voice that emerges from Polydorus's tomb is divorced from the substance that oozes from the branches, as though the purity of the signifying speech must remain separated from any contaminating contact with the substantive blood, in Dante's *Commedia* blood and voice have instead, as Spitzer showed, been "fused together" in "the single phrase *usciva insieme parole e sangue* . . . : there gushes forth a stream of 'speech-endowed blood,' of 'bleeding screams'—a hideous revelation of the hybrid which we must accept as a unit-manifestation, because of the singular verb *usciva*."[17] The hidden, mysterious causes that Aeneas desperately sought have here been unified and realized into a sign of God's judgment on a sinner.

In the *Inferno*, the Incarnation is the transcendent controlling model of meaning, and it exerts its force with a vengeance, through the inversion of *contrapasso*; in this episode it makes the word not flesh but blood. Yet despite this transformation, Virgil's proof, which the overseeing poet stages, controls, and dramatizes, is directed not so much against the text of

---

16. As Giuseppe Mazzotta succinctly notes in terms congenial to this reading, "Virgil, who has described the scene in the *Aeneid* and now asserts his authorship ('ciò c'ha veduto pur con la *mia* rima'), is himself perplexed by the experience he confronts (ll.50–51), as if the reality they witness exceeds his language" (*Dante, Poet of the Desert: History and Allegory in the "Divine Comedy"* [Princeton: Princeton University Press, 1979], 189; Mazzotta's emphasis). Mazzotta's observations derive in part, as do Sarolli's in a much more direct fashion, from Spitzer's note in his seminal article on the thirteenth canto, in "Speech and Language," 83. Teodolinda Barolini has a brief, incisive reading of the episode in her *Dante's Poets*, 212.

17. Spitzer, "Speech and Language," 88.

the *Aeneid* (here in truth fulfilled) as against the author of the *Aeneid,* to take possession of his poem. Though Virgil ostensibly conducts his demonstration for the benefit of the wayfarer, the poet of the *Commedia* has fashioned out of Virgil's demonstration a dramatic proof for the poet of the *Aeneid.* Virgil's proof has in effect turned back on itself and revealed that even the most outrageous events of the *Aeneid* have a fulfillment in the otherworld that exceeds his ken, vision, and language. In the thirteenth canto, Virgil becomes just one more reader of his own poem, and as such, he turns out to be less than reliable in his response to a thoroughly reliable prophetic poem, once that poem, torn from its original owner, belongs to Dante.

This is not the only time that Virgil misreads. In another passage from the opening of the thirteenth canto, after the wayfarer halts in the woods, the poet recalls,

Cred'ïo ch'ei credette ch'io credesse
che tante voci uscisser, tra quei bronchi,
da gente che per noi si nascondesse.

(13.25–28)

[I believe that he believed that I believed that all those voices from amid the trunks came from people who were hidden from us.]

The poet's words in this tercet refuse to guarantee a stable understanding of what either Virgil or the wayfarer thought.[18] The verse *cred'ïo ch'ei credette ch'io credesse* cannot be reductively equated—as it so often is—with the phrase *the wayfarer believed.* The subjunctive mood of the final verb, *credesse,* defines the overall atmosphere of uncertainty. The phrase *I believe he believed I believed* articulates not a stable passage of thought but

---

18. The rhetorical play of the repeated verb *credere* has often been taken as a proleptic echo of Pier della Vigna's manner of speech. The poet, following a widespread practice in the *Commedia* of historical characterization, anticipates Pier della Vigna's presence by deliberately imitating his voice. Yet by such a reading alone, the verse *cred'io . . . ,* in furnishing a linguistic portrait, only has significance through form; along these lines, some seek to base the meaning of the verse on a sympathetic or unsympathetic reading of Pier della Vigna's style, a meaning that often tends to rest in turn on a prior decision as to whether the poet shares the wayfarer's sympathy toward the sinner. Spitzer, "Speech and Language," 18, instead considers "the verse *cred'io . . .* to be the 'onomatopoeic' rendering of [the wayfarer's] mental state of estrangement and confusion"; he assumes the words have meaning, but he also seems to assume that the poet's thoughts faithfully reproduce the wayfarer's state of mind and that the structure of the verse reproduces the wayfarer's estrangement rather than the poet's irony.

a highly ironic sequence of misinterpretations, with Virgil as the disruptive mediating link. The poet is reading Virgil's mind, who has in turn misread the wayfarer's mind, attributing to him the uncertain belief that the voices emerging from the trees belong to people hiding behind them.[19] The poet believes this to be the case. Though it may not be so, the poet offers this as a plausible explanation as to why Virgil at first had the wayfarer break the branch: "Però disse 'l maestro . . ." [Therefore the master said . . .] (13.28).

Virgil's insistence makes the gesture of breaking into an interpretive act, much as it was for Aeneas, who sought deep hidden causes:

> "Se tu tronchi
> qualche fraschetta d'una d'este piante,
> li pensier c'hai si faran tutti monchi."

> (13.28–30)

["If you break off a little branch from one of these plants, the thoughts you have will all be cut short"]

Only by rending ("tronchi"), Virgil claims, will the wayfarer's thoughts ("pensier") be "cut short" [monchi]. By contrast with Aeneas's repeated and aggressive rending of the branch, the wayfarer's violence in the thirteenth canto has been reduced to a bare minimum; but its effect has been amplified. It is as though the causes the wayfarer seeks are apparent, so apparent that only a superfluous effort is required to reveal them. He grips a twig ("ramicel"), and the immediacy of the spirit's reaction, expressed by the repeated "e . . . e" at the beginning of verses 32 and 33, implies that only a narrow interval of time has elapsed between the breaking of the branch and the spirit's cry, as though the two acts were in fact simultaneous. No sooner has the wayfarer plucked ("colsi," 13.32) than the stub cries ("e 'l tronco suo gridò," 13.33) and bleeds profusely: "Da che fatto fu poi di sangue bruno" (13.34). The violence inflicted on Pier della Vigna is at once evident.

But the violence in this scene, though enacted by the wayfarer and inflicted on Pier della Vigna, is ultimately directed back on Virgil through

---

19. To my knowledge, the only scholars to have commented on this fact, both of whom have contributed to my understanding of the passage, are Umberto Bosco, "Il canto dei suicidi (XIII dell'*Inferno*)," in *Dante vicino* (Caltanisetta and Rome: Salvatore Sciascia, 1966), 261; and, in a highly suggestive and convincing manner, Sebastiano Agliano, "Lettura del canto XIII dell'*Inferno,*" *Studi danteschi* 33 (1955): 152–53.

the poet's irony. Virgil has the wayfarer break a plant to cut short thoughts. In doing so, however, he has the wayfarer reenact Aeneas's interpretive violence to eliminate thoughts that may well never have even been there to begin with. We do not know what the wayfarer thought. Yet when he holds out his hand to break the branch, he extends it hesitantly, "un poco avante" [a little forward] (13.31).[20] If understanding requires an act of violence, the wayfarer may be said to have here probed with the reserve of someone who already knows. Virgil has the wayfarer reenact Aeneas's interpretive gesture to seek deep hidden causes, yet everything about this cautious gesture implies that the wayfarer has already anticipated the result. The gesture signals, in its tentativeness, recognition.

The poet's assimilation of the marvel of the Polydorus episode in the *Commedia* thus becomes an index of Virgil's blindness and the wayfarer's insight. Just as the marvels in the *Aeneid* repeatedly reflect Aeneas's inability to comprehend the drama he must enact, so Dante retroactively uses Virgil's marvel against the poet of the *Aeneid* to reflect Virgil's blindness to the true prophetic power of his poem. At the same time, when the poet composes the *Commedia,* he in turn represents the fabulous event not as a marvel that takes away his power of speech but as a credible historical fact demonstrated by Virgil and dimly foreseen by the wayfarer, who hesitatingly holds out his hand. In this way, whereas Virgil in the *Aeneid* permits history to give meaning to the marvel of the Polydorus episode through a distanced allusion to the founding of Rome in the sprouting of Romulus's spear on the Palatine hill, Dante transforms Virgil's marvel into an event that actually took place, an event that can only find its true full meaning in his *Commedia.*

Dante's poetic strategy throughout the *Commedia* is to historicize the marvelous, to assert repeatedly that everything that takes place in this voyage must be understood as credible and real, in part because everything exists in a universe ordered by God, but above all because the poet, as the wayfarer, witnessed these events and has returned to tell us about them. For example, when the poet recalls how he beheld Geryon, the fabulous hybrid creature that rose out of the abyss of lower hell (*Inf.* 16.124–36), he hesitates, wondering whether he should narrate the truth ("ver," 124) of what he saw even if it should seem a lie ("menzogna," 124). But he cannot be silent, and he swears by the notes of his own "comedia" (128) that what he saw was truly there. What the poet recalls here is "marvelous" [ma-

---

20. The observation of hesitancy is Singleton's in Dante Alighieri, *The Divine Comedy,* 1:207.

ravigliosa] (132). But his reaction is the opposite of Virgil's at revisiting his own marvel in Dante's poem. In the thirteenth canto, Virgil refuses to speak, indicating that his language, within the *Commedia* as in the *Aeneid,* fails to represent the incredibile. The poet of the *Commedia,* however, recalls Geryon and insists that he is compelled to speak: "qui tacer nol posso" [But here I cannot be silent] (16.127). His insistence, which has no other justification than the poet's own authorial claim, assures us that his language is somehow sufficient to represent what he assumes everyone would deem "maravigliosa."[21] The poet's rhetorical strategy in both the thirteenth and sixteenth cantos, however, is essentially the same. The poet points back to his own text—in the thirteenth canto through Virgil's demonstration—as the source that self-sufficiently generates and encloses its own meaning, as well as the meaning of Virgil's poem. The poet may rely on his own text, not so much because he has been commanded to write it by Beatrice and Cacciaguida, but because he is the same person who saw the things about which he tells. In doing so, he has written, at least according to the definition of Hugh of St. Victor, *historia,* much as "Mandeville" will later do by inversely yoking a patent falsehood in content ("menzogna") onto the familiar genre of historical truth ("ver"). To ask, then, why we believe, or are asked to believe, in the events of the *Commedia* is to inquire why we believe, or are asked to believe, in any self-authenticating medieval "travelogue" that chronicles wondrous events witnessed by a pilgrim on a voyage through strange and unfamiliar lands.[22]

If there is a single, overriding event that therefore sustains and guarantees the historical validity of all that occurs in the *Commedia* (no matter how incredible the poet's vision becomes), it is the poet's self-authenticating, autobiographical claim that he actually undertook a voyage through the otherworld. No event in the entire poem consistently evokes such wonder from the sinners and the repentant who occupy the first two realms of

---

21. For readings of Geryon as an emblem of the *Commedia* within the *Commedia,* see Barolini, *The Undivine "Comedy,"* chap. 3; Zygmunt Barański, "The 'Marvellous' and the 'Comic': Toward a Reading of *Inferno* XVI," *Lectura Dantis: A Forum for Dante Research and Interpretation* 7 (1990): 72–95, which gives particular attention to issues of the marvelous; and Franco Ferrucci, "Comedia," *Yearbook of Italian Studies* 1 (1971): 29–52. My own reading has been strongly shaped by the observations of Mazzotta, *Dante, Poet of the Desert.*

22. On medieval travelogues as a genre, see the introduction and first chapters of Campbell, *The Witness and the Other World;* and the first chapter of Greenblatt, *Marvelous Possessions,* which contains a discussion of Mandeville in particular. On the marvelous in medieval thought, see Le Goff, *L'imaginaire médiéval.*

the otherworld. "Qual maraviglia!" [What a marvel!] (15.24), Brunetto Latini cries out upon fixing Dante with his squinting, piercing gaze and seizing the hem of his Florentine robe. The sinners in the *bolgia* (ditch) of the seditious momentarily forget the lacerating pain of their punishments when they hear Virgil inform them that Dante, still in his body, is on a journey through the Inferno "per dar lui esperïenza piena" [in order to give him full experience] (28.48). Pier da Medicina, his throat pierced, his nose lopped off, and one ear missing, pauses in the *bolgia* of the seditious "a riguardar per maraviglia / con li altri" [with the rest to gaze in astonishment] (28.67–68). In the second canto of the *Purgatorio,* the souls newly arrived on the shore recognize that Dante breathed and "maravigliando diventaro smorte" [marveling grew pale] (2.69). A canto later, a throng of late-repenters, after being likened to timid sheep, step back in fright when they notice the light broken on the ground by the wayfarer's side. Virgil, seeing their timid amazement, assures them that there is no reason to marvel ("Non vi maravigliate," 3.97), for the wayfarer voyages alive in the world of the dead by divine will. Under nearly identical circumstances, the wayfarer is singled out in the fifth canto of the *Purgatorio:* "e vidile guardar per maraviglia / pur me, pur me, e 'l lume ch'era rotto" [and [I] saw them gazing in astonishment at me alone, at me alone, and the light that was broken] (5.8–9). In the fourteenth canto of the *Purgatorio,* two repentant sinners on the terrace of the envious marvel with upturned faces after overhearing the wayfarer's assertion to Sapia that he is moving through the otherworld in his actual bodily form (14.13–15). In the sixteenth canto of the *Purgatorio,* on the terrace of the wrathful, the wayfarer self-confidently lures an unseen repentant sinner to follow him with the assurance "maraviglia udirai" [You will hear a marvel] (16. 33). The marvel the repentant Marco Lombardo will hear is that the wayfarer has traveled in bodily form through the Inferno and now is on his way to God's realm, "per modo tutto fuor del moderno uso" [in a manner wholly outside modern usage] (16.42). Time and again, the marveling of the sinners in hell and the repentant in purgatory affirm the historical validity of the *Commedia* by reenforcing the corporeal reality of the wayfarer. That is Dante's surest means of preserving and evoking wonder.

What sort of wonder is this, then? Indeed, what sorts of wonder govern the *Commedia* generally?[23] To answer these questions, we may begin by

23. Some of these questions have been addressed by Patrick Boyde in *Dante Philomythes and Philosopher: Man in the Cosmos* (Cambridge: Cambridge University Press, 1981), 43–56.

turning to the second book of the *De monarchia,* where Dante argues along Aristotelian lines that marveling and ignorance are related:[24]

Sicut ad faciem cause non pertingentes novum effectum comuniter admiramur, sic, cum causam cognoscimus, eos qui sunt in admiratione restantes quadam derisione despicimus. (*Mon.* 2.1.2)

[Just as we marvel at a new effect [or fact], not being able to perceive the cause, so, as soon as we know the cause, we look down with a certain disdain at those who continue in their marveling.][25]

The awareness of underlying causes instantaneously puts a stop to wonder and inspires disdain toward those who continue to wonder. Yet disdain, Dante insists, dissipates under the warmth of man's natural love, giving way to a didactic desire to reveal the truth through edifying treatises, such as the *De monarchia,* and to illumine the minds of those who remain ignorant (2.1.5–6).[26]

To dispel the wayfarer's false beliefs, his ignorance, and his marveling—to reveal the "causes of things" no matter how novel the effects of the otherworld may seem—is just one of Virgil's functions in the poem as the wayfarer's guide, a function that is often as humanely endearing as it is abstractly and schematically allegorical. But some events stubbornly remain marvels for Virgil. The fulfillment of the Polydorus episode in a

---

24. See, for the Aristotelian text, *Metaphysics* 982b9–10. Boyde, *Dante Philomythes,* is particularly good on this, but he also has, to my mind, an overly felicitous view of Dante's appropriation of the *Metaphysics:* disdain, which does not enter into Aristotle's philosophy with respect to the marvelous, has a large role to play in Dante's theology and aesthetics. For its transmission through the Middle Ages as an "aesthetic," see Cunningham, *Woe and Wonder.*

25. Dante's language is deliberately harsh here. He speaks of looking down ("despicimus") with a certain disdain ("quadam derisione") because he is about to deride the Guelph propagandists of the times who contumaciously persist in asserting that the Roman race occupied the world by force while, in the meantime, having fixed the eyes of his mind deeply into the problem and no longer superficially, Dante had come to perceive a divine plan: "Sed postquam medullitus oculos mentis infixi et per efficacissima signa divinam providentiam hoc effecisse cognovi, admiratione cedente, derisiva quedam supervenit despectio, cum gentes noverim contra romani populi preheminentiam fremuisse, cum videam populos vana meditantes, ut ipse solebam, cum insuper doleam reges et principes in hoc unico concordantes: ut adversentur Domino suo et Uncto suo, romano principi" (*Mon.* 2.1.3–4).

26. This happy passage of thought, in which disdain dissipates as truth is unveiled, functions well in theory but never quite in practice in Dante's *De monarchia.* Dante not only edifies but also continues to passionately deride and disdain those who stubbornly persist in their false beliefs regarding the divine right of the Roman Empire.

Christian universe pains Virgil even after he has urged the wayfarer to learn and experience the truth. In *Inferno* 23, Virgil learns who Caiaphas is and why he suffers; yet after learning the "causes of things" here, Virgil still marvels:

Allor vid' io maravigliar Virgilio
sovra colui ch'era disteso in croce
tanto vilmente ne l'etterno essilio.

(23.124–26)

[Then I saw Virgil wonder over him who was thus outstretched, as on a cross, so vilely in the eternal exile.]

Virgil's reason—his "natural light," to borrow Singleton's adaptation of scholastic terminology[27]—does not allow him to penetrate the novelty of Christian history and the sign of the cross. Certain causes, certain truths, remain marvels over which Virgil can only puzzle, however admiringly, without ever reaching full understanding. So, too, in a poignant moment, Virgil marvels as *his* journey to Beatrice ends. In the Garden of Eden, a sudden brightness floods the forest, melodic music passes through the luminous air, and seven monumental candlesticks—seeming like seven gold trees at first—advance. The symbolic pageant preceding Beatrice's advent has just begun, and the wayfarer, full of wonder, turns to Virgil, whom he discovers to be no less amazed at the sight of these wondrous new things:

Io mi rivolsi d'ammirazion pieno
al buon Virgilio, ed esso mi rispuose
con vista carca di stupor non meno.

(29.55–57)

[I turned round full of wonder to the good Virgil, and he answered me with a look no less charged with amazement.]

The next time the wayfarer turns to speak to Virgil, in *Purgatorio* 30, his guide has disappeared, for Beatrice has arrived.

---

27. In Charles S. Singleton, *Journey to Beatrice* (Baltimore: Johns Hopkins University Press, 1977).

Though there is no patent derision of Virgil's marveling in the *Commedia,* Dante's disdain is latent in his strategy of authorial subversion. Consider how the poet registers Virgil's amazement by means of a subtle echo from the *Aeneid.* Not only is the word *stupor* used in the very last description of Virgil in the *Commedia,* but that word, used sparingly before in the poem (*Purg.* 15.12, 26.71), is applied to Virgil here for the very first time. The word may thus here echo Virgil's descriptions of Aeneas as "stupet inscius" (10.249)—Aeneas is so described, for example, when he stands in ignorance before the omen of the ships turned into nymphs—or Virgil's application of the closely related word *obstipescere* to Aeneas on a variety of occasions (1.513; 2.560, 774; 3.48, 298; 5.90). With Beatrice's advent, Virgil is ironically presented, now for the first and last time, as he repeatedly presented Aeneas—as always at the edge of a truth, as at best cheered by the omen of the marvels he sees but does not understand, just as Aeneas was cheered when he saw the nymphs.

Here as elsewhere in the *Commedia,* Virgil's marveling remains ignorant, cut off from the source of truth's revelation, trapped, as in the Polydorus episode, within an inadequate language never quite sufficient to represent things the way they were or are. He perceives Christian truths through a glass darkly and is forever perplexed by the novel reality of Christian history. Marveling, to borrow from Albert the Great's definition, is here a "suspensionem cordis in stuporem prodigii magni in sensum apparentis" [suspension of the heart caused by amazement at the sensible appearance of something portentous, great, and unusual]. Yet marveling in this instance is also a suspension that never seems to move Virgil beyond stupor into knowledge. It is a marveling that also characterizes the realm, likewise constructed "ex suspensione," to which Virgil must and will return: limbo.[28] Not surprisingly, the closer Virgil approaches Beatrice, the more he marvels, in the generative wonder of a soul seeking a truth it will never fully apprehend. He is therefore last described in the

---

28. I cite the translation of Albert the Great from Cunningham, *Woe or Wonder,* 79, and the Latin from Albertus Magnus, *Opera Omnia,* ed. Augustus Borgnet (Paris: Ludovicus Vives, 1890), 6:30: "Admirationem autem vocamus agoniam et suspensionem cordis in stuporem prodigii magni in sensum apparentis, ita quod cor systolem patitur. Propter quod etiam admiratio aliquid simile habit timori in motu cordis, qui est ex suspensione. Hujus igitur motus admirationis in agonia et systole cordis est ex suspensione desiderii ad cognoscendam causam entis quod apparet prodigii: et ideo a principio cum adhuc rudes philosophari inceperunt, mirantes erant quaedam dubitabilium quae paratiora erant ad solvendum." That Dante understood wonder to operate in this fashion is evident from *Par.* 32.92 and, in particular, *Par.* 20.86–87: "lo benedetto segno mi rispuose / per non tenermi in ammirar sospeso."

Commedia as "carca di stupor" [charged [or, more precisely, burdened] with stupor], a state defined in Dante's *Il convivio* as

uno stordimento d'animo per grandi e maravigliose cose vedere o udire o per alcuno modo sentire: che, in quanto paiono grandi, fanno reverente a sè quelli che le sente; in quanto paiono mirabili, fanno voglioso di sapere di quelle. (4.25.5–6)[29]

[a bewilderment of the spirit from seeing or hearing or in some way perceiving great and marvelous things, which, inasmuch as they seem great, make reverent those who perceive them, inasmuch as they seem wondrous, induce the desire to know about them.]

Virgil, as Dante's definition avers, has, with Beatrice's advent, been permitted to witness things that appear marvelous ("paiono mirabili"). But in his suspended wonder, Virgil may only marvel in reverent awe, "voglioso di sapere" [desirous to know], at the preparation for the revelation that is about to descend.

The blessed, by contrast, will never wonder in "stupor," for there are no marvels for those who know the truth. The wayfarer indeed wonders initially about the things that he sees. In the first canto of the *Paradiso,* he is filled with "grande ammirazion" [great wonder] (1.98) at his ascent, and he marvels how he can pass through the light bodies of heaven (1.8–9). In canto 2 he beholds as a "mirabil cosa" [wondrous thing] his entrance into the gleaming, polished body of the moon, which curiously lacks the dark spots seen from the outside down on earth (2.25). He later marvels, as the starry eagle acknowledges, over the salvation of the pagans Trajan and Ripheus (20.87, 101). And he marvels as he had never marveled before over the Virgin Mary enthroned at the zenith of the celestial rose (32.91–92). The wayfarer wonders in paradise, yet time and again his wondering must be cut short.[30] To wonder is to confess ignorance, though an

---

29. All citations of Dante's *Il Convivio* are Dante Alighieri, *"Il Convivio" ridotto a miglior lezione e commentato,* ed. G. Busnelli and G. Vandelli, vols. 4–5 of *Opere di Dante,* vol. 4 ed. Michele Barbi; vol. 5 ed. Vittore Branca, Francesco Maggini, and Bruno Nardi, Fondazione Giorgio Cini (Florence: Le Monnier, 1934 and 1954). See in particular the note ad locum for further references to Aquinas.

30. He must not wonder over his ascent, for it would be a marvel instead, Beatrice claims, had he drifted down below (1.139–40). Nor must he marvel that the moon's dense body is a shining penetrable globe unmarred by the dark spots viewed from earth (2.56–57). "Non ti maravigliar," Beatrice insists when she smiles at his confusion (3.25); "non ti maravigliar," she

ignorance that may propel an inquiring mind, such as the wayfarer's, on a voyage toward knowledge. As Albert the Great wrote:

Qui autem dubitat et admiratur, ignorans videtur: est enim admiratio motus ignorantis procedentis ad inquirendum, ut sciat causam ejus de quo miratur: cujus signum est, quia ipse Philomithes secundum hunc modum Philosophus est: quia fabula sua construitur ab ipso ex mirandis. Dico autem Philomiton poetam amantem fingere fabulas. *Miton* enim, prima producta, fabulam sonat, et *Philomiton* sonat amatorem fabularum si penultima producatur: sicut enim in ea parte *logicae,* quae poetica est ostendit Aristoteles, poeta fingit fabulam ut excitet ad admirandum, et quod admiratio ulterius excitet ad inquirendum: et sic constet philosophia, sicut est de Phaetonte, et sicut de Deucalione monstrat Plato: in qua fabula non intenditur nisi excitatio ad mirandum causas duorum diluviorum aquae et ignis ex orbitatione stellarum erraticarum provenientium, ut per admirationem causa quaeratur, et sciatur veritas.[31]

[Now the man who is puzzled and wonders apparently does not know. Hence wonder is the movement of the man who does not know on his way to finding out, to get at the bottom of that at which he wonders and to determine its cause. A token in proof is that the famous Philomithes according to this way of looking at the matter is a Philosopher, for he constructed his stories out of wonderful events. I hold that Philomithes was a poet who loved to fashion stories: for *mithes,* with the first syllable long, is the word for stories, and *Philomithes,* then, means a lover of stories, if you make the penultimate syllable long. Thus Aristotle shows in that branch of logic which is called poetic that the poet fashions his story for the purpose of exciting wonder, and that the further effect of wonder is to excite inquiry. Such is the origin of philosophy, as Plato shows with respect to the stories of Phaeton and Deucalion. The single purpose of these stories is to excite one to wonder at the causes of the two deluges of fire and of water (which issued from the circuit of wan-

---

again urges when the wayfarer cannot endure her sight (5.4); "non ti maravigliar," Peter tells him, as the saint blushes in shame at the degradation of the Church he founded (27.20). The wayfarer wonders in paradise, but he must not wonder since the "causes of things" are continually being revealed to him.

31. Albertus Magnus, *Opera Omnia,* 6:30; translation is from Cunningham, *Woe or Wonder,* 80.

dering stars), so that through wonder the cause would be looked for, and the truth discovered.]

The poet of the *Commedia,* who is surely aware of all the Phaeton-like risks encountered "on the way to finding out" [procedentis ad inquirendum], will always rhetorically insist that he is not ignorant of the existence of truth, the "deep hidden causes" governing the Christian cosmos and its eternal laws.[32] As the wayfarer, he has passed through all the realms of the otherworld, gazed into Beatrice's eyes, and glimpsed the source of truth, when he beheld God and the effigy of humankind shimmering through the center of the empyrean. In theory, at least, the marvelous in the *Commedia* should therefore never become a means for arriving at some half-envisioned yet ungraspable truth; it should never be a sign of what St. Thomas Aquinas defined as *stupor* rather than *admiratio.*[33] The wonder generated by marvels should always yield to a movement into the demystifying knowledge and experience of a theological truth. Marveling out of ignorance indeed gives way to astonished admiration of truth witnessed as a concrete signifying reality in God's universe. In this way, marveling has moved from the subjective intellectual yearning before something "wondrous to tell" to the admiring appreciative gaze at the existence of something "wondrous to behold." As such, when the repentant marvel over the wayfarer's presence, their marveling soon gives way to shock and admiration at perceiving God's will, the very substance of His power. What results from the act of marveling among the saved is simply the distilled recognition that the wayfarer is the literal expression of God's power at which they may gaze in reverence.

So, too, though in a far more ethereal context, in *Paradiso* 28, after

---

32. On Phaeton, see Kevin Brownlee, "Phaeton's Fall and Dante's Ascent," *Dante Studies* 102 (1984): 135–44; Barolini, in *The Undivine "Comedy,"* 48, 51, and 64, postulates Phaeton as a surrogate for Ulysses as the type and antitype of the poet.

33. "Admirans refugit praesenti dare judicium de eo quod miratur, timens defectum, sed in futurum inquirit. Stupens autem timet et in praesenti judicare et in futuro inquirere. Unde admiratio est principium philosophandi, sed stupor est philosophicae considerationis impedimentum" (Thomas Aquinas, *Summa Theologiae,* 61 vols. [New York: McGraw-Hill, 1964–81], 1–2, Q. 41, art. 5, resp. 5). Dante does not appear to adhere to Aquinas's distinctions in the *Commedia,* though the word *stupor* often carries with it a greater sense of shock. With regard to *stupor,* Aquinas, for example, writes: "RESPONSIO: Dicendum quod nomen stultitiae a *stupore* videtur esse sumptum: unde Isidorus dicit, *Stultus est qui propter stuporem non movetur.* Et differt stultitia a fatuitate, sicut ibidem dicitur, quia stultitia importat hebetudinem cordis et obtusionem sensuum; fatuitas autem importat totaliter spiritualis sensus privationem" (2–2, Q. 46, art. 1, resp.).

Beatrice describes the organizing hierarchy of the angelic realm, she concludes by saying:

> Questi ordini di sù tutti s'ammirano,
> e di giù vincon sì, che verso Dio
> tutti tirati sono e tutti tirano.

(28.127–29)

[These orders all gaze upward and prevail downward, so that toward God all are drawn, and all do draw.]

The reflexive *s'ammirano* expresses above all the primacy and importance of vision, but, as Charles Singleton notes, "the suggestion here is that each order looks with ecstasy or wonder ('s'ammirano') on the next *higher* order."[34] Marveling, far from a sign of ignorance, is in paradise the outpouring and overpouring of knowledge accumulated and transferred. Yet as the reflexive *s'ammirano* also indicates, these angelic creatures, as well as passing knowledge through an admiring, uplifting vision, are wondering at each other, admiring each other, as God's creatures. Their replenishing gaze is at once transparent and reflective, communicative and self-fulfilling. In this respect, marveling is not just an admiring vision but a fulfilling *experience* that moves back and forth between the subject and the object, an experience of truth in contact with a reality that is palpable through vision alone. The wayfarer earlier shares with the griffin this experiential vision of admiration, a "stupor" that, while rendering him "voglioso di sapere," replenishes his desire for knowledge with a reverent self-fulfilling gaze (*Purg.* 31.127–29). The poet of the *Commedia* seeks to recall this same vision of wordless contact and communion at the end of his poem, when the wayfarer, fixed and motionless, lifts his eyes and at last beholds God.[35]

---

34. Singleton's commentary in Dante Alighieri, *The Divine Comedy*, 3:460; Singleton's emphasis.

35. Singleton, in his commentary of *Paradiso* 33.95–96, took note of this with words that are here worth recalling: "The verb *mirare*, here stressed by repetition, can always connote 'marvel,' as it does in this case, and for a moment now the wayfarer remains 'fixed' and 'motionless' in his contemplation of the marvel that is disclosed to him: God in His perfection, as containing all things within Himself." The previous tercet includes the description of "la 'mpresa / che fé Nettuno ammirar l'ombra d'Argo" in Dante Alighieri, *The Divine Comedy*, 3:580. The passage from Neptune's "ammirar" to the wayfarer's "mirar" marks the passage from the poet's task of representation to the fulfillment of the wayfarer's vision.

The wayfarer has passed through the three realms of the otherworld and envisioned God, yet the poet's appreciative marveling, unlike the speechless, though communicative marveling of the angels, is finally expressed in and through language. Insofar as Dante repeatedly recognizes that the marvelous in his poem exists in and through language, he has also partly retained the Virgilian reflexivity of locating the marvelous in the act of representing. But unlike Virgil, Dante relentlessly claims that his act of representation will always succeed by comparison, even when he grants its inadequacy. In canto 13, when Dante has Virgil point back to the *Aeneid* within the *Commedia,* the highly controlled, staged experience of a "poétique de la démonstration" accentuates the learned, reflexive bookishness of Dante's text. But the overall aim of this metatextual *demonstratio* is to fulfill Virgil's pagan marvel, thereby acknowledging the superior power of Dante's Christian art to represent adequately the marvelous. Similarly, when Dante swears by the notes of his own "comedia" (*Inf.* 16.128) that the "maraviglios[o]" (132) Geryon exists, he obliquely reveals how the opacity of language, in the form of the notes ("note," 16.128) composing the song of his *cantica,* mediates his infernal representation of this figure of errancy at all times.[36] The rhetorical intention behind this reflexive act, however, is to present the marvel of Geryon to the reader as a historical fact previously witnessed by the poet in person. If, as Marcia Colish claims, words for Dante "are accurate but imperfect indices of their objects,"[37] the poet of the *Commedia* here suggests that language operates transparently in the representation of Geryon in the very same moment that he discloses how words in their density not only describe things but are things in and of themselves.

"Oh maraviglia!" [O marvel!] (*Purg* 1.134), Dante exclaims as he remembers how the rush on the shore of Mount Purgatory grew back as soon as it had been plucked. In doing so, the poet of the *Commedia* simultaneously recalls Virgil's golden bough and represents his own fully Christianized "marvel" as an objective entity. For Dante, the rush is indeed neither *mirabile visu* (wondrous to behold)[38] nor *mirabile dictu* (wondrous to tell); it is simply a marvel: "Oh maraviglia!" And while the exclamation

---

36. See in particular John Kleiner, *Mismapping the Underworld: Daring and Error in Dante's "Comedy"* (Stanford: Stanford University Press, 1994) for a study of Geryon as a figure of romance errancy and transgression.

37. Colish, *The Mirror of Language,* 247.

38. The formula is, as mentioned in note 4 of the introduction, more Homeric than Virgilian, but it does appear in the *Aeneid,* as in 7.78.

belongs to the poet and lacks quotation marks in modern editions, it could easily be voiced by the wayfarer. The rush on the shore is a marvel for both the wayfarer and the poet, in a temporal suspension that conflates their voices, experiences, and visions. What the wayfarer sees and experiences, the poet sees and experiences. This is perhaps the closest Dante ever comes to writing in the *style indirect libre* (free indirect discourse). Like most self-conscious realists, Dante avoids the conflicting claims of a vision beheld within the narrative ("Oh maraviglia!" with quotes implied) and of the author's vision narrated (Oh maraviglia! without quotes), by omitting, in a Virgilian context, any explicit reference either to the act of seeing (*visu*) or to the act of telling (*dictu*). If the elision of the Virgilian formulas minimizes authorial intrusion, the absence of quotation marks in contemporary editions of the *Commedia* nonetheless reminds the reader that the representation of the marvel as a real historical fact witnessed by the wayfarer is predicated on the graphic presence of the poet's apostrophe on the page.

Wherever the marvelous appears in the *Commedia*, Dante's language never permits it to intrude and *singularly* call attention to the "fictionality" of his poem. He often goes one step further and asserts, as with the ecphrasis on the first terrace of Mount Purgatory, that his marvels are real, sometimes more real than reality.[39] In this respect, the essential problem for the poet of the *Commedia* is how to represent as credible and historically real the astonishing truths he perceived, even though what he knows and remembers may at times appear too incredible to be believed. What fails him, he claims, is never his awareness of the existence of truth or the causes of the things that he saw, but his memory and his language. Yet even in the last moment of the poem, when the poet strains to describe the ineffable and yearningly strives to recall his vision of God, his failing memory and language may still be understood as the assurance that he, in fact, was there.

Not without a certain anxiety, intellectuals in the Renaissance debate over the *Commedia* perceived with querulous acuity that the entire poem is predicated on the marvel of the wayfarer's passage through the otherworld, the passage of not a semi-god or even a saint but simply an ordinary man, a certain Dante Alighieri. Castravilla, the pseudonymous author of a

---

39. For a recent reading of this, see Barolini, *The Undivine "Comedy,"* chap. 6. Barolini's two book-length studies are a sustained attempt to squarely confront the duplicity of Dante's truth claims and credibility, an attempt preceded by the work of Mazzotta. I emphasize, along these lines, that Dante does indeed foreground often the fictionality of his poem, but always with the aim of recuperating frames within frames as an authenticating device.

pamphlet that initiated the entire debate over Dante in the Renaissance, claimed that the wayfarer is so sinful and full of flaws that it is impossible to ever believe that he might have undertaken the voyage "through the special grace of God, as with Saint Paul."[40] It was Bellisario Bulgarini, however, a hard-nosed Aristotelian long thought to have been Castravilla himself, who persistently refuted any claim that the voyage was verisimilar. He rejected even those explanations that turned to the credibility of God's capacity and will to intervene as the ultimate guarantee that the wayfarer's voyage could indeed have taken place.[41] The wayfarer's voyage, Bulgarini declared, "does not come from anything other than from the assertion alone, and from the pure and naked will of Dante himself."[42] To be sure, the wayfarer's passage, in purely secular terms, originates in the poet's will; and the force and worldliness of the poet's will, though sometimes disguised, is always present in his representation of the marvelous. When Virgil marvels over the fulfillment of his "mirabile monstrum" in the thirteenth canto or over the pageant for Beatrice, the poet of the *Commedia* has manipulated Virgil into marveling over the superior

---

40. Castravilla [pseud.], *Discorso di M. Ridolfo Castravilla,* ed. Mario Rossi, vols. 40–41 of *Collezione di opuscoli danteschi inediti o rari,* ed. G. L. Passerini (Città di Castello: Lapi, 1897), 25–26 and 28.

41. Among which were the explanations of Filippo Sassetti, *Sopra Dante di Filippo Sassetti,* vols. 40–41 of *Collezione di opuscoli danteschi inediti o rari,* ed. G. L. Passerini (Città di Castello: Lapi, 1889), 74–78 (Sassetti considered this the most important issue); Lelio Marretti, "Avvertimenti del Sig. Lelio Maretti," on fols. 446–48 in MS H.VI.19, Biblioteca comunale, Siena; Iacopo Mazzoni, *Discorso di Giacopo Mazzoni,* 64; and Mazzoni, *Difesa di Dante* (Cesena: Bartolomeo Rauerij, 1587), 626.

42. Bellisario Bulgarini, *Repliche di Bellisario Bulgarini alle risposte del Sig. Orazio Capponi sopra le prime cinque particelle delle sue considerazioni, intorno al discorso di M. Giacopo Mazzoni, composto in difesa della "Comedia" di Dante* (Siena: Luca Bonetti, 1585), 134. See also his *Alcune considerazioni di Bellisario Bulgarini, gentilhuomo sanese, sopra 'l discorso di M. Giacopo Mazzoni, fatto in difesa della "Comedia" di Dante* (Siena: Luca Bonetti, 1583), 49–50; his marginalia in Marretti, "Avvertimenti," fols. 446–48; and his *Risposte di Bellisario Bulgarini a' ragionamenti del Sig. Ieronimo Zoppio, intorno alla "Commedia" di Dante* (Siena: Luca Bonetti, 1586), 44. Oratio Capponi, in his response—*Risposte del Sig. Oratio Capponi alle prime cinque particelle delle considerazioni di Bellisario Bulgarini sopra 'l discorso del Sig. Giacopo Mazzoni,* MS G. IX, Biblioteca comunale, Siena—finds himself straddling both sides of the issues and comes down on neither side, because he emphasizes his own will as a reader in believing (fols. 50–60). ["Difesa di Dante"], MS 2435, Biblioteca Riccardiana, Florence, attributed by Weinberg to Francesco Bonciani, recognizes the problem without providing a solution (fol. 118). For an overview of the debate, see the relevant chapters in Bernard Weinberg, *A History of Literary Criticism;* Michele Barbi, *Della fortuna di Dante nel secolo xvi* (Florence: Fratelli Bocca, 1890); Aldo Vallone, *L'interpretazione di Dante nel cinquecento: Studi e ricerche* (Florence: Olschki, 1969); and Vallone, *Aspetti dell'esegesi dantesca nei secoli xvi e xvii attraverso testi inediti* (Lecce: Milella, 1966).

power of a Christian poet's art. To the extent that the marvels in the *Commedia* originate in God's will, the God of the *Commedia* has also been constrained to operate, in Francesco Patrizi's Neoplatonic definition of the poet, as a "facitore del mirabile" [maker of the marvelous].[43]

Nowhere is this more strangely evident than in paradise. Here the blessed are both fabric and fabricators of marvels, appearing in a onetime "command performance" for the wayfarer.[44] They continue to orchestrate out of themselves the most artfully outrageous events for his benefit, in a *cantica* filled with the marvels of cosmic skywriting, a ladder leading to heaven, and a shimmering star-spangled eagle that not only flaps its wings but talks as it wheels above the wayfarer's admiring gaze. We might justify Dante's marvels in paradise by inferring, along with Charles Singleton, that if Dante's poem imitates "God's way of writing," then, by analogy, Dante's marvels may be understood as an imitation of God's miracles.[45] Thus, like the individual letters temporally and spatially spread out across the heavens, Dante's marvels may be read temporally and spatially as signifiers throughout paradise, leading the wayfarer "voglioso di sapere"—and the poet and the reader as well—toward the final vision of the poem. As an imitation of God's miracles, Dante's marvels consequently have a didactic function: they are there not only to be enjoyed, in Augustinian terms, but to be used.

However, such an explanation fails to account for how the marvels in the *Paradiso* completely operate. In this most doctrinal of *cantiche,* the marvels provide one of the few sources of sheer poetic diversion, so much so that they sometimes appear extraneous in relation to the didactic exemplary role that they are no doubt meant to play. One may rationalize the imperial eagle's presence as entirely appropriate in the sphere of Jupiter, but does the eagle really have to whirl about the wayfarer's head as it sings ("roteando cantava") [wheeling it sang] (20.97)? Though all the marvels of paradise have a rational meaning in their specific context, and though all may be construed as didactically meaningful or thematically justified, Dante's God also sometimes displays in select, concentrated moments an egregious excess in paradise, a willful overabundance in his capacity to represent and in his desire to make the wayfarer lift up his brow in admi-

---

43. Patrizi da Cherso, *Della poetica,* 271.

44. The quoted phrase is so applied by Freccero, in his "*Paradiso* X: The Dance of the Stars," in *Dante: The Poetics of Conversion,* ed. Rachel Jacoff (Cambridge: Harvard University Press, 1986), 211.

45. Singleton, *Dante's "Commedia,"* 15.

ration and awe. Moreover, unlike the "gran maraviglia" of Satan (who is condemned eternally to the center of hell, 34.37), the "maraviglia" of the rush on the shore of Mount Purgatory (1.134), or the "cosa incredibile" of the bleeding branch in the *Inferno* (13.50), the marvels of paradise have no prior claim to historicity. This is the only time these marvels will ever appear. Like the eagle within which all the souls experience "dolce *frui*" [sweet fruition] (19.2, emphasis in text), the marvels of paradise seek to inspire—unlike Dante's own Geryon, who likewise circles about as a figure of poetic transgression—not fear but a "dolce amor che di riso [s]'ammanti" [sweet Love, that mantlest [itself] in a smile] (20.13). And like the "maraviglia" of the wayfarer himself, the marvels of paradise are there only because the wayfarer is there. They are there because of his transitory presence, a presence that has no other guarantee than the poet's insistent, and often self-astonished, claim that he, in fact, was there:

Se i barbari, venendo da tal plaga
    che ciascun giorno d'Elice si cuopra,
    rotante col suo figlio ond' ella è vaga,
veggendo Roma e l'ardüa sua opra,
    stupefaciensi, quando Laterano
    a le cose mortali andò di sopra;
ïo, che al divino da l'umano,
    a l'etterno dal tempo era venuto,
    e di Fiorenza in popol giusto e sano,
di che stupor dovea esser compiuto!

                      (31.31–40)

[If the Barbarians, coming from such region as is covered every day by Helice, wheeling with her son whom she delights in, when they beheld Rome and her mighty work, when Lateran rose above all mortal things, were wonder-struck, I, who to the divine from the human, to the eternal from time had come, and from Florence to a people just and sane, with what amazement must I have been full!]

To completely lose faith in this dimension of the poem, in the poet's guarantee of presence and in the fulfillment of his voyage as history, to lose faith in the poet's *Commedia* as Virgil in the thirteenth canto accused the wayfarer of having lost faith in his *Aeneid,* is to have already initiated a movement toward the highly skeptical, demystified prose of the

Decameron. Indeed, from the outset of Boccaccio's text, both history and the marvelous have been conflated in a direct, eyewitness chronicle report of things now wondrous "to hear": "Maravigliosa cosa è a udire quello che io debbo dire" [A marvelous thing is it to hear what I have to relate] (1 intro. 16). What the chronicling narrator insists he must tell ("debbo dire"), much as Dante insisted that he had to speak of Geryon (*Inf.* 16.127), is the unexpected death of two pigs from a diseased man's clothes. But unlike Dante's self-authenticating solitary claim, this is a marvel witnessed by others too (*Dec.* 1 intro. 16). History, both as a category of thought and as distinct social practice, has become rhetorical, a contact zone for cohesion, consensus, and, above all, exchange. What is "wondrous to tell" has for Boccaccio become the work of the community engaged in transacting shared knowledge.

The world of the *Decameron* is constructed on multiple processes of communal exchange, from those produced by the plague in the introduction, where the disease is visibly ("visibilmente," 17) passed on from one person like a florin in the marketplace, to the exchange of stories told by the noble *brigata* (party) in different gardens. Such a world of constant exchange, already implicit in Boccaccio's youthful epic-romance in prose, the *Filocolo,* does not mark a denial, much less an evasion, of history's deeper truths. Nor does it deny the philosophical properties of the marvelous as a cognitive act. It does, however, indicate a refusal to move beyond the living world—the banks of the Mugnone, a fabulous springtime garden flowering in the heart of winter—toward the causes that move the cosmos for both the living and the dead. With the *Filocolo,* where the marvelous already begins to operate as an object of exchange itself, we begin to enter a world grounded on humankind's capacity to transform itself through labor and sociability rather than on God's ability to transform humankind through grace and the Word made flesh.

Chapter 3

The Value of Marvels

Denari fanno l'omo comparére;
denari el stolto fingono scienziato;
denari cómpreno zascun peccato;
denari mostran spendere e tenere;
   denari dánno donne per godere;
denari tengon l'anemo beato;
denari lo vile mantèn en stato;
denari gli enemici fan cadere.
   E senza loro onn'omo par assiso:
ch'igli reze lo mondo e la fortuna,
e, se tu vòi, te manda en paradiso.
   Unde sazo me par chi gli raúna:
ché quigli soli, plú d'atra vertute,
contra melanconia rende salute.

                —Messer Niccolò del Rosso

If I long for a particular dish or want to take the mail-coach because I am not strong enough to go by foot, money fetches me the dish and the mail-coach: that is, it converts my wishes from something in the realm of imagination, translates them from their meditated, imagined or willed existence into their *sensuous, actual* existence—from imagination to life, from imagined being into real being. In effecting this mediation, money is the *truly creative* power.

                —Karl Marx

The "Neapolitan" Idalogo: On the Margins of the Marketplace

Toward the beginning of the fifth and last book of Boccaccio's lengthy epic-romance *Filocolo,* Florio and Biancifiore, now married and returning on their homeward voyage from the east, decide to linger for several days in the rich city of Naples, enjoying themselves as well as pursuing more ennobling activities (5.5.1).[1] In their edifying *otium,*[2] both Florio and Biancifiore lose sight of their original goal to see the aging king before he dies. Captivated by the many things to do, they take a tour of the classical past. They visit the tomb of Misenus, the cave where Aeneas descended into the underworld, the ruins of Cumae, Pozzuoli with its relics, "e ancora quante cose mirabili in quelle parti le reverende antichità per li loro autori rapresentano" [and still so many marvelous things in those places that the revered antiquities represent through their authors] (5.5.2). Each day brings a new delight for the two lovers, as "essi tal volta guardando l'antiche maraviglie vanno e negli animi come gli autori di quelle diventano magni" [they sometimes go gazing at the ancient marvels and become in their spirits as great as the authors of them] (5.5.3). Florio and Biancifiore do not, however, *only* go sightseeing. As part of their serious recreation, which consists of bathing, sailing, and fishing, they also go hunting in a woods near Naples. There, one day, while shooting at a deer, Florio accidentally strikes the edge of a tall pine, chipping away a piece of the bark, "at which," the narrator writes,

> sangue con dolorosa voce venne appresso, non altrimenti che quando il pio Enea del non conosciuto Polidoro, sopra l'arenoso lito, levò un ramo. (5.6.3)

> [there came forth blood and a grieving voice, not unlike the time when pious Aeneas took a branch from the unrecognized Polydorus on the sandy shore.]

The casual viewing of ancient ruins, which leads up to and prepares for Boccaccio's revision of the marvel of the bleeding branch from the *Aeneid,* takes place as a digression, one of many in a text that already runs some six

---

1. The epigraphs heading this chapter are, in order, from Aldo Francesco Massèra, ed., *Sonetti burleschi e realistici dei primi due secoli,* revised by Luigi Russo (Bari: Laterza, 1940), 212; and "The Power of Money in Bourgeois Society," in the *Economic and Philosophic Manuscripts,* in *The Marx-Engles Reader,* ed. Robert C. Tucker (New York: Norton, 1972), 82 (Marx's emphasis). Citations from the *Filocolo* and *Decameron* are from Giovanni Boccaccio, *Tutte le opere,* vols. 1 and 4, ed. Vittore Branca (Milan: Mondadori, 1967 and 1976); all translations are, with only slight modifications, from Boccaccio, *Il filocolo,* trans. Donald Cheney, with an introduction by Thomas G. Bergin (New York: Garland Publishing, 1985), and *The Decameron,* trans. G. H. McWilliam (Middlesex: Penguin, 1972).

2. On the positive and (primarily) negative values associated with *otium,* see the synthetic study by Brian Vickers, "Leisure and Idleness in the Renaissance: The Ambivalence of *Otium,*" *Renaissance Studies* 1 and 2, no.4 (1990): 1–37 and 107–54.

hundred pages longer than the work on which it is modeled. Yet in this particular digression, as Florio and Biancifiore visit *anticaglie* (old curiosities), *guasti luoghi* (ruined places), or other sites that fall under the rubric of *antichità* (antiquities), they display a desire and a mentality long associated with both Petrarch and the beginning of humanism, which advocated the slow steady reacquisition of the classical past through its ruins.[3] Both in substance and in detail, Florio's and Biancifiore's touring cannot compare with the immense archeological enterprise that Petrarch, led by his historical imagination, conducted to locate and make meaning out of overgrown landscapes.[4] There is no powerful historical imagination at work in Boccaccio's text, nothing to equal Petrarch's archeological walk with Giovanni Colonna through the wilderness of Rome, no rigorous reconstruction of Rome like that Petrarch later sought to accomplish in his unfinished epic *Africa*. The *Filocolo*, which freely conflates Angevin Naples with the time of early Christianity, cannot be said to reveal a rigorous historical mentality that confronts the otherness of the past. Like the author of the medieval *Mirabilia urbae Romae*, a tour guide still in vogue in Petrarch's time, Boccaccio calls his ruins "marvels" [maraviglie], a lexical choice that indicates how much we are still within the framework of a medieval mind.[5]

Yet the spirit that motivates the desire in Florio and Biancifiore to tour the marvels of antiquity, and by that touring to "become in their spirits as great as the authors of them," remains Petrarchan. Moreover, in contrast with the anonymous *Mirabilia urbae Romae* and its disorganized compendium of ruins, Boccaccio's brief list of ruins—the tomb of Misenus, the lake of Avernus, the cavern of the sibyl of Cumae—has a focus, dominated by the presence of Virgil. More important, these marvels are worth seeing, according to the narrator, because such authors as Virgil put them there: "quante cose mirabili in quelle parti le reverende antichità *per li loro autori rapresentano*." Without the descriptions and records of these authorities, there would exist no knowledge that such places were worth seeing, much less worthy of being revered. To be in contact with a world that authors recorded and helped fashion permits observers in the present to participate in, and be uplifted by, their greatness and their deserved glory. Authors

---

3. See the succinct remarks of Antonio Enzo Quaglio in his notes to the *Filocolo* in vol. 1 *Opere*. Other examples include 3.33.8 and 4.73.

4. Thomas Greene, *The Light in Troy: Imitation and Discovery in Renaissance Poetry* (New Haven: Yale University Press, 1982), 90.

5. Greene, *Light in Troy*, 90, discusses this with respect to Petrarch, citing Peter Burke, *The Renaissance Sense of the Past* (London: Arnold, 1969), 2.

are shapers of both antiquities and marvels, "autori di quelle [antiche maraviglie]," and their fame rests in part on their ability to make those monuments of the past endure as marvels for future generations. The humanists' desire to accomplish this same feat in their own time partakes of a drive that recovers, in the very moment that it discloses the inability to fully reproduce, the authority and permanence of classical epic.

Even though Florio and his companions have just visited many Virgilian "maraviglie" in their sightseeing tour about the environs of Naples, they nevertheless perceive the marvel of the bleeding branch with full-blown literary naïveté, experiencing shock, surprise, and horror (5.6.4). For them this is an authentic marvel and, presumably, one without precedent. The narrator of the *Filocolo,* by contrast, enlists the Polydorus episode as part of the vast intertextual world that makes up his epic-romance ("non altrimenti che"). The marvel of Virgil's episode makes claims on the narrator's imagination not just because it elicits surprise but because it serves as a familiar model of epic authority. It is, like the "maraviglie" Florio and Biancifiore have just seen, a kind of revered, classical literary ruin buried in Boccaccio's text. In the Virgilian phrase, this marvel is "wondrous to say" (*mirabile dictu*) precisely because it has been said by a canonical "author" before.

However, the actual resemblance between Boccaccio's and Virgil's episodes, though accurate in the main, is nevertheless slight in the particular. Conspicuously lacking in the Boccaccian text is the Virgilian emphasis on struggle and repetition. Aeneas uproots not one branch, as Boccaccio asserts ("levò *un* ramo"; my emphasis), but three branches. The bleeding branch speaks not immediately but only with the third vigorous try. However, in canto 13 of Dante's *Inferno,* as in the *Filocolo,* the branch once broken bleeds immediately, the violence inflicted is reduced to a bare minimum, and the voice that emerges from the twig mingles with the blood to form a single compound.[6] Like Florio, who aims at a moving deer but pierces instead the pine tree placed exactly in between (5.6.2), Boccaccio targets the classical authority of Virgil with his explicit reference to the Polydorus episode yet strikes (in this instance not accidentally) the intermediating—but by now, for Boccaccio, canonical—text of Dante's *Inferno.*

In privileging *Inferno* 13 as a literary model for his own revision of the Polydorus episode, Boccaccio may well have had in mind the common

---

6. Quaglio, in the notes to his edition, vol. 1 *Opere,* identifies the more pervasive Dantean echoes throughout.

theme of faith in both his and Dante's texts. Just as Pier della Vigna insists that he never broke faith with his lord ("mai non ruppi fede," *Inf.* 13.74), so Idalogo, the spirit trapped within the tree in the *Filocolo,* foregrounds the risks and value of his own faithfulness in a world composed largely of deceivers and fraud. There are, indeed, few men or women of true faith in Idalogo's tale. His own father, Eucomos, betrays Gannai, the princess he has falsely wooed and flattered (5.8.14); Idalogo himself is betrayed in turn by the woman he loves. In rounding out the story of his life, Idalogo then provides Florio and Biancifiore with the following moral observation: "Potete adunque per le mie parole e per me comprendere quanta poca fede le mondane cose servino agli speranti, e massimamente le femine" [Therefore you can comprehend through my words and through my nature how little faith worldly things keep with those trusting in them, and especially women] (5.8.46). Of course, Biancifiore stands out as the one woman exempt from blame; her faithfulness, as Idalogo soon makes plain, is the model for all others in the world: "Or se' tu—disse Idalogo—quella Biancifiore per la quale il mondo conosce quanto si possa amare, o essere con leale fede amato? Se' tu colei la quale, secondo che tutto il mondo parla, è tanto stato amata da Florio figliuolo dell'alto re di Spagna, e che, per intera fede servargli, se' nimica della fortuna stata" ["Are you, then," said Idalogo, "that Biancifiore by whom the world knows how much one can love, and be loved with a loyal faith? Are you she who (from what everyone says) has been so loved by Florio, son of the mighty king of Spain, and has made herself the enemy of Fortune by keeping perfect faith with him"] (5.9.5). Unlike Dido, characterized at *Inferno* 5.61–62 as "colei che . . . ruppe fede" [she who . . . broke faith], and thus the very opposite of Pier della Vigna, Biancifiore is universally recognized in the *Filocolo* as the ideal woman who has adhered to the pact of love despite all the woes that love may bring.

While at one level faith binds Dante's poem to Boccaccio's *Filocolo,* at another level avarice, the one sin increasingly privileged during the "commercial revolution,"[7] separates Virgil's Polydorus episode from Boccaccio's revision of it. As both a mythographer and a compiler of mythographies, Boccaccio would have known Bernardus Silvestris's medieval allegory that traces, as Fulgentius did earlier, the maturation of the human psyche in the first six books of the *Aeneid.* In allegorizing the *Aeneid* in his

---

7. See Lester K. Little, "Pride Goes before Avarice: Social Change and the Vice in Latin Christendom," *American Historical Review* 76 (1971): 16–49; and Little, *Religious Poverty and the Profit Economy in Medieval Europe* (Ithaca: Cornell University Press, 1978).

commentary, Silvestris etymologizes Polydorus's name as "Polydoris, multa amaritudo" and interprets Thrace, where Polydorus is slain on account of Polymestor's greed, as the moral landscape of "avarice" from which Aeneas is told to flee: "fuge litus auarum" (*Aen.* 3.44). Both Anthony Cassell and William Kennedy have shown that Dante made use of Silvestris's allegory to highlight the role of the sin of avarice in Pier della Vigna's decision to commit suicide.[8] The presence of avarice as a contributing factor in Pier della Vigna's death further reminds us that issues of economic value lie at the heart of *Inferno* 13. These issues are evident in the form of the spendthrifts, who destroy their property as the suicides destroy their own lives,[9] and in the form of Pier della Vigna, who functions as a figural "type" of Judas, the archsinner whose final act was to kill himself after having sold Christ for gold.

Boccaccio, for whom matters of exchange were always of great concern, calls attention in his revision of the Polydorus episode not to the role of avarice but to the conspicuous absence of it. Idalogo, born a shepherd, describes how he turned away from the worldly practices of his father (the shepherd Eucomos) to pursue the ideals of scholarly learning, true love, and poetry embodied in the figure of his aristocratic mother (Gannai, the princess of France). In the same way, Boccaccio, we are led to believe through a thinly veiled allegory, left behind the avaricious world of commerce to follow a longing—no doubt attributed to the fabled aristocratic blood of his Parisian mother—to become a learned poet and a noble lover.[10] In Idalogo's abandonment of the "pastorale via," Boccaccio alludes to his own abandonment, as Quaglio points out in his commentary, of "la mercatura."[11] Polydorus and Pier della Vigna may have been

---

8. Cassell, "Pier della Vigna's Metamorphosis," 45–46; William Kennedy, "Irony, Allegoresis, and Allegory," 127, from whom I quote Silvestris. Giorgio Padoan, "Tradizione e fortuna del commento all'‘Eneide’ di Bernardo Silvestre," *Italia medioevale e umanistica* 3 (1960): 227–40, has documented the widespread circulation of Silvestris's commentary in the Middle Ages.

9. I thank Albert Ascoli for this connection and for drawing my attention to the issues of economic exchange already inscribed into Dante's treatment of the marvelous in canto 13.

10. For a synthetic review of the autobiographical elements, see in particular Salvatore Battaglia, "Elementi autobiografici nell'arte del Boccaccio," in *Giovanni Boccaccio e la riforma della narrativa* (Naples: Liguori, 1969), 123–24. On Boccaccio's artful refashioning of his biography, which was for so long taken at face value, see Giuseppe Billanovich, *Restauri boccacceschi* (Rome: Edizione di Storia e Letteratura, 1945); and see, above all, Vittore Branca's "Profilo biografico," in Giovanni Boccaccio, *Tutte le opere,* ed. Branca (Milan: Mondadori, 1967), 1:3–203; and Branca's "Schemi letterari e schemi autobiografici," in *Boccaccio medievale e nuovi studi sul "Decameron,"* 5th ed. (Florence: Sansoni, 1981), 191–249.

11. Quaglio, *Filocolo,* 1:924.

undone by greed, but Idalogo, born of nobility, is greedy for knowledge, love, and honor alone:

La genitrice di me misero mi diede per padre un pastore chiamato Eucomos, i cui vestigii quasi tutta la mia puerile età seguitai; ma poi che la nobiltà dello 'ngegno, del quale natura mi dotò, venne crescendo, torsi i piedi dal basso calle, e sforzandomi per più aspre vie di salire all'alte cose. (5.6.8)

[The mother of this wretched being gave me as father a shepherd named Eucomos, whose footsteps I followed for almost all my childhood. But when the nobility of intellect with which nature endowed me began to mature, I turned my feet from the low path and forced myself to ascend by more difficult ways to higher matters.]

The *Filocolo,* though written in prose rather than poetry, is surely meant to stand as the triumphant testimony to the author's, alias Idalogo's, success in escaping the "basso calle" of his father's calling and in elevating his mind to "alte cose." The *Filocolo* is prompted by and dedicated to the royal Fiammetta, the fictionalized Maria d'Aquino, illegitimate daughter of the king of Naples. It is also an encyclopedic work filled with Boccaccio's learning: myriad erudite classical allusions and imitations (the Polydorus episode being one of a plethora), invented local mythological lore, arcane asides, rhetorical embellishments, and lengthy displays of astronomical knowledge.[12] However, one obvious element dis-

---

12. On the evident erudition, see Antonio Enzo Quaglio, *Scienza e mito nel Boccaccio* (Padua: Liviana, 1967); Quaglio, "Tra fonti e testo del *Filocolo,*" parts 1 and 2, *Giornale storico della letteratura italiana* 139 (1962): 321–69, 513–40; and 160 (1963): 321–63, 489–551; Francesco Bruni, "Il *Filocolo* e lo spazio della letteratura volgare," in *Boccaccio e dintorni* (Florence: Olschki, 1983), 1–21; James McGregor, *The Image of Antiquity in Boccaccio's "Filocolo," "Filostrato," and "Teseida"* (New York: Peter Lang, 1991); and Steven Grossvogel, *Ambiguity and Allusion in Boccaccio's "Filocolo"* (Florence: Olschki, 1992). Situating it in terms of Boccaccio's development, see Branca in Boccaccio, *Tutte le opere,* 1:43–48. As far back as Francesco De Sanctis, *Storia della letteratura italiana* (Milan: Rizzoli, 1983), 1:366–68, scholars have reacted with a sense of tedium to the willful display of erudition in the *Filocolo.* On this see Battaglia, *Giovanni Boccaccio,* 156–57, who nevertheless responds with a positive, balanced recognition of Boccaccio's youthful, and culturally rewarded, enthusiasm for encyclopedic knowledge (158). See as well Nicholas J. Perella, "The World of Boccaccio's *Filocolo,*" *Publications of the Modern Language Association* 76 (1961): 330–39. Discussions of the *Filocolo* have attempted to locate large-scale structural designs within the text, though they have not completely dispelled the sense of tedium associated with it. See, for

tinguishes Idalogo from the author, or rather from the historical Boccaccio who wrote the text (as opposed to the fictive "I" who narrates it). Rather than being noble, Boccaccio, for all the nobility of his mind, was the legitimized bastard son of a bourgeois Florentine parvenu who had made, and continued to make, his living as a representative of the great Bardi Bank. Understandably, this is something that Boccaccio, as he aspires to be embraced by the nobility of Angevin Naples by writing the *Filocolo,* consciously attempts to disguise.[13] As a result, Boccaccio not only ennobles a popular romance by alluding to Virgil's epic but covertly ennobles his own origins as well in a fantasy that can only be construed in retrospect as a classic example of the Freudian "family romance." In revising the Polydorus episode, Boccaccio has selectively revised his lineage too.

As in the case of Boccaccio's re-presentation of himself through the figure of Idalogo, the courtly aristocratic world of Angevin Naples dominates the *Filocolo* ideologically, even though commercial activity occupied much of Boccaccio's experience as a youth in the city. Knights, such as Fileno, may therefore desire within the nobility to rise above their normal allotted station in the *Filocolo.* But in the many pages that comprise this epic-romance, the only merchants—besides those masquerading as shepherds in the allegory of Idalogo's tale—are the ones who sell the noble Biancifiore for a substantial profit. This does not reflect very well on their profession. There are no bankers, usurers, or money changers. Accordingly, all the processes of exchange, both between the king and the merchants and between the merchants and the sultan, take place without money.

We are, in short, very distant from the rich and varied social worlds of the *Decameron,* a work written in the commercial banking center of Flo-

---

example, Victoria Kirkham, "Reckoning with Boccaccio's *Questioni d'amore,*" *Modern Language Notes* 89 (1974): 47–59; Janet Levarie Smarr, *Boccaccio and Fiammetta: The Narrator as Lover* (Urbana and Chicago: University of Illinois Press, 1986), 34–60; James McGregor, *The Shades of Aeneas: The Imitation of Vergil and the History of Paganism in Boccaccio's "Filostrato," "Filocolo," and "Teseida"* (Athens: University of Georgia Press, 1991); and Grossvogel, *Ambiguity and Allusion,* who also provides a critical survey of the scholarship on the *Filocolo* in his introduction. It should be clear from my previous statements that I do not place Boccaccio's "archeological" work in the *Filocolo* on a par with the Petrarchan humanist program of heuristic imitation discussed by Thomas Greene in *The Light in Troy.*

13. Vittore Branca has written well on this in connection with Boccaccio's relationship with Niccola Acciaiuoli, in Boccaccio, *Tutte le opere,* 1:26–28. Thomas Bergin, *Boccaccio* (New York: Viking, 1981), provides a good summary (88–90).

rence and hailed by Vittore Branca as a "mercantile epic" because it was largely composed of and for the newly arrived bourgeoisie.[14] Yet of all Boccaccio's early works, the *Filocolo* also contains within it features that were later adopted in the *Decameron*. First and foremost is the convention of having a group of noblemen and noblewomen gather together to tell and share stories in order to take their minds off the heat of the day. This storytelling activity takes place in the *Filocolo* not as a respite from a plague but as an extended interlude in Filocolo's delayed search for Biancifiore; moreover, following each story, the *brigata* turns to debate "questions of love," which are then finally decided by the ruling queen, Fiammetta.[15] Nevertheless, of all the stories told in the *Filocolo,* two were eventually carried over into the *Decameron* itself.

One of those stories—the story of the "mirabile" garden that flowers in the dead of winter—was later substantially revised as the fifth novella of day ten in the *Decameron*.[16] I argue that by moving from one to another

---

14. For Vittore Branca's discussion of the mercantile basis of the *Decameron,* see his "L'epopea dei mercatanti" in *Boccaccio medievale,* 134–64. See also much of the work of Giovanni Getto, *Vita di forme e forme di vita nel "Decameron"* (Turin: Petrini, 1958). Giuseppe Mazzotta, *The World at Play in Boccaccio's "Decameron"* (Princeton: Princeton University Press, 1986), 75, notes, for example: "It is certainly undeniable that the marketplace, the art of the city where goods are exchanged, prices are fixed, money is alternately made and lost and, more generally, a utilitarian morality holds sway, is a privileged space of Boccaccio's imagination. In fact there is so little in the *Decameron* that is not absorbed within the nomenclature of economics or is not, at least, affected by it, that the 'ragion di mercatura' is taken to be nothing less than the ground of all values, the implied paradigm by which loyalties, social bonds, love and even literature itself are appraised." See also Mario Baratto, *Realtà e stile nel "Decameron"* (Vicenza: Pozza, 1970), passim. For the readership of the *Decameron,* see the opening pages to "Tradizione medievale" in Branca, *Boccaccio medievale.* Like Branca, Giorgio Padoan has traced the ideological shift in Boccaccio's art as he moved from Naples to Florence; see his "Mondo aristocratico e mondo comunale nell'ideologia e nell'arte di Giovanni Boccaccio," in *Il Boccaccio, le muse, il parnaso e l'arno* (Florence: Olschki, 1978). For Florentine writers and merchants, see Christian Bec, *Les marchands écrivains: Affaires et humanisme à Florence, 1375–1434* (Paris: Mouton, 1967).

15. For discussions of the "questioni d'amore," see Victoria Kirkham, "Reckoning with Boccaccio's *Questioni d'amore*"; Paolo Cherchi, "Sulle 'quistioni d'amore' nel *Filocolo,*" in *Andrea Cappellano, trovatori e altri temi romanzi* (Rome: Bulzoni, 1979); and Pio Rajna, "L'episodio delle questioni d'amore nel *Filocolo* del Boccaccio," *Romania* 31 (1902): 28–81.

16. Francesco Guardiani has already treated some salient aspects of this shift in his "Boccaccio dal *Filocolo* al *Decameron:* Variazioni di poetica e di retorica dall'esame di due racconti," *Carte Italiane: A Journal of Italian Studies* 7 (1985–86): 28–46; and now see Grossvogel, *Ambiguity and Allusion,* 206–29. For a reading of the version in the *Decameron,* see Millicent Joy Marcus, "An Allegory of Two Gardens: The Tale of Madonna Dianora (*Decameron* X, 5)," *Forum Italicum* 14 (1980): 162–74.

version of the same story, Boccaccio incorporates the marvelous into different processes of social and economic exchanges.[17] These same processes of exchange are further reflected in the values toward work and wealth that undergird the economies in which Boccaccio composed these respective literary texts: the land-based, feudal wealth of aristocratic Angevin Naples and the money-based wealth of bourgeois, mercantile Florence. At the same time, in the discussion over the novella of the marvelous garden that takes place in the frame of the *Filocolo,* a voice emerges that attempts to justify the existence of parvenus in society. This voice, though quickly quashed in the same debate, nevertheless anticipates the *Decameron* by advocating a vision of the world that legitimates social change through the sudden acquisition of immense, and hence seemingly marvelous, wealth.

From the *Filocolo* to the *Decameron:* The Evolving Value of Marvels

This is the story told by Menedon in book 4 of the *Filocolo.* An unnamed noblewoman finds herself courted by a knight named Tarolfo, who, amid his many devices for wooing, sends messengers often to his beloved, "forse," the narrator informs, "promettendole grandissimi doni" [perhaps promising her great gifts] (4.31.3). The indication of the possibility that the lady's love might be exchanged in a process of gift-giving, largely in accordance with the proper behavior prescribed in Andreas Capellanus's *The Art of Love,*[18] anticipates the noblewoman's strategy for ridding herself of her suitor. The noblewoman's "sottile malizia" [shrewd trick] (4.31.7) of which the narrator speaks consists in her decision to engage her suitor in a process of exchange only to put an end to the normal function of that process through the use of the marvelous. Where Tarolfo perhaps promises great gifts in exchange for sexual gratification, the noblewoman

---

17. For issues of the marvelous in the *Decameron,* see the many comments interspersed throughout the study of Baratto, *Realtà e stile,* especially on pages 36, 42, 44, 56, 91, 108–9, 114, 117, and 137, where he elaborates on his concept of the "meraviglioso terreno," a concept that easily lends itself to the "marvelous garden" here discussed; M. H. Bailet, *L'homme de verre: Essai d'interprétation thématique* (Padua: Studio Bibliografico Antenore, 1972); and Marga Cottino-Jones, "Magic and Superstition in Boccaccio's *Decameron,*" *Italian Quarterly* 18 (1975): 5–32.

18. In *The Art of Courtly Love,* trans. John Jay Parry (New York: Norton, 1969), Andreas Capellanus, in practical-minded fashion, moves back and forth in his position, accepting and promoting the transfer of gifts (in chapter 2, "Between What Persons Love May Exist") and attacking it (in chapter 9, "Love Got with Money").

binds herself to her suitor with a sworn agreement of her own. She requests, in sure exchange for her love, a gift so great that it is impossible to either acquire or produce. Her worth, so she deems, is nothing less than the traditional *locus amoenus* where Venus dwells in winter or in spring. Manipulating the language of courtly love, the noble lady thus agrees that she will become Tarolfo's Venus if he can materialize the traditional metaphor and provide the actual place: a springtime garden flourishing in the middle of the winter.

The noblewoman's pact, transmitted through a third-party messenger, at once binds her to the suitor. But the marvel of the "impossible task" [cosa impossibile] (4.31.8) polarizes their relationship, distancing and forever separating them.[19] She has struck up a deal whose terms can never be met because the value of the Venereal habitat equated with her love presumably exceeds the normal boundaries of what man or nature can ever produce. The marvelous, here gendered as feminine, acts for the noblewoman as a deterrent of both further contact and eventual exchange.

Tarolfo, however, whose love for the noblewoman knows no bounds (4.31.3), does not find the price too high. He knows full well that he is being thwarted, but thanks to the bargain, he transforms the noblewoman's rejection into a knightly test: "ancora che impossibile gli paresse e che egli conoscesse bene perché la donna questo gli domandava, rispose che già mai non riposerebbe né in presenza di lei tornerebbe, infino a tanto che il dimandato dono le donerebbe" [although it seemed impossible to him and he well understood why the lady had asked it of him, he replied that he would never rest or return to her presence until he gave her the gift she had asked] (4.31.9). The nature of the transaction agreed on permits Tarolfo to wax heroic and fashion his behavior as though he were acting on his lady's, rather than his own, desire. The noblewoman has requested the paradise of a goddess, and Tarolfo deems this to be fair value. Bound by the service of love, Tarolfo thus sets out on a courtly quest.

Seeking to fulfill his beloved's desire in a quest for a gift she does not really want, Tarolfo travels about the world until he arrives at the plain where the battle of Pharsalia once took place. There he meets a poor, short, bearded, middle-aged wizard called Tebano, an appropriate name because he comes from Thebes. On seeing the poverty of the shabbily dressed Theban, who is going about digging up weeds, Tarolfo soon

19. For the topos of *similitudo impossibilium* see Ernst Robert Curtius, *European Literature and the Latin Middle Ages,* trans. Willard R. Trask (New York: Harper & Row, 1953), 95–96.

bluntly declares his social status and wealth: "Io sono dell'ultimo ponente assai ricco cavaliere" [I am a wealthy knight from the distant West] (4.31.14). He then announces that he has a "project," an "impresa." The poor wizard, after hearing of Tarolfo's desire to create a lush springtime garden in the winter, nevertheless seizes on the opportunity by asking: "Ma che doneresti tu a chi quello che tu vai cercando ti recasse ad effetto?" [But what would you give to someone who brought to fulfillment what you are looking for?] (4.31.19). Even if the language is one of gift-giving, the process is now more openly one of barter. A deal is in the making, and Tarolfo responds to the poor man's practical request with a solid offer: "Io signoreggio ne' miei paesi più castella, e con esse molti tesori, i quali tutti per mezzo partirei con chi tal piacere mi facesse" [In my land I rule over many castles, and with them much treasure, both of which I should divide equally with whoever might do me such a favor] (4.31.19).

Compared to the verbal exchange between Tarolfo and the noble-woman, which is the exchange between two social equals governed by the proper mediating channels of third-party messengers, the extended direct conversation between Tarolfo and the poor wizard appears at times almost crass and comical in the way it highlights the absolute disjunction in their worldly stations. The poor man momentarily chides the nobleman with a moral message about appearances and essences (4.31.18). But the practical side of life soon gets the better of Tebano. What, the wizard inquires, will his services reap? In the brief dialogue that concludes the pact between the two men, their conversation contrasts the quick calculations of a man who ordinarily has to work for his living with the self-assurance of a nobleman who has lived in the lap of luxury all his life:

"Certo," disse Tebano, "se questo facessi, a me non bisognerebbe d'andare più cogliendo l'erbe." "Fermamente," disse Tarolfo, "se tu se' quelli che in ciò mi prometti di dare vero effetto, e davelo, mai non ti bisognerà più affannare per divenire ricco." (4.31.19–20)

["Indeed," said Tebano, "if I did this, I would no longer have to go gathering herbs." "Definitely not," said Tarolfo; "if you are the one who promises me to bring this to fulfillment, and if you do it, you will never more have to labor to become rich."]

Although Tarolfo initially fears on seeing the wizard that he has come upon a fearful shade (4.31.12), he soon discovers that he is in fact dealing with a man who in social station is a sort of itinerant peasant. Tarolfo and the wizard could not come from more diverse social worlds. Their difference in social status is emphasized in the contrast between, on the one hand, the "erbe" that the poor wizard gathers out of medical necessity and, on the other hand, the expendable luxury of the lush garden that the beloved lady requests (though neither needs nor wants) and that Tarolfo then seeks to procure at all costs. "Per questo piano," the wizard informs Tarolfo, "vo cogliendo queste erbe, acciò che de' liquori d'esse faccendo alcune cose necessarie e utili a diverse infermità, io abbia onde vivere, e a questa ora necessità e non diletto mi ci costringe di venire" [I am going over this plain collecting these herbs so that by making things necessary and useful for various infirmities out of their liquors, I may find means to live; and it is need and not pleasure that constrains me to come here at this hour] (4.31.13). Evidently, noblemen and noblewomen wander in pleasure through manicured gardens. Laborers and peasants have contact with soil, roots, and dirt because of basic, economic necessity.

In terms of the overall economics of exchange, Tarolfo's pact with the wizard draws the traditional language and imagery of courtly love down to a more practical, worldly level. Earlier, the noblewoman's love and beauty were measured according to the gift of the marvelous, which finds its proper realm in the impossible. The landscape in which the noblewoman fittingly belongs, and shrewdly places herself, is a Venereal bower. But as one process of worldly exchange leads to another, and as social relations shift from a mediated deal between two distanced nobles to a practical face-to-face swap between a wealthy landholder and a poor man plucking herbs, the narrator finally reveals in crude material terms just how much the lady's love is actually worth to Tarolfo: not all but half of his worldly possessions.[20]

Marvels, it would seem, can be bought, and the noblewoman's lack of foresight into this matter leads to the climax of the tale. The initially pro-

---

20. A true lover, Andreas Capellanus points out at the beginning of his *De arte honeste amandi*, should be prepared to give up everything, but a wise lover, whom Tarolfo in this context appears to be, should carefully work out his expenditures in advance: "A true lover would rather be deprived of all his money and of everything that the human mind can imagine as indispensable to life rather than be without love, either hoped for or attained. For what under heaven can a man possess or own for which he would undergo so many perils as we continually see lovers submit to of their own free will? We see them despise death and fear no threats, scatter their wealth abroad and come to great poverty. Yet a wise lover does not throw away wealth as a prodigal spender usually does, but he plans his expenditures from the beginning in accordance with the size of his patrimony" (Capellanus, *The Art of Courtly Love*, 30).

posed, yet obstructed, process of exchange between the nobleman and the noblewoman can now go forward because the marvelous itself has been drawn into a secondary—now triangular—process of exchange. The noblewoman's love is no longer worth only a marvelous garden. The garden is now simultaneously worth half Tarolfo's possessions, which in turn can always be exchanged for something else. Through this simple act of substitution, the value of the noblewoman, who was effectively "commodified" from the moment she placed herself in a process of exchange, has entered into a potentially ever-widening network of social and economic exchanges. Her value no longer exists in one single unifying object of her own choosing, but constantly, relativistically, and alienatingly in other objects, in whatever Tarolfo's possessions can at any given moment buy. In terms neatly set out by Jean-Joseph Goux, we have moved from an initial simple phase of equivalence, of "elementary or accidental form of value," in which "a commodity is declared identical to another commodity," to the following phase of "ambivalence" or pluri-valence, of "the total or extended form of value," in which "a commodity cannot express its value once and for all, cannot fix its own price in an absolute universal estimate."[21] It is, according to this design of material-historical progression, only a matter of time before the noblewoman's love is exchanged for money, the one universal object of exchange.

For the moment, however, the magician has only bargained for half of Tarolfo's possessions. Once he has furnished this garden, Tarolfo, in the words of the noblewoman, has "earned" his lady's love ("guadagnato avete l'amore mio," 4.31.41). The observation is soon reiterated by the noblewoman's wealthy husband (4.31.2), who commands his wife to keep to her original pact with Tarolfo: "Va, e copertamente serva il tuo giuramento, e a Tarolfo ciò che tu promettesti liberamente attieni: egli l'ha ragionevolmente e con grande affanno guadagnato" [Go, secretly keep your oath, and give Tarolfo what you promised freely; he has earned it fairly and with great labor] (4.31.44). In both instances, the word *guadagnare*, used to express the concept of "winning," neatly recalls the language of the chivalric ideal. The verb models Tarolfo as the noble knight who has set out on a quest and through "grande affanno" rightly ("ragionevolmente") deserved his lady's love. Tarolfo frames his performance in much the same way when he informs the noblewoman that her

---

21. Jean-Joseph Goux, *Symbolic Economies: After Marx and Freud,* trans. Jennifer Curtiss Gage (Ithaca: Cornell University Press, 1990), 13, 16, and 15.

request has at long last been fulfilled: "Madonna, dopo lunga fatica io ho fornito quello che voi comandaste" [My lady, after long labor I have provided what you asked] (4.31.37). What the noblewoman's husband calls a "grande affanno," Tarolfo instead terms a "lunga fatica." Like so many knights in chivalric romances before him, Tarolfo has only obeyed his lady's command. The language of earning and the language of labor, freely employed by the noblewoman, the noblewoman's husband, and Tarolfo, together reflect the ideals of chivalry and of the social world of the aristocracy to which that language and the three speakers belong.

Yet the same language bears no relation to the actual events themselves. Tarolfo has performed no great feats of conquest in his "impresa." He has battled no giants, wrestled to the ground no horrible monsters, defeated no fearsome foes. His quest—his "grande affanno" and "lunga fatica"—in truth entails a long voyage, which the narrator dismisses in a short sentence: "E partitosi della terra con quella compagnia che a lui piacque di prendere, tutto il ponente cercò per avere consiglio di potere pervenire al suo disio; ma non trovato lui, cercò le più calde regioni, e pervenne in Tesaglia, dove per sì fatta bisogna fu mandato da discreto uomo" [Leaving the country with the companions he chose to take, he scoured all the western world for advice as to how he might attain his desire; but not finding it, he sought out the hotter regions, and came to Thessaly, where he had been sent by a wise man, for such a need as his] (4.31.9). Moreover, the climax of Tarolfo's "impresa," to which the narrator instead devotes ample attention, hardly involves a heroic confrontation. When the poor wizard observes Tarolfo wandering alone over "lo misero piano che già tinto fu del romano sangue" [the wretched plain [of Pharsalia] that was once stained of Roman blood] (4.31.10), he inquires circumspectly: "Non sai tu la qualità del luogo come ella è? Perché inanzi d'altra parte non pigliavi la via? Tu potresti di leggieri qui da furiosi spiriti essere vituperato" [Don't you know what kind of place this is? Why didn't you choose some other place to wander? Here you could easily be attacked by angry ghosts] (4.31.15). Yet, rather than engaging in a heroic confrontation with the fierce ghost of a soldier on the epic battlefield of Pharsalia, Tarolfo concludes his lonesome quest by making a simple transaction with a poor man. The desire for wealth, inveighed against as the "seeds of war" [belli / semina] in Lucan's *Pharsalia* (1.158),[22] becomes on this former battlefield

---

22. Lucan, *The Civil War* (Cambridge: Harvard University Press, 1969). I would like to thank one of the Press's anonymous readers for this connection to Lucan.

a blessing for Tarolfo, who can now succeed in his amorous quest for romance precisely because the wizard wishes to get rich. In terms of the chivalric ideal, Tarolfo has not so much earned his lady's love as bought it. Nor has he labored much at all; instead he has traded a portion of his wealth for the wizard's labor. "Non ti travagliare," the wizard informs Tarolfo as they conclude their deal (4.31.21). The verb *travagliare* clearly means "worry," but we may be justified in taking it to signify that the nobleman will henceforth not have to lift a finger. At the risk of exaggeration, it is as if Dante, to win the love of Beatrice in the garden of Eden, had paid a plebian to undergo the voyage in his stead.

Though the wizard fabricates a garden that "parve alla donna bellissima cosa e mirabile" [seemed to his lady both beautiful and marvelous] (4.31.41), the exchange between Tarolfo and the poor man never takes place. On seeing the generosity of the noblewoman's husband (who gives up his wife) and the generosity of Tarolfo toward his beloved (the knight releases the noblewoman from her obligation), the wizard decides that he should be no less generous in turn. He therefore liberates Tarolfo from the terms of their prior agreement. At this point, Menedon, who has just concluded his tale, asks the *brigata*—though more specifically Queen Fiammetta, who decides all such *questioni d'amore* in the *Filocolo*—which of the three men was the most generous (4.31.54–55). Not unexpectedly, Menedon excludes from consideration the obvious "generosity" of the woman, for in having initially accepted Tarolfo's offer of a gift in exchange for her love, the noblewoman has become, by the end of the novella, an effaced object of exchange in an economy of male desire. In the ensuing debate, the issue of generosity thus turns on the husband's desire for honor, the sacrifice of sexual gratification by Tarolfo, and the giving up of riches by Tebano.

Valuing honor above all, Fiammetta argues that Tebano proved the least generous of the three because his hunger for riches is not worthy "con ciò sia cosa che esse sieno le più volte a virtuosa vita noiose, e possasi con moderata povertà vivere virtuosamente" [inasmuch as it is usually disruptive of the virtuous life, and one can live virtuously with a certain amount of poverty] (4.32.4). Inverting Fiammetta's judgment, Menedon then insists that the wizard was the most generous of them all. In doing so, his rebuttal can also be read as a powerful defense of parvenus. He champions the wizard's "ardente disio" [eager longing] (4.33.4) to flee from the trials of poverty, and he maintains the fundamental right humans have to the wealth they gain through hard work: "quanto deono elle piacere e essere care a chi in modo debito le guadagna e possiede!" [how pleasant and precious must wealth be when one earns and possesses it in a proper fashion!] (4.33.6). So distressful is poverty to the universal well-being of all men that some in fact steal "per vivere splendidamente in riposo" [to live splendidly in repose] (4.33.5), perhaps finding no other alternative for acquiring riches. But those who earn a living and through their honest labors come to possess great wealth are justified in rejoicing over it and keeping it. Parvenus, such as Boccaccio and his father and their fellow bankers in aristocratic Angevin Naples, could find in Menedon's rebuttal a voice legitimating their existence among aristocrats, their right to acquire through hard work a lifestyle of splendor. "Io sono vivuto," the fifty-year-old Boccaccio would in fact recall at the height of his literary career and fame, "dalla mia puerizia infino in intera età nutricato, a Napoli ed intra nobili giovani meco in età convenienti, i quali, quantunque nobili, d'entrare in casa mia né di me visitare si vergognavano. Vedevano me . . . assai dilicatamente vivere, sì come noi fiorentini viviamo; vedevano ancora la casa e la masserizia mia, secondo la misura della possibilità, splendida assai." [I lived from my childhood to man's estate, nourished in Naples and amongst noble youths of my own age who, although noblemen, were not ashamed to enter my house nor visit me. They saw me . . . living a very refined way, the way we Florentines live; in addition they saw my house, its furnishings and fittings, within the measure of my means, very splendid indeed.][23]

If Fiammetta, on the one hand, measures generosity according to an aristocratic hierarchy without referring to any events in the novella, Menedon, by contrast, responds by paying attention to narrative details that he marshals for the defense of his interpretation. He stresses how Tebano was repeatedly characterized in the novella as poor, and he further indicates that Tebano went to great lengths to escape his poverty as he labored to acquire his wealth: "egli di Tesaglia infino in Ispagna venne, mettendosi per li dubbiosi cammini e incerti dell'aere alle pericolose cose per fornire la 'mpromessa fatta da lui" [he came from Thessaly to Spain, and set off on dangerous and uncertain aerial roads toward dangerous things, in order to supply what he had promised] (4.33.7). Thus, although Menedon works the particular into a universal assumption about the ideological good of wealth, his interpretation still rests on the details of the story he himself narrated. By the time we arrive at Fiammetta's concluding rebuttal, how-

---

23. Cited by Branca in Boccaccio, *Tutto le opere*, 1:20; the translation is from Vittore Branca, *Boccaccio: The Man and His Works*, trans. Richard Monges (New York: New York University Press, 1976), 19.

ever, the novella has been rewritten altogether. The wizard was not generous, Fiammetta now informs the *brigata*. He merely feared being slain by
Tarolfo, who, in the meantime, has evidently grown eager to retrieve his
lost riches:

> Apertamente si pare che da voi è mal conosciuta la povertà, la quale
> ogni ricchezza trapassa se lieta viene. Tebano già forse per l'acquistate
> ricchezze gli pareva esser pieno d'amare e di varie sollecitudini. Egli già
> imaginava che a Tarolfo paresse avere mal fatto, e trattasse di
> ucciderlo per riavere le sue castella. Egli dimorava in paura non forse
> da' suoi sudditi fosse tradito. Egli era entrato in sollecitudine del go-
> vernamento delle sue terre. Egli già conoscea tutti gl'inganni apparec-
> chiati da' suoi parzionali di farli. Egli si vedea da molti invidiato per le
> sue ricchezze, egli dubitava non i ladroni occultamente quelle gli le-
> vassero. Egli era ripieno di tanti e tali e sì varii pensieri e sollecitudini,
> che ogni riposo era da lui fuggito. Per la qual cosa ricordandosi della
> preterita vita, e come sanza tante sollecitudini la menava lieta, fra sé
> disse: "Io disiderava d'arricchire per riposo, ma io veggo ch'elli è
> accrescimento di tribulazioni e di pensieri, e fuggimento di quiete." E
> tornando disideroso d'essere nella prima vita, quelle rendé a chi gliele
> avea donate. ... e però se Tebano si levò questo stimolo da dosso, non
> fu liberale, ma savio. In tanto fu grazioso a Tarolfo, in quanto più
> tosto a lui che ad un altro gli piacque di donarlo, potendolo a molti
> altri donare. (4.34.10–15)

[Obviously it appears that you do not understand well the nature of
poverty, which surpasses all wealth if it comes happily. Perhaps
Tebano saw that because of the wealth he had obtained he was full of
various bitter cares. Already he imagined that Tarolfo thought he had
done wrong, and was arranging to kill him to regain his property. He
lived in fear lest perhaps he might be betrayed by his subjects. He had
entered into the cares of governing his property. Already he was aware
of all the snares his sharecroppers had prepared for him. He saw himself envied by many for his wealth, and he feared that thieves would
stealthily take it from him. He was so full of various thoughts and worries of this sort that all repose eluded him. And for this reason he
recalled his past life, and how he had led it happily without all these
worries, and said to himself, "I wanted to become wealthy so as to find
repose, but I see that wealth means an increase of tribulations and

cares, and a flight from calm." And wanting again to return to his earlier life, he gave that wealth back to the person who had given it to him. . . . And so if Tebano freed himself from such a nuisance, he was not generous but wise. He was gracious to Tarolfo to the degree that he chose to give it to him rather than another, since he could have given it to many others.]

Clearly, for Fiammetta the nobility is never so wise as the poor man who gives up his possessions. All the fears attributed to the wizard—the dread of governing lands, the terror of thieves, the suspicion of underlings, the imagined cheating of sharecroppers—do not, nor it seems ever did, plague Tarolfo, who is only too happy to regain his property. No doubt this is the case because the wizard's sagacity does not derive from a spontaneous recognition of the virtues of poverty. It derives instead from the structure of a society that mystifies, through the familiar language of Christian stoic philosophy as expressed by Fiammetta, the ideology of a deeply ingrained aristocratic disdain toward a poor man who suddenly acquires the substance of a nobleman's wealth. The natural order of social relations must therefore be preserved and justified in this particular novella at all costs, just as, in the larger narrative, Filocolo's mother and father instinctively find themselves compelled to oppose the marriage between a king's son and a woman presumed to be a mere plebian. Judging from Fiammetta's response and its tacit acceptance by all the storytellers, moreover, the elite circle of the noble *brigata* debating these questions in their own garden wishes to distance itself from any association with parvenus. What, after all, would be more out of place in the *Filocolo* than the transformation of a poor, short, bearded man, accustomed to dirtying his hands in a peasantlike fashion by pulling up roots, into a nouveau riche who dresses not in tattered rags but in the crimson robes of a lord with a lord's treasures, and who sits by a noblewoman's side in a landed estate or garden of his own?

This situation is, however, quite different when Boccaccio takes up the novella again in the *Decameron* where—new names given and old names taken away—a discussion once more follows. There he writes:

Chi potrebbe pienamente raccontare i varii ragionamenti tralle donne stati, qual maggior liberalità usasse, o Giliberto o messer Ansaldo o il nigromante, intorno a' fatti di madonna Dianora? Troppo sarebbe lungo. (10.6.2)

[Who could fully recount the various discussions that now took place amongst the ladies as to whether Gilberto or Messer Ansaldo or the magician had displayed the greater liberality in the affair of Madonna Dianora. It would take too long to tell.]

The "question," as Vittore Branca notes, "is exactly the same . . . that is developed in the *Filocolo*."[24] Yet the debate, which is not recorded and is therefore deferred to the reader, is inconclusive.[25] It is inconclusive in this case, I suspect, because the social relations governing the novella have changed the terms of the debate, and because there is a fundamental difference in the nature of the wealth acquired and the modes of behavior that are now associated with it.

The poor wizard of the *Filocolo* knows how the world works, with all its attendant social hierarchies and cultural codes. He discerns the features of a nobleman at first glance, and he recognizes that the rags he wears are "vilissimi" [most base] (4.31.18). More important, he is cognizant and resentful of the way cultural attitudes predetermine assumptions about inner value. Finally, he knows how to make a deal to acquire wealth. Yet, as a solitary man in a deserted area of the world, the wizard appears asocial. To the extent that he goes about digging up dirt and plucking herbs to cure his own ailments and prolong his own life, he further appears self-sufficient. He uses magic in his isolation to meet his most basic, specific personal needs (health and longevity), not to pursue personal profit within a narrow or broad network of social and economic exchanges. Thus, working against Tarolfo's assumption that the wizard has always labored to get rich ("non ti bisognerà più affannare per divenire ricco," 4.31.20) is the truth that this wizard has positioned himself in a region far from commercial activity or any social base where his skill as a magician might be rewarded. The wizard of the *Filocolo* has lucked into, as it were, a one-shot deal that will lift him from poverty to wealth, from work to pleasure, from *negotium* to *otium*. He is fortunate, but his Fortune is only partially characteristic of the *Decameron*. It is a chance opportunity that a clever, socially adept individual seizes to get what he wants at one extraordinary moment in time.[26]

---

24. Branca in Boccaccio, *Tutte le opere*, 1518, vol. 4, "E' proprio la 'questione' che si sviluppa nel *Filocolo*."

25. For an alternate reading, see Guardiani, "Boccaccio dal *Filocolo*," 40–41.

26. For observations regarding "Fortune" in the *Filocolo* see Perella, "The World of Boccaccio's *Filocolo*," passim.

Missing from this definition is the element of strategy celebrated in the *Decameron,* the ability to put oneself in the right place at the right time, the merchant's ability to work the far-flung networks of commercial activity— the ports, cities, highways, and crossroads of the world. The wizard of the *Decameron* is distinguished from Tebano precisely because he possesses a degree of that mercantile ability. He is not just socially aware but socially active. No longer a poor rustic root-picker wandering on the edge of the civilized world, this wizard has instead become a kind of skilled artisan ever open to temporary gainful employment, responding to a worldwide call in order to sell his craft ("arte") for cash in an urban setting:

> Il cavaliere, udita la domanda e la proferta della sua donna, quantunque grave cosa e quasi impossibile a dover fare gli paresse e conoscesse per niun'altra cosa ciò essere dalla donna addomandato se non per torlo dalla sua speranza, pur seco propose di voler tentare quantunque fare se ne potesse e in più parti per lo mondo mandò cercando se in ciò alcun si trovasse che aiuto o consiglio gli desse; e vennegli una alle mani il quale, dove ben salariato fosse, per arte nigromantica profereva di farlo. Col quale messer Ansaldo per grandissima quantità di moneta . . . (10.5.9–10)

> [On hearing about the lady's proposition, the gentleman naturally felt that she was asking him to do something very difficult, or rather wellnigh impossible, and realized that her only reason for demanding such a thing was to dash his hopes; but nevertheless he resolved that he would explore every possible means of furnishing her request. He therefore sent inquiries afoot in various parts of the world to see whether anyone could be found to advise and assist him in the matter, and eventually a man came into his hands who offered to do it by magic, provided he was well-enough paid. So Messer Ansaldo agreed to pay him a huge sum of money . . .]

From the *Filocolo* to the *Decameron,* the desire for sexual gratification is managed through wealth. In the later text, however, magicians are no longer recognizably poor, filthy, and peasantlike. And marvels, the products of magic, are sold in an effort to obtain not the worldly possessions of the landed nobility but the circulating power of money in the marketplace as an agent of further exchange. We have, in short, entered a brave new world dependent on the very processes of exchange governed by currency that was shunned by the noble-minded Idalogo of the *Filocolo,* who had been transformed into a tree.[27] And in such a world, with its presumed extended networks of economic exchanges and rapidly growing communes, Menedon's argument in defense of parvenus suddenly rings true. The introduction of money implicitly injects into the earlier version of the novella the inevitable breakdown of an agrarian, feudal society divided between, on the one hand, the pleasures of the nobility who barter for their marvels and, on the other, the needs of poverty-stricken people who toil for their livelihood with what they can gather from the soil. By the time we have come to the *Decameron,* the autobiographically authorial figure of Idalogo, whose name is loosely translated in Boccaccio's Greek as "voice from the woods," has taken off his pastoral garb and grown distinctly, though not exclusively, urban in spirit and in tone.

The "Florentine" Calandrino: A Market of Marvels

For the wizards of both the *Decameron* and the *Filocolo,* the making of marvels constitutes a source of income. A fabulous garden costs something, whether it is measured in terms of feudal estates or great sums of money. Magicians may therefore have extraordinary powers, but in no way do these powers release them from the underlying structures of the economies in which they live. Tebano, despite his impressive ability to transform a frozen plot of grass by the shore into a springtime garden, cannot seem to transform his own peasantlike rags into the robes of a nobleman. Likewise, the nameless wizard of the *Decameron* exercises his magic for financial gain, presumably because he relies on money, rather than magic, to procure the things he needs or desires. The ability of magicians to transform the world about them does not serve them well when it comes to dealing with the material demands of their daily lives. Magic is always a means, never a substitute, for the wizard's private acquisition of wealth: it is a skill like any other, a legitimate form of work rewarded in cash.

Such an approach to magic and its marvelous effects reverses a romance practice in which the concentrated power of magic often operates

---

27. As a result, the suitor of the *Decameron,* while evidently "per arme e per cortesia conosciuto per tutto" [known for feats of arms and deeds of courtesy by all] (10. 5.4), is therefore a man who presumably conducts himself according the chivalric code of honor, and he now sees no real reason to set out on a courtly quest as Tarolfo did; the knight, having grown sedentary and calculatingly bourgeois in manner, now allows money, in the form of "currency," to run about the world for him.

as a disguised substitute for a collective social workforce. In romances palaces brimming with servants and feasts often appear and disappear with none of the fatigue that accompanies the construction of magnificent edifices, let alone the energy required to maintain their opulence. From this perspective, the marvelous in romance often reflects a happy vision of the lifestyle of the wealthy, ordinarily (though not necessarily, as Eugene Vance has shown) the landed aristocracy enjoying their *otium*. All this is neatly accomplished, moreover, without ever having to account for the social and economic systems producing such wealth and sustaining such habits of leisure.[28] Magicians, far from operating as skilled artisans (as they do in the novella of the *Decameron*), achieve with a whoosh of their wands what skilled and unskilled laborers normally labor to do over a pro-tracted period of time. The power of magic operates in such instances as the power of riches, and in a society based on a market system, power of this kind is inevitably grounded in the fluid power of money.

We may explore this connection between money and the magic of the marketplace, the identification of money as the source of the happy world of romance *otium,* by examining briefly the third novella of day eight of the *Decameron.*[29] In this famous novella concerning Calandrino in search of the heliotrope, the romance quest for marvels becomes a quest for money by a character who is a failed parvenu and whose journey is a mock-Dantean descent. Calandrino is repeatedly represented as con-stantly going down: "in giù della pietra cercando" [looking down there for the stone] (8.3.39); "giù per lo Mugnone" [down along the Mugnone] (8.3.43).[30] In this way he recalls the sinners of the seventh *bolgia* of Dante's *Inferno,* thieves with no place to hide from the punishment of those chas-ing after them: "sanza sperar pertugio o elitropia" [without hope of hiding place or heliotrope] (24.93). There is, of course, no Dantean otherworld in

---

28. See Vance, "Chrétien's *Yvain* and the Ideologies of Change and Exchange," in *Mervelous Signals.* Vance is concerned with uncovering not the feudal agrarian basis of mag-ical powers but the discourse of nascent capitalism in Chrétien's treatment of magic and mar-vels: "The marvels of capital money and commerce," he writes, "are at the very heart of Chré-tien's romanesque *merveilleux* in *Yvain*" (129). I have benefited as well from the discussion of R. Howard Bloch, *Etymologies and Genealogies: A Literary Anthropology of the French Mid-dle Ages* (Chicago: University of Chicago Press, 1983), in particular 165–74.

29. Amid the many discussions dedicated to Calandrino, those that have most influenced my reading are: Luigi Russo, *Letture critiche del "Decameron"* (Bari: Laterza, 1956), 278–300; Carlo Muscetta, *Giovanni Boccaccio* (Bari: Laterza, 1972), 192–99; Mazzotta, *The World at Play,* 188–94; and Millicent Joy Marcus, *An Allegory of Form: Literary Self-Con-sciousness in the "Decameron"* (Saratoga: Anma Libri, 1979), 79–92.

30. I owe this observation to Wayne Rebhorn. My translation.

this novella, just this world. And there is no marvel that is not here grounded conceptually in the power of money, "that solid piece of metal," as Marx wrote, in which "all the physical wealth evolved in the world of commodities is contained in a latent state."[31] What Calandrino thus unwittingly wishes to become, as a distant harbinger of Don Quixote, is the prosaic hero of the bourgeois world, capable of descending into hell to retrieve a fabled gem and acquire fabulous wealth as a result of his "quest." He aims to acquire the mythic power to change himself in society by possessing all the goods produced and distributed beneath the sun.

A Florentine painter who originally came from the outlying countryside, Calandrino does not give the impression that he has been a singularly successful artist. At one point in this novella he describes the act of painting as "avere tutto dì a schiccherare le mura a modo che fa la lumaca" [to daub walls all the time like a lot of snails] (8.3.29). Painters, with this metaphor, have been likened to snails that leave behind, in the slow tedious progression of their lives, not beauty but slime. In short, painting is an inherently filthy activity, no different than work on the farm, the kind of work the country-based Calandrino perhaps knew best. It is also, for that matter, no different than the kind of work the wizard of the *Filocolo* was engaged in when Tarolfo came upon him picking weeds. Not surprisingly, then, Calandrino, who has logically come to the city in search of better prospects, is immediately taken in by Maso del Saggio's description of Bengodi, with its overflowing cornucopia of goods, its happy productivity and fertility, and its utopian communal wealth (8.3.18). Bengodi is not a lush springtime garden exchanged for love (Tarolfo) or for socially valuable labor time (Tebano); it is, instead, the peasant's droll vision of what a *locus amoenus* should be: the land of Cockaigne as the typical medieval and Renaissance dreamland of endless conspicuous consumption.

Calandrino, however, now lives permanently in Florence, and for a newly urbanized man, who has "fatti" [affairs] to attend to on a daily basis, the land of Bengodi is too far away. Calandrino therefore informs Maso del Saggio, who has been pretending all along to be a great lapidary, that "Troppo ci è di lungi a' fatti miei" [It's too far away for my affairs] (8.3.18). Immediate gratification in the land of plenty must consequently give way to the realities of daily urban life, where all the objects of consumption to be found in the land of Bengodi cost money, and where

---

31. Karl Marx, *A Contribution to the Critique of Political Economy*, with an introduction by Maurice Dobb, trans. S. W. Ryazanskaya (New York: International Publishers, 1970), 124.

Calandrino earns money by pushing slime across walls. This then brings Calandrino back to the original question: "Ma dimmi," he asks Maso del Saggio, "che lieto sie tu, in queste contrade non se ne truova niuna di queste pietre così virtuose?" [But do please tell me, are there none of these magical stones to be found in this part of the world?] (8.3.18). In responding to Calandrino's question, Maso del Saggio tells him of two stones, one of which is the heliotrope, which can be found in the nearby Mugnone.

Though the heliotrope's traditional power to render its possessor invisible has been explicitly denied by Maso del Saggio, Calandrino nevertheless believes that he has at last found the instrument—not a paintbrush, but a fabled gem—that will allow him to effect a radical metamorphosis in his life. Hurrying off, he announces to Bruno and Buffalmacco what he plans to do with the heliotrope once he has found it:

> Compagni, quando voi vogliate credermi, noi possiamo divenire i più ricchi uomini di Firenze: per ciò che io ho inteso da uomo degno di fede che in Mugnone si truova una pietra, la qual chi la porta sopra non è veduto da niuna altra persona; per che a me parrebbe che noi senza alcuno indugio, prima che altra persona v'andasse, v'andassimo a cercar. Noi la troverem per certo, per ciò che io la conosco; e trovata che noi l'avremo, che avrem noi a fare altro se non mettercela nella scarsella e andare alle tavole de' cambiatori, le quali sapete che stanno sempre cariche di grossi e di fiorini, e torcene quanti noi ne vorremo? Niuno ci vedrà; e così potremo arricchire subitamente. (8.3.28–29)

[Pay attention to me, my friends, and we can become the richest men in Florence, for I have heard on good authority that along the Mugnone there's a certain kind of stone, and when you pick it up you become invisible. I reckon we ought to go there right away, before anyone else does. We'll find it without a doubt, because I know what it looks like; and once we've found it, all we have to do is to put it in our purses and go to the money changers, whose counters, as you know, are always loaded with groats and florins, and help ourselves to as much as we want. No one will see us; and so we'll be able to get rich quick.]

Though the urbanized Calandrino earlier concluded that the land of bounty was too far away, he has now located a nearby substitute in the marketplace. The prospects of conspicuous consumption in the land of Bengodi—with all its wondrous goods, such as mountains of parmesan cheese, countless sausages, and rivers of good fresh wine—are never too far away as long as one has access to an endless supply of gold and silver florins.

The introduction of the heliotrope thus suddenly offers Calandrino not just the immediate gratification of desire but the more lasting, and therefore infinitely more gratifying, prospects of economic and social success in an urban setting. As a source of almost unlimited wealth produced without labor, the marvel of the heliotrope holds out to Calandrino the possibility of permanently escaping one mode of worldly existence for another. With the heliotrope, Calandrino can go from being a painter who dirties walls to being a kind of gentleman whose maximum effort consists in casually counting stolen coins. What Calandrino obviously wants, and what he has been denied because of his lack of skill as a workman, is a piece of the action that the other "nuove genti" [new people] (8.3.4) arriving from the *contado* [countryside] have acquired. The enthusiasm with which Calandrino therefore scurries about the banks of the Mugnone already anticipates how he plans to hop "now here now there" [or qua or là saltando] (8.3.39), from one money changer's table to another, gathering into the folds of his uplifted apron countless florins until he can hold no more. The stones in his apron are as good as cash, and with so much money, Calandrino will be able to step out of his customary existence and enter the world of leisure. Instantly ("subitamente"), he will be lifted above the social world of those who operate a mechanical trade, propelled even beyond the social world of the burghers whose "sùbiti guadagni" [sudden gains] Dante so deplored (*Inf.* 16.73–75).[32]

But therein lies the problem. Rich or poor, Calandrino is destined to remain the town jerk, mocked by the companions whom he even seeks to cheat. Money refashions appearances, but never, in Boccaccio's *Decameron,* essences. Forever cheap, avaricious, and inept in artistic ability and manners, Calandrino, with his "nuovi costumi" [strange customs] (8.3.4), will always lack the ability to produce things of either temporary or lasting value, just as he will always lack the knowledge, in the words of Giovanni Getto, "to live well."[33] In early, protocapitalist Renaissance Flo-

---

32. The verses from the *Commedia* read: "La gente nuova e i sùbiti guadagni / orgoglio e dismisura han generata, / Fiorenza, in te, sì che tu già ten piagni." Marcus, *Allegory of Form,* 82, emphasizes this passage in her discussion of Calandrino; the same passage clearly subtends Muscetta's discussion as well. See also Franco Fido, "Dante, personaggio mancato del *Decameron,*" in *Le metamorfosi del centauro: Studi e letture da Boccaccio a Pirandello* (Rome: Bulzoni, 1977).

33. Getto, *Vita di forme.*

rence, which promises rewards and limited upward mobility for artistic labor, Calandrino is forever stuck being Calandrino. He cannot, for all the wealth in the world, escape being boorish. For this reason, either Calandrino must learn to know his place in society, or else he will be put back into his place, a place suited to both his wit and capacities. What matters most, then, is not how much money Calandrino has or might ever have. What matters most is the social value of what Calandrino produces (which money in turn may or may not accurately measure) and how, in the daily operations of monetary transactions, human transactions are also always taking place.

The structured irony of the novella, which makes Calandrino the butt of an elaborately staged hoax, reveals that the word *heliotrope* has no referential value. It is an empty sign pointing to the emptiness of Calandrino, who would seek all the wealth in the world in order to compensate for his own inept artistry, and to the consummate artistry of the tricksters who place the word *heliotrope* under erasure in what Millicent Marcus has called their "self-canceling rhetoric."[34] The heliotrope, in terms of the age-old relationship of *nomina* and *res,* is only wondrous to speak of (*mirabile dictu*). It is part of the rhetoric of the marvelous supremely practiced by other tricksters in Boccaccio's work, such as Frate Cipolla and Ser Cepparello. Like the monetary sign in the 1300s, the heliotrope has here become a *flatus vocis,* "cut off from its roots in physical property or weight"; it is an agent of exchange used by tricksters for mere pleasure rather than profit.[35] Yet because the heliotrope is a sign with no real referential value, Calandrino's quest for it reflects a broad basic assumption, made familiar through the flourishing genre of venality satire in the later Middle Ages, that money, whether we are speaking of *Regina Pecunia, Dea Moneta, Dan Denier, Herr Pfenninck,* or simply a personified *Nummus,* can in fact buy anything and everything.[36]

---

34. Marcus, *Allegory of Form,* 84.

35. The quote is from Bloch, *Etymologies,* 170. Over *rhetoric of the marvelous,* Bailet, *L'homme de verre,* prefers the phrase *language of the marvelous.* I have here tried to emphasize the important rhetorical aim behind the use of this language in the *Decameron.* There is, in short, always an attempt to persuade. For discussions of the marvelous in the rhetoric of Frate Cipolla and others in the *Decameron,* see in particular Marcus, *Allegory of Form.*

36. John A. Yunck, *The Lineage of Lady Meed* (Notre Dame: University of Notre Dame Press, 1963). For discussions of attitudes toward money in the age of the "commercial revolution," see—along with Lester Little, "Pride Goes before Avarice"—Lauro Martines, *Power and Imagination: City-States in Renaissance Italy* (New York: Knopf, 1979), in particular 79–93; and, specifically for Florence, Carlo M. Cipolla, *The Monetary Policy of Fourteenth-Century Florence* (Berkeley: University of California Press, 1982). I have also benefited

"Florins clear your eyes and give you fires," the Sienese Cecco Angolieri sarcastically wrote, "turn to facts all your desires / and into all the world's vast possibilities" [[I fiorini] ti fanno star chiaro e pien d'ardire, / e venir fatti tutti i tuoi talenti, / che si pôn far nel mondo né seguire].[37] By the time we have come to the quest for the heliotrope in the *Decameron,* all that is seemingly impossible to achieve, as Calandrino comically reveals in his inability to achieve the ends he pursues, may be actually bought by the parvenus alike through the magical—in the Marxian sense, the "truly creative"—power of money. From this perspective, which is a perspective Boccaccio shared in his concern for the use of signs and symbols in human transactions, the lands of pleasure and pure wish fulfillment do not only exist in or through the language that represents them. They also exist in and through the universal equivalent of money, which, unlike the heliotrope, has the power to render invisible not the individual who holds it but the concentrated labor-time for which money is constantly, if not always consciously, exchanged.

In this light, Boccaccio, with his novella of Calandrino, bequeaths to the modern world a notion of the marvelous radically grounded in social and economic reality and hence a marvelous far more verisimilar than what any of the writers examined in this study could ever produce, despite their serious musings on the subject. Readers never expect Calandrino to locate the heliotrope any more than we imagine that Tasso's Tancredi in the *Liberata,* for example, penetrating the enchanted woods to chop down a tree, will witness just the oozing forth of sap. For something so truly commonplace and verisimilar to occur, we must move beyond Tasso's forest to Cervantes' plains, where no enchanters exist and where all the marvels are lodged in the brain of a maddened hidalgo from La Mancha. But the practical social value of the marvelous, so comically dramatized in Calandrino's narcissistic quest for the heliotrope as a substitute for all the

---

from John McGovern, "The Rise of New Economic Attitudes—Economic Humanism, Economic Nationalism—during the Later Middle Ages and the Renaissance, A.D. 1200–1550," *Traditio* 26 (1970): 217–53; and Peter Spufford, *Money and Its Use in Medieval Europe* (Cambridge: Cambridge University Press, 1988). For a semiotic reading of monetary theory in the Middle Ages, see Bloch, *Etymologies.*

37. Massèra, *Sonetti burleschi,* 100. The translation by Lauro Martines, though not a word-for-word rendering, nevertheless captures the spirit of these verses; it comes from his *Power and Imagination,* 79. On Cecco Angolieri in the context of venality satire, see the remarks by Mario Marti in *Cultura e stile nei poeti giocosi del tempo di Dante* (Pisa: Nistri-Lischi, 1953). Yunck is not helpful for venality satire in Italian literature, which he concludes "was not especially popular" (*The Lineage of Lady Meed,* 274).

money in the world, nevertheless remains a central issue in Ariosto's *Furioso* too. In the *Furioso,* a work likewise indebted to totalizing quests for single objects of universal value, the marvelous embodies once again the desire for the impossible plentitude of an absolute, though this time in a society ruled by the interrelated powers of magic and military might rather than by money as a mystifying agent of normal, everyday exchange.

Chapter 4

Ariosto, Power, and the Desire for Totality

Au-delà de l'agrément, de la curiosité, de toutes les émotions que nous donnent les récits, les contes et les légendes, au-delà du besoin de se distraire, d'oublier, de se procurer des sensations agréables ou terrifiantes, le but réel du voyage merveilleux est, nous sommes déjà en mesure de le comprendre, l'exploration plus totale de la réalité universelle.

—Pierre Mabille

Astolfo's Quest

In the sixth canto of the *Orlando furioso,* the hippogriff travels nonstop for three-thousand miles in a straight line and then settles down with Ruggiero on an island of exotic beauty.[1] As soon as the hippogriff has neared this land, Ruggiero jumps off and ties the winged horse to a myrtle between a laurel and a pine. He faces the breeze, drinks water from a fountain, and bathes his hands. But the hippogriff suddenly turns to flee, startled by a presence that darkens the forest and makes the animal shy. What frightens the hippogriff the narrator cannot say. It is a "non so che" [I don't know what] (6.26). But this "non so che" has textually maneuvered the *Furioso* in relation to the thirteenth canto of Dante's *Inferno.*[2] Fleeing,

---

1. The epigraph heading this chapter is from Pierre Mabille, *Le miroir du merveilleux,* with an introduction by André Breton (Paris: Minuit, 1962), 24. Citations from the *Orlando furioso* are from Ludovico Ariosto, *Orlando furioso,* ed. Emilio Bigi, 2 vols. (Milan: Rusconi, 1982); all translations are, with minor modifications, from Ariosto, *The "Orlando Furioso" of Ludovico Ariosto,* ed. Stewart A. Baker and A. Bartlett Giamatti, trans. William Stewart Rose (Indianapolis: Bobbs-Merrill, 1968). Citations from the *Cinque canti* and the *Satire* are from Ariosto, *Opere minori,* ed. Cesare Segre (Milan: Ricciardi, 1954); translations of the former are from Ariosto, *Five Cantos,* trans. Leslie Z. Morgan (New York and London: Garland Publishing, 1992).

2. On the linguistic traces and stylistic importance of Dante in the *Furioso,* see Cesare Segre, "Un repertorio linguistico e stilistico dell'Ariosto: La *Commedia,*" in *Esperienze ariostesche* (Pisa: Nistri-Lischi, 1966), 51–83; Luigi Blasucci, "La 'Commedia' come fonte linguistica e stilistica del 'Furioso,'" in *Studi su Dante e Ariosto* (Milan: Ricciardi, 1969),

the hippogriff overturns the myrtle to which it was tied, releasing in turn a human voice—the voice of Astolfo—in a manner overtly drawn from Dante's simile of the hissing, burning branch:

> Come d'un stizzo verde ch'arso sia
> da l'un de' capi, che da l'altro geme
> e cigola per vento che va via,
> sì de la scheggia rotta usciva insieme
> parole e sangue.
>
> (*Inf.* 13.40–44)

[As from a green brand that is burning at one end, and drips from the other, hissing with the escaping air, so from that broken twig came out words and blood together.]

> Come ceppo talor, che le medolle
> rare e vote abbia, e posto al fuoco sia,
> poi che per gran calor quell'aria molle
> resta consunta ch'in mezzo l'empia,
> dentro risuona, e con strepito bolle,
> tanto che quel furor truovi la via;
> così murmura e stride e si coruccia
> quel mirto offeso, e al fine apre la buccia.
>
> (6.27)

[As in a stick to feed the chimney rent,
Where scanty pith ill fills the narrow sheath,
The vapour, in its little channel pent,
Struggles, tormented by the fire beneath;
And, till its prisoned fury find a vent,
Is heard to hiss and bubble, sing and seethe:
So the offended myrtle inly pined,
Groaned, murmured, and at last unclosed its rind.]

In elaborating on Dante's simile, Ariosto has taken a little over four verses from the *Commedia* and doubled them into an extended rewriting

---

121–62; and now, in particular for its thematic relevance rather than simply its stylistic presence, the many observations of Albert R. Ascoli in *Ariosto's Bitter Harmony: Crisis and Evasion in the Italian Renaissance* (Princeton: Princeton University Press, 1987).

that comprises an entire octave unto itself.[3] But Ariosto's reelaboration of Dante's simile is not just a "filling out," an *amplificatio*. It is also, and above all, an act of liberation.[4] Ariosto has extracted from Dante's simile the image of combustion and wind, liberating it of all its infernal qualities: the darkness, the gloom, the blood. In the same way, he has transformed Dante's zone of the suicides into a pleasance of singing birds and verdant trees, of courteous knights who fall in love and talk with "espedita e chiarissima favella" [very clear and quick speech] (6.28). Within the larger narrative of the *Furioso*, this same act of liberation finds its extended analogue through the figure of Astolfo here released. The emergence of Astolfo's voice with Ariosto's rewriting of Dante's simile marks the inscription into the *Furioso* of a *viator* who adores traveling so much that he will eventually descend into hell and fly up to the terrestrial paradise. With the emergence of Astolfo's voice, Ariosto has transformed the wayfarer's spiritual quest for God in the *Commedia* into a spirited romance desire to see the many marvels that are scattered about the world.

Ariosto may have picked up this notion of liberation from Dante's own oblique revision of canto 13 in the *Purgatorio*. In canto 25, just before turning to his extraordinary invention of the aerial bodies of the otherworld, Dante alludes to Meleager—the boy who wastes away as a stick burns—to express through Ovidian myth the separation (rather than conflation, as in the Polydorus episode) of sign and referent, body and spirit. In purgatory, unlike hell, metamorphosis is ideally that of the cocoon, and spirit is conceptually released from, though still mimetically attached to, the body.[5] Yet the desire for the marvelous as expressed by Astolfo in the *Furioso* also already began to govern Astolfo's last appear-

---

3. Blasucci, *Studi*, has written well on this: ". . . egli tende a completare, per dir così, gli spunti brachilogici e fulminei di Dante. Per quel che riguarda quest'ultimo aspetto, che interessa più da vicino il nostro assunto, ci basterà ricordare a puro titolo di campione il paragone famosissimo di VI, 27 . . . , che riprende e sviluppa con analitica ampiezza la similitudine dantesca dello 'stizzo verde' (*Inf.*, XIII, 40–2), ma insieme ne stempera l'intensa icasticità espressiva ('geme / e cigola') in fluente dinamicità ritmica ('così murmura e stride e si coruccia'). E tuttavia, qui e altrove, pur nella radicale rielaborazione dello spunto originario, alcuni persistenti richiami verbali oppure la stessa conservazione delle rime, come osserva Segre, dichiarano ancora il rapporto dell'Ariosto con la sua fonte (nel nostro esempio è da notare tra l'altro il riscontro delle rime *sia: via*)" (157–58).

4. For an alternative reading, see the final pages of Daniel Javitch, "The Imitation of Imitations in *Orlando furioso*," *Renaissance Quarterly* 38 (1985): 215–39. See Ascoli for observations on the importance of the many Dantean subtexts in *Ariosto's Bitter Harmony*, passim.

5. I thank one of the Press's readers for drawing my attention to Dante's Ovidian revision of the Polydorus episode in purgatory and its relevance to Ariosto here.

ance in Boiardo's poem, a poem itself deeply indebted to Ovidian mythology. In particular, in the second book of the *Orlando innamorato,* Astolfo, as he returns home with Dudone and Ranaldo, comes upon the fay Alcina, who has been luring toward the shore with words alone some of the strangest fishes ever seen, among which is even a whale that is like a two-mile-long island (2.13.57–58). Angered that these men have found her at her task, Alcina decides to open the land beneath their feet. Love unexpectedly triumphs in a Boiardian world, however, and Alcina soon finds herself inflamed with a great desire for Astolfo (2.13.59–60).[6] Calling out, she entices the barons to venture beyond the shore on the isle of the whale's back and see a "gran meraviglia" [great marvel], knowing perhaps that only Astolfo, nearest the shore, would actually go:

> —Bei baroni, or che chiedete?
> Se qua con meco vi piace pescare,
> Bench'io non abbia né laccio né rete,
> Gran meraviglia vi potrò mostrare

> (2.13.61)

[Well barons, what now do you seek? If you don't care to fish with me, even though I don't have either a hook or a net, I will show you all a great marvel.]

In the *Furioso,* Astolfo tells much the same story to Ruggiero. He does not, however, simply summarize his last appearance. He instead refashions the desire imputed to him from the Boiardian narrator's distanced point of view, making it the guiding heartbeat to his existence. In Ariosto's retelling of the tale, the point of view has noticeably shifted—Astolfo is speaking, not the narrator—and with this interiorized shift of perspective the marvelous of the *Innamorato* suddenly takes on a specificity that is at once both highly personal and charged with emotion. Where Astolfo in the *Innamorato* is, among other things, a handsome clownish braggart and a knight who sometimes fights, in Ariosto's *Furioso* he has almost singularly become a figure in quest of the marvelous.[7] Ariosto took Boiardo's

6. All citations of the *Orlando innamorato* in my text are from Boiardo, *Orlando innamorato,* ed. Aldo Scaglione, 2 vols. (Turin: Unione Tipografico-Editrice Torinese, 1951). Translations are my own.

7. For an account of Astolfo in previous works, including Boiardo's, see Giuseppe Guido Ferrero, "Astolfo (Storia di un personaggio)," *Convivium* 29 (1961): 513–30; and Mario Santoro, "L'Astolfo ariostesco: *Homo fortunatus,*" in *Ariosto e il Rinascimento* (Naples: Liguori,

final cue and turned Astolfo's yearning for a "great marvel" into a powerful abstraction that represents, as in Jacques Lacan's description of the nature of "demand," the desire for "an impossible plenitude."[8]

In recalling Boiardo's marvel of the two-mile whale, Astolfo in the *Furioso* does not begin with an initial unamazed perception of the whale as an island. He retrospectively dwells on this enormous whale as a marvel, inverting the actual chronological sequence by first reconstructing the recognition and then offering the initial deceptive impression. In Astolfo's memory the whale takes shape as the very image of something, in the Homeric phrase, "wondrous to behold." "Veggiamo una balena," he tells Ruggiero, "la maggiore / che mai per tutto il mar veduta fosse" [There we behold a mighty whale, of size / The hugest yet in any waters seen] (6.37). While the Boiardian narrator's whale is enormous among others kept under Alcina's spell ("Tra le balene vi era una maggiore" [among the whales, there was a greater one] [2.13.58]), Astolfo's in the *Furioso* is the largest in the entire sea. Boiardo's whale is one among many, a marvel among others in a sea where there exist even bigger whales than those enchanted to Alcina's shore. Such a whale is built out of a comparison: it

<hr />

1989). Most critical readings have tended to envision Astolfo as a thematized "figure of the poet," most notably in recent times Giamatti, *The Earthly Paradise*, and David Quint, "The Figure of Atlante: Ariosto and Boiardo's Poem," *Modern Language Notes* 94 (1979): 77–91. Peter DeSa Wiggins, *Figures in Ariosto's Tapestry: Character and Design in the "Orlando furioso"* (Baltimore: Johns Hopkins University Press, 1986), has a fine critique of these readings; he notes they begin with early commentaries of the *Furioso*. But as the title to his chapter "Il Lucido intervallo" indicates, and as in fact happens, Wiggins also tends to develop Astolfo as an analogue of the poet. Peter V. Marinelli, *Ariosto and Boiardo: The Origins of "Orlando furioso"* (Columbia: University of Missouri Press, 1987), for whom Astolfo still "sees what his poet-creator sees" (180), provides an interesting reading through Lucian. Perhaps the best caveat to any attempt to read Astolfo in such a manner is the study of Robert Durling, *The Figure of the Poet in Renaissance Epic* (Cambridge: Harvard University Press, 1965). But see also Ascoli, *Ariosto's Bitter Harmony,* who manages to avoid superimposing Ariosto on the poet.

For readings of the marvelous in the *Furioso* that have contributed to my own, see Guido Almansi, "Tattica del meraviglioso ariostesco," in *Ludovico Ariosto: Lingua, stile, e tradizione. Atti del congresso organizzato dai comuni di Reggio Emilia e Ferrara (12–16 ottobre 1974),* ed. Cesare Segre (Milan: Feltrinelli, 1976), 175–93; Riccardo Bacchelli, "Orlando fatato e l'elmo di Mambrino: Saggio di idee sul meraviglioso in Ariosto e per Cervantes," in *La congiura di Don Giulio e altri scritti Ariosteschi* (Milan: Garzanti, 1958); and Attilio Momigliano, *Saggio sull' "Orlando furioso"* (Bari: Laterza, 1928).

8. I quote from Elizabeth Grosz, *Jacques Lacan: A Feminist Introduction* (London: Routledge, 1990), 62, who provides an excellent discussion of this difficult key concept in Lacan's thought (59–64). For a Lacanian reading of the *Furioso* to which I am indebted, see Deanna Shemek, "That Elusive Object of Desire: Angelica in the *Orlando furioso,*" *Annali d'italianistica* 7 (1989): 116–41.

is bigger, not the biggest—a foretaste of bigger whales, and bigger marvels, yet to come.[9] Astolfo's whale, by contrast, exists as a superlative, an absolute. It is not simply bigger, but "la maggiore" [the biggest], and this superlative stands not in relation to those few swimming around Alcina's shore but in relation to all the whales ever seen "per tutto il mar" [in the entire sea]. Astolfo's claim is for a superlative exceptionality amid a totality of experiences. This claim reflects not so much the actual reality of the whale, however, but its power, then and now, as an object of desire within the realm of the absolute. Singled out, Astolfo's whale is in a class by itself. It is a marvel that cannot portend other, greater whales, because it is the greatest among them all in the entire sea—a sort of "Angelica" of whales.

Astolfo will eventually sit on the huge back of this whale, but he is lured for other reasons. As in the *Innamorato,* Alcina draws Astolfo beyond the shore to ride on the whale's back. But when Astolfo in the *Furioso* recalls Alcina's offer to reveal all kinds of fish, her claim suddenly takes on a greater specificity. Rather than grouping fish into the three generic sizes ("di forme grande e piccole e mezane") [of large, small, and medium forms] (2.13.61), Alcina's description in the *Furioso* moves from the commonplace to the exotic, from the everyday occurrence of fish with scales to the more peculiar concept of fish that are soft, only to hold out as bait at the end of a lure the remarkable image of fish that even have hair. Furthermore, unlike Boiardo's Alcina, who only offers all the fish in the sea, Ariosto's Alcina promises that they will see more fish than all the stars in the sky. Alcina's offer in the *Innamorato* is built out of an equation. She can offer "quante ne ha il mare" [as many as the sea contains] (2.13.61). Alcina in the *Furioso* instead holds out an offer that moves beyond the parity of an equation to the promise of something even more: "e saran più che non ha stelle il cielo" [more in number than the stars of night] (6.39).[10] Astolfo's Alcina moves from the normal to the exotic to arrive finally at the abstract in the realm of the absolute. She has offered Astolfo more than the sea can offer by offering even more than the cosmos can give. The

---

9. Along these lines, the marvelous of the *Innamorato* may be said to function, as does the narrative process itself, in a manner that is additive, always leaving on the horizon another marvel to be seen, to carry the knights into another adventure. On the marvelous in the *Innamorato,* see Eduardo Saccone, "Boiardo, o dell'altra orbita," in *Il soggetto del "Furioso" e altri saggi tra quattro e cinquecento* (Naples: Liguori, 1974).

10. "Le merveilleux," Mabille writes along these lines, "exprime le besoin de dépasser les limites imposées, imposeés par notre structure, d'atteindre une plus grande beauté, une plus grande puissance, une plus grande jouissance, une plus grande durée" *Le merveilleux,* with an introduction by Luc de Heusch (Paris: Pierre Jean Oswald, 1977), 69.

final image she holds out, consequently, is of an upward glance toward the stars in the sky. This glance, which already begins to move in the direction of Astolfo's lunar flight, posits the marvelous as a movement built out of a yearning for more, a movement that can begin with the typical and can gradually progress toward the impossible plenitude of an absolute.

This is the movement that culminates in Alcina's promise that they will see and hear a siren beyond the island of the whale's back: "E volendo vedere una sirena / che col suo dolce canto acheta il mare, / passian di qui fin su quell'altra arena" [And would you hear a mermaid sing so sweet, / That the rude sea grows civil at her song / Pass with me where she sings the shoals among] (6.40). By pointing toward the siren, moreover, as Albert Ascoli observed, Alcina leads Astolfo toward herself.[11] Like the siren, Alcina sits by the seashore, and though she does not quiet the waves with a spellbinding song, she enchants all the fish with "semplici parole e puri incanti" [simple words and by mere magic lore] (6.38). Like the siren that could soothe the turbulence of the sea, Alcina, once on her island, quiets in Astolfo every last desire, in this way operating as a vanishing point for desire itself:

> pareami aver qui tutto il ben raccolto
> che fra i mortali in più parti si smembra,
> a chi più et a chi meno e a nessun molto;
> né di Francia né d'altro mi rimembra:
> stavomi sempre a contemplar quel volto:
> ogni pensiero, ogni mio bel disegno
> in lei finia, né passava oltre il segno.
>
> (6.47)

> [I weened that I each separate good had won,
> Which to mankind is dealt in different measure,
> Little or more to some, and much to none.
> I evermore contemplated my treasure,
> Nor France nor aught beside I thought upon:
> In her my every fancy, every hope
> Centered and ended as their common scope.]

---

11. Ascoli, *Ariosto's Bitter Harmony,* 139, makes note of this and incorporates it into an argument of narrative seduction, of which the siren figure is part of a larger intertextual web.

Like the child's circular gaze with the mother in the Lacanian realm of the Imaginary, the fulfillment of Astolfo's totalizing experience, represented as the gathering into a single body of all the good scattered about the forgotten world, does not mean that Astolfo's love for Alcina has, once and for all, taken over his prior yearning for the marvelous. Rather, Astolfo's memory of his love for Alcina indicates that his prior longing for a "great marvel" was, and still very much is, a passion for an absolute: "pareami aver qui *tutto* il ben raccolto."

Not surprisingly, after expressing such a passion for the marvelous, Astolfo soon accrues marvels at an extraordinarily rapid rate, once he has been transformed by the good fay Melissa back into human form. He acquires first a magical sword, then a book of counterenchantments, and finally a fabulous horn. Astolfo then leaves Alcina's island with Rabicano, Boiardo's "destrier meraviglioso" [marvelous horse] (*Inn.* 1.13.24), a horse that eventually leads Astolfo into Atlante's castle and there to Ariosto's "alta maraviglia" [great marvel] (6.4), the hippogriff. At this point, Astolfo, who has been chasing after Rabicano as his own elusive object of desire, could not be happier (22.26). But for all his happiness, Astolfo does not now know what to do with Rabicano. He may have come upon an animal of superior qualities, but he has no intention of simply abandoning his own horse on the road for the first passerby to seize. After some consideration, Astolfo decides to wait until he can offer Rabicano as a gift to a deserving friend. He waits, but nobody comes; the stars fill the sky, and still nobody arrives. With his book, horn, Rabicano, hippogriff, and lance, Astolfo is overwhelmed with marvels to the point that he can no longer move. He has two marvelous horses—one that appears to fly (15.40) and one that does indeed fly—but he can only ride one horse at a time.

While there is a rapid concentration of marvels in Astolfo's possession from the moment he is transformed back into human form, Ruggiero, by contrast, cannot seem to hold on to those that he obtains.[12] The magic ring, which Melissa gave him, he loses to Angelica; moments later he loses the hippogriff as well (11.14). Ruggiero, it would seem, is destined not to have marvels. Unlike Astolfo, who gradually takes on the characteristics of being the figure of the marvelous in the poem, Ruggiero must preserve the features of a hero patterned from an epic cast and must consequently learn to get on in life by the power of his sword alone. This being the case,

12. On the pairing of Ruggiero and Astolfo see Ascoli, *Ariosto's Bitter Harmony;* and Marianne Shapiro, *The Poetics of Ariosto* (Detroit: Wayne State University Press, 1988), chap. 3.

Ruggiero, after inadvertently winning a knightly combat through the blinding light of Atlante's shield, throws his last remaining marvel into a well. He does this precisely in the moment when Astolfo, unable to ride two horses at the same time, stands waiting to give away Rabicano, his fabulous "destrier meraviglioso." The culmination of Astolfo's rapid acquisition of marvels perfectly corresponds to Ruggiero's depletion of the limited few he manages to obtain. By calculated symmetry, the two heroes, whose inception into the poem as full-fledged characters begins in canto 6, follow completely contrary patterns of development. Whereas Astolfo accrues marvels and uses them liberally whenever any danger arises, Ruggiero uses them so sparingly that he is finally compelled to lose or discard them.

Astolfo, however, is prepared to give away a marvel. He has been waiting all day and evening to hand his Rabicano over "[come] mancia" ("as a gift," 22.29). But when Bradamante finally arrives the next morning, Astolfo has changed his mind. He is overjoyed, not merely because his cousin will take good care of his fabulous horse, but because in handing Rabicano over to Bradamante, Astolfo knows that he will then be able to ask for his horse back when he returns. So Astolfo tells Bradamante:

> che le volea
> dar Rabican, che sì nel corso affretta,
> che, se scoccando l'arco si movea,
> si solea lasciar dietro la saetta;
> e tutte l'arme ancor, quante n'avea,
> che vuol che a Montalban gli le rimetta,
> e gli le serbi fin al suo ritorno;
> che non gli fanno or di bisogno intorno.
>
> (23.14)

> [he will bestow
> His Rabican; so passing swift of kind,
> That, if the courser started when a bow
> Was drawn, he left the feathered shaft behind;
> And will as well his panoply forego,
> That it may to Mount Alban be consigned:
> And she for him preserve the martial weed;
> Since of his arms he has no present need.]

Astolfo, who yearns for the marvelous and gathers marvels at an increas-
ingly rapid rate, is, despite his clownish past in previous romances, no fool.
Marvels are difficult to come by, limited in number, and powerful things.
Only heroes who have to prove their epic stature willingly toss them away.
Astolfo therefore hands Rabicano over to Bradamante. Yet before leaving
on his tour "dei pennati . . . paese" [of the winged people's land] (23.12),
Astolfo decides to take further advantage of the occasion, to liberate him-
self of even more marvels so that he may voyage lighter:

> Volendosene andar per l'aria a volo,
> aveasi a far quanto potea più lieve.
> Tiensi la spada e 'l corno, ancora che solo
> bastargli il corno ad ogni risco deve,
> Bradamante la lancia che 'l figliuolo
> portò di Galafrone, anco riceve;
> la lancia che di quanti ne percuote
> fa le selle restar subito vote.
>
> (23.15)

> [Bent, since a course in air was to be flown,
> That he, as best he can, will make him light.
> Yet keeps the sword and horn; although alone
> The horn from every risque might shield the knight:
> But he the lance abandons, which the son
> Of Galaphron was wont to bear in fight;
> The lance, by which whoever in the course
> Was touched, fell headlong hurtling from his horse.]

Midway into the *Furioso,* at a juncture in the poem when both central
and subordinate characters reach decisive turning points—Ruggiero
throws Atlante's shield away and relies on his valor alone, Orlando goes
stark raving mad, Bradamante exacts from Ruggiero his pledge, and
Isabella recovers Zerbino and Zerbino Isabella—Astolfo comes to a decisive turning point and makes a decisive choice as well. In unburdening
himself for his voyage, Astolfo has significantly kept for himself all the
Ariostan marvels (the book, the horn, and the hippogriff) and relieved
himself of all the marvels of his Boiardian past (Rabicano and the golden
lance). From this moment on, as Astolfo steps onto the hippogriff, he has
become—like Orlando who "per amore venne in furore e matto" [for love

became both full of fury and mad]—a fully Ariostan creation. Relieved and lightened of his past, Astolfo may now rise up and begin his voyage about the world on the hippogriff's back. The marvelous creature that first released Astolfo into the poem has, at long last, become Astolfo's own:

Salito Astolfo sul destrier volante,
lo fa mover per l'aria lento lento;
indi lo caccia sì, che Bradamante
ogni vista ne perde in un momento.

(23.16)

[Backed by Astolpho, and ascending slow,
The hippogryph through yielding aether flew;
And next the rider stirred the courser so,
That in a thought he vanished out of view.]

The Hippogriff and a Ptolemaic Map

While constructed in part on Boiardo's Rabicano,[13] the hippogriff, as so many readers have noted, is far more conspicuously modeled on Pegasus, the winged horse that produced through an accidental blow of its heal the fountain of the Muses. The classical allusion at once serves to figure the hippogriff as an emblem of poetry within the text, the *vis imaginativa* that needs, as in Plato's description of the twin horses guiding the chariot in the *Phaedrus,* the restraint of reason to become the controlled fantasy of poetry. But what constitutes this poetic vision? Is it, as Eugenio Donato argues, one of pure textual self-referentiality and thus of signs pointing to more signs that never even begin to gesture toward the "outside world"?[14] Or is it, as Albert Ascoli contends, a vision placed "squarely between the world of nature and that of poetic fantasy as a way of showing how equivocal are all mediations of imagination between the two—suggesting both that nothing is more *natural* to humankind than evasive flights of imagination and that the artifice of imagination always works upon materials derived from the real and inevitably (if involuntarily) reflects back upon

---

13. As Pio Rajna intuited in *Le fonti del "Orlando furioso,"* 2d ed., ed. Francesco Mazzoni (Florence: Sansoni, 1975).

14. Eugenio Donato, "'Per selve e bosherecci labirinti': Desire and Narrative Structure in Ariosto's *Orlando furioso,*" in *Literary Theory/Renaissance Texts,* ed. P. Parker and D. Quint (Baltimore: Johns Hopkins University Press, 1986).

them?"[15] Extending these observations into the realm of cartography and the wonder of exploration, I argue that Ariosto offers through the hippogriff a vision of a totality anachronistically mapped out in the poem through the successive flights of the creature's riders, though a totality that Renaissance discoveries, which Ariosto mentions in the final version of the poem, defies.

The very first rider of the hippogriff, Atlante, in many ways indicates, through his movements, much of what Ariosto means to offer through his vision of this "alta maraviglia." Early in canto 2, Atlante flies until he arrives where eagles hardly go (2.49); he then dashes headlong to earth, only to rise up and wheel about in wide, spacious circles (2.53). These acrobatic movements take place from noon to sundown. Though Atlante's movements are superfluous within the overall conflict—indeed, he wins the battle only by revealing his blinding shield when it finally gets too dark to fly—they nonetheless permit Atlante to test the vertical and horizontal frontiers of the space in which he lives. Moreover, by stretching out his space, Atlante is further stretching out time, in a typically Ariostan strategy of narrative diversion.

The space Atlante explores, we soon learn, lies somewhere in a valley of the Pyrenees (4.7), precisely where a peak reaches up to reveal both Spain and France (4.11). This is a wide region with a vast panoramic vision, and as Pinabello makes plain, Atlante scours this entire region night and day. He flies near Rodonna to seize Pinabello's beloved; and somewhere near Bordeaux, where the proprietor of canto 4 has his inn (3.71, 75), Bradamante beholds Atlante on the hippogriff, whereupon the innkeeper informs Bradamante that the wizard often passes that way (4.4–6). The space Atlante explores is thus relatively large, though it is, for the most part, restricted and substantially indistinct as well. He visits Rodonna (2.37)—perhaps the Ptolemaic Rhodamnus;[16] other than that, the narrator does not give any additional localized indication as to where Atlante goes. He peruses the surrounding counties, ventures upward and downward, circles round-and-about from day until night, but he is also compelled to return to his castle in the Pyrenees, for that is where Ruggiero is,

15. Ascoli, *Ariosto's Bitter Harmony,* 256; see 246–57. For other readings of the hippogriff, see Shapiro, *The Poetics of Ariosto,* chap. 3; and Valerie Merriam Wise, "Ruggiero and the Hippogriff: The Ambiguities of Vision," *Quaderni d'italianistica* 2 (1981): 39–53.

16. That Ariosto is referring to the Ptolemaic Rhodamnus is maintained by Michele Vernero, *Studi critici sopra la geografia dell' "Orlando furioso"* (Turin: Tipografia Palatina di Bonis e Rossi, 1913).

and that is where Atlante must bring the damsels he has captured. There are, in short, recognizable constraints placed on Atlante, or at least Atlante has willfully placed constraints on himself for the love of his Ruggiero. He only explores what is at hand.

Despite these restrictions, Atlante's world is nevertheless symbolically complete. From his castle, constructed in a valley on the highest peak in the Pyrenees, Atlante may view both France and Spain, even to the point of visually embracing two littorals. Such a view, reminiscent of Petrarch's description of his encompassing perspective from Mont Ventoux, takes in two extremes, the Spain of the infidels, representing the east, and the Christians of France, representing the west, the shore of the Atlantic and the shore of the Mediterranean. Situated in the exact center, in the dividing chain of mountains and on the highest peak, Atlante's view unites not only opposing shores and countries but opposing civilizations. In this way Atlante's view expresses a desire for a totality: a vision that can unite opposites. As limited as Atlante's space may be, it is thus symbolically complete; and within that space Atlante travels and explores his world on the hippogriff's back.

Once he has learned to control the hippogriff, Ruggiero, unlike his protector, aims to circumnavigate the entire globe (10.70). After leaving Alcina's island, he therefore flies over Catai and then travels north by northwest over the mountain range of Imavo. He then turns south to Sarmazia, only to swerve back north to visit Russia ("Russi"), Prussia ("Pruteni"), and Pomerania ("Pomeria," 10.71).[17] At this point, Ruggiero believes he should return to Bradamante soon ("presto," 72). But sitting on the hippogriff inevitably instills in Ruggiero the desire to explore. So rather than directly flying to Bradamante, Ruggiero travels south to Poland and Hungary, then back north to Germany and the icy "boreale orrida terra" [horrid, northern land] (10.72), then south to England, north to Ireland, south to Ibernia, and back north to Ebuda (10.93), where his voyage finally stops. The moral consequence of this meandering, as Albert Ascoli has shown, occurs only at the very end, when Ruggiero, who has already digressed in his errant path to Bradamante, lapses momentarily and lusts after the naked Angelica whom he has freed. But for all Ruggiero's winding ways, Ariosto has endowed his voyage with a direction. By the time Ruggiero has reached the end of his journey, which began with Catai in the Orient, he has traveled beyond the "ultima terra" [distant

---

17. I have rapidly synthesized the observations of Vernero, *Studi*, 77–78.

land] of England and arrived at Ebuda, which, according to the narrator, lies "nel mar di tramontana inver l'occaso, / oltre l'Irlanda" [in the great northern sea, toward the west, / Green Ireland past] (8.51).

To understand how Ariosto could have ever located Ebuda beyond Ireland as an extreme point in the northwest, one may look at an early Ptolemaic map. In the codex acquired by Borso d'Este in 1466, and from which was later derived the printed Ulm edition of 1482, one may pinpoint Ebuda situated in the top left corner, precisely where Ptolemy indicated the island should be: "Hiberiae superiacent parvae quinque insulae Ebudae nomine; quarum occidentalior vocatur Ebuda" [Five little Hibernian islands by the name of Ebuda lie beyond, of which the most western is called Ebuda] (*Geogr.* 2.2).[18] And no sooner has one glanced at any of these early Ptolemaic maps than it becomes clear that Ariosto has made Ruggiero follow a highly deliberate course. Ruggiero, in moving high and low, has gradually drawn a visible arc around half the world as represented on the Ptolemaic map. His twists and turns, errant movements south and north, skirt the center of the world—the Mediterranean basin, Greece, Italy, and France—and hug a conceptual circumference. Through Ruggiero's wanderings, Ariosto has touched the extreme contours of the northern hemisphere. In doing so, he has already begun to embrace the world by drawing a wavering line about the top half of the Ptolemaic map.

The remaining contours of the world are tracked on the Ptolemaic map in Astolfo's two separate voyages. In the first, Logistilla decides to send Astolfo back home from Alcina's island "per la via più espedita e più sicura" [by the securest and the freest track] (15.10). The quickest and most direct way, as Logistilla knows, is to move back over the lip of the globe and down the "boreal pelago" [boreal place] (15.12), where harsh winds blow over the arctic sea, and where there is little sun most of the time (15.12). Needless to say, apart from being dangerous, traveling over the glacial sea would not be much fun. So rather than sending Astolfo over the northern, nocturnal, windy lip of the globe ("Più tosto . . . che per quel

---

18. Cited in Vernero, *Studi,* 80. On the Estense acquisition of maps, see Luciano Serra, "Da Tolomeo alla Garfagna: La geografia dell'Ariosto," *Bollettino storico reggiano* 28 (1974): 151–84; and Claudio Greppi, "Una carta per la corte: Il viaggiatore immobile," in *The Renaissance in Ferrara and Its European Horizons,* ed. J. Salmons and Walter Moretti (Cardiff: University of Wales Press, 1984). In Francesco Berlinghieri, *Geographia* (Florence: n.p., 1482), with the designs of Nicolo Tedeschi, taken by Serra to be one of the sure works consulted by Ariosto, one reads: "Ebude isole cinque a siti iberni / sopra stanno & di loro ebuda e decta / Quella che uerso occaso piu discerni" (17v).

boreal pelago vada" [Rather than for that Boreal place steer] [15.12]),
Logistilla decides to send Astolfo back the sunny, southern way.

To travel over the glacial sea means following a path that is "espedita"
[without impediments] (15.10). It is the kind of quick, lone, linear path that
Ruggiero was first obliged to follow when he was carried on the hippogriff's back "per linea dritta e senza mai piegarsi" [on a straight path
without a single bend] (6.19). To travel the long way, however, implies the
very opposite kind of movement. In his *Dizionario della lingua italiana,*
Niccolò Tommaseo provides a definition of the word *volteggiare* that
encapsulates the overall controlled, deviating movement of the *Furioso:*
"Girare o Voltarsi in qua e in là" [To move or turn about here and
there].[19] Ships are said to "volteggiare" in this sense, and for Astolfo to
return by ship "volteggiando" (15.12) signifies that he has returned home
"here and there," much as Ruggiero did on the hippogriff. If Logistilla has
reasoned thus in sending Astolfo home by such a long path
"volteggiando," her reasoning ultimately lies in Ariosto's plan. For by the
time Astolfo has disembarked in Arabia, he has, after traveling along the
Asian coast, traced an undulating line around three-quarters of the world
on the Ptolemaic map.

Astolfo is a veritable voyager, and his means of traveling in the *Furioso*
consistently become more uplifting. He emerges out of his Boiardian past
on a whale's back, he sails home on a fairy-guided ship, he trots on a horse
that almost flies, and at last he acquires the hippogriff. As a man with
some traveling experience, Astolfo is naturally overjoyed when he first
obtains the hippogriff. Ariosto's "alta maraviglia," the hippogriff—more
than the whale, the ship, or Rabicano—will serve him well as he moves
about. Wherever and whenever Astolfo's desire commands, the hippogriff
will take him, and Astolfo's aim, like Ruggiero's before him, is to circumnavigate the entire globe:

Non potrebbe esser stato più giocondo
d'altra aventura Astolfo, che di questa;
che per cercar la terra e il mar, secondo
ch'avea desir, quel ch'a cercar gli resta,

---

19. The emphasis is mine. On the controlled oscillating "qua e là" movement of the
Furioso, see D. S. Carne-Ross, "The One and the Many: A Reading of *Orlando furioso,* Can-
tos I and VIII," *Arion* 5 (1966): 195–234; Eduardo Saccone, *Il soggetto; Patricia Parker,*
"Ariosto," in *Inescapable Romance: Studies in the Poetics of a Mode* (Princeton: Princeton
University Press, 1979).

e girar tutto in pochi giorni il mondo,
troppo venia questo ippogrifo a sesta.

(22.26)

[At nought Astolpho could more joyous be
Than this; of all things fortunate the best:
In that the hippogryph so happily
Offered himself; that he might scower the rest,
(As much he coveted) of land and sea,
And in a few days the ample world invest.]

In his third satire, Ariosto expresses much the same desire, claiming in poetry that he aims to see all the world—all, that is, that remained for Ariosto to see, so long as he did not have to budge too far from Ferrara. Ariosto will remain in his "contrada" [county], and explore ("cercando") through his imagination "il resto" [the rest] by following the Ptolemaic map ("con Ptolomeo").[20] He will move not in a straight path but exactly as Astolfo is said to have moved on his ship: "volteggiando" (*Sat.* 3.66). Like Atlante, Ruggiero, and Astolfo, Ariosto will move back and forth in an exploratory movement of "qua e là" [here and there]. Yet it is a planned movement all the same. Aiming for completion, Ariosto, who has already seen something of the world, intends to see the rest.

Ariosto accomplishes this imaginative voyage in his poem through the combined movements of the hippogriff's three consecutive navigators. For while the marvel of the hippogriff instills the desire to travel and explore, it also repeatedly instills in its riders the desire for a totality, an absolute.

---

20. The verses from which these citations are drawn are as follows:

Chi vuole andare a torno, a torno vada:
  vegga Inghelterra, Ongheria, Francia e Spagna;
  a me piace abitar la mia contrada.
Visto ho Toscana, Lombardia, Romagna,
  quel monte che divide e quel che serra
  Italia, e un mare e l'altro che la bagna.
Questo mi basta; il resto de la terra,
  senza mai pagar l'oste, andrò cercando
  con Ptolomeo, sia il mondo in pace o in guerra;
e tutto il mar, senza far voti quando
  lampeggi il ciel, sicuro in su le carte
  verrò, più che sui legni, volteggiando.

(*Sat.* 3.55–66)

Atlante, within his limited domain, scours everything: "Tutto il paese giorno e notte scorre" (2.43); Ruggiero wants to circle the entire globe: "finir tutto il cominciato tondo" (10.70); and Astolfo plans to circumnavigate the whole world as well: "e girar tutto . . . il mondo" (22.26). The Ariostan marvelous, symbolized in the "alta maraviglia" of the hippogriff, is not a desire for a partial vision. This is a vision that "demands," in the very sense of the term that Lacan ascribes to the noun, everything. Atlante, Ruggiero, and Astolfo, all of whom travel on the hippogriff, time and again express through their movements a desire to embrace the impossible plenitude of an absolute. Yet in the end, they are all deprived of the fulfillment of that very desire.

Atlante, though he sees everything in his circumscribed domain, only sees a small portion of the world. He is compelled to return time and again to the Pyrenees Mountains. He may see the two opposite littorals from his enchanted castle and embrace two nations with a symbolic view, but he cannot, despite the loftiness of his vision, see the two distant shores of the Atlantic and the shore beyond Catai. Nor can he embrace in a unifying vision the east and the west, the north and the south, Asia and Europe and Africa and "quella boreale orrida terra" [that horrid, northern land] (10.72). Atlante's world is ultimately a small world that stands as a metaphor for the larger one outside. Ruggiero, by contrast, aims to circle the entire globe, and he almost accomplishes that impressive task. Swept away on the hippogriff's back in the Pyrenees, he flies beyond the straits of Hercules. Moving west, he then travels as far as Ebuda, whereupon, circling south, he heads for the "minor Bretagna" [small Britain], even though he planned to circle all of Spain next (10.113). Had Ruggiero adhered to his original plan, he would have surely completed his navigation of the entire globe. But Ruggiero's lusting after Angelica compels him to settle down near Normandy, and there, just short of his circumnavigation of the world, he loses the hippogriff.[21] Finally neither does Astolfo, the greatest traveler of them all, manage to fulfill his quest to see what remains of the world. He completes Ruggiero's unfinished circumnavigation instead. Passing over the Pyrenees, which was the point of Ruggiero's initial departure, Astolfo moves to Spain, exactly where Ruggiero had planned to travel next, traversing the country from one corner to another (33.97). He then crosses the Mediterranean and comes to the straits of Hercules. At this point, just where Ruggiero was carried west (6.17),

---

21. See Ascoli, *Ariosto's Bitter Harmony,* 185–87, 226–28.

Astolfo decides to turn east, planning to see Africa (33.98). Traveling high and low along the northern coastline, Astolfo then follows the Nile down to the mountain of the moon, where his zigzagging voyage about the world finally stops, his circumnavigation left unfinished.

Only Ariosto, charting the movements of Ruggiero and Astolfo on a Ptolemaic map, is permitted a total vision of the world. By the time Astolfo has arrived at the base of the mountain to the moon, Ariosto has drawn a conceptual circle around the Ptolemaic map and further linked both easterly and westerly extremes—from the straits of Hercules to Catai—through Ruggiero's flight across the Atlantic Ocean. Yet in doing so, Ariosto has also significantly left something out: a world that Renaissance explorations were gradually rendering obsolete, and a world about which Ariosto had sure knowledge long before he even began working on the *Furioso*. As early as 21 April 1493, only two months after Columbus was obliged to disembark in Lisbon after completing his first voyage on 4 March, Ercole I received a copy of a letter written from his correspondent Annibale Gennaro, who claimed to have read Columbus's own summary of his voyage.[22] With words that inadvertently evoke Ruggiero's initial flight "per linea dritta" [in a straight line] (6.19) across the Atlantic, Gennaro tells how Columbus sailed across the ocean "per dritta linea" until he came to the Orient. Gennaro's letter no doubt nourished Ferraran interest in worldly explorations. Ercole I immediately requested more information through his correspondent in Milan and, if possible, a copy of Columbus's summary itself so that he might better know more about those "nuove isole" [new islands] discovered. But Gennaro's letter, which also spoke at the end in Mandevillian terms of "la provincia dove nascino li homini con coda" [the province where men with tails are born], also fed a highly cultivated Ferraran taste for tales of voyages through the Orient in search of marvels, tales found, for example, in Marco Polo's *Milione* and Jean de Mandeville's travels, both of which were contained in the Duke's rich library.[23]

---

22. On the immediacy with which news of Renaissance explorations reached the court of Ferrara, and the interest it excited from the outset, see the fascinating documentation in Domenico Fava and Carlo Montagnani, eds., *Mostra colombiana e americana della R. biblioteca estense* (Modena: Società Tipografia Modena, 1925).

23. Cited in Greppi, "Una carta per la corte," 201–2. On the Estense library, see Giulio Bertoni, *La biblioteca estense e la cultura ferrarese ai tempi del duca Ercole I (1471–1505)* (Turin: Loescher, 1903).

It was not until the final 1532 edition of the *Furioso* that Ariosto enlarged the geographical space of his romance to include Renaissance discoveries. In canto 15, Astolfo learns from Andronica about the epic-making navigators of the Renaissance, those "nuovi Argonauti e nuovi Tifi" [New Argonauts put forth, and Tiphys new] (15.21), who will one day venture beyond the straits of Hercules and discover seafaring passages to the Orient by coasting around Africa or, much as Ruggiero did in his voyage to Alcina's island, by traveling due west. There is no radical conception of a "new" world here. Columbus and Vasco de Gama have only reached the Orient. But Ptolemy's world, through Renaissance explorations of "nuove terre e nuovo mondo" [new lands and new creations] (15.22), has at once been enlarged with vast expanses of oceans and territories undiscovered, thereby rendering the classical worldview of the Ptolemaic map, if not anachronistic or obsolete, at least partly unreliable. Nevertheless, this newly expanded vision still retains a sense of its own totality in Ariosto's poem. For as the vatic Andronica augurs, along with explorations, there will be military conquests; green shores staked out with crosses and imperial banners; men elected to possess lands; hundreds of people uprooted by no less than ten; the suppression and subjection of lands beyond India to Aragon; conquistadors, such as "Hernando Cortese," who have placed under imperial edict kingdoms in the Orient (15.23–27). Explorers in Andronica's disclosure of the future have gradually ceded to military captains who reconstitute a sense of totality in the world by making the whole world obedient ("Tutto il mondo ubidiente") to a monarch's militarized force (15.29). This new world is not one that Ariosto explicitly chose to circumscribe when he first wrote his poem. Yet once mentioned, the world redefined by Renaissance explorations nevertheless remains a totality in the *Furioso* by being ruled, however it is finally mapped out, by a single temporal authority and his comprehensive use of military power. It is to the uses and abuses of that military power, then, and the way in which power is reconfigured within the realm of the marvelous, that we turn in the final section of this chapter and in the final version of the *Furioso*.

Marvels and "abominosi ordigni"

In the 1532 version of the *Furioso*, Orlando comes upon a remarkable form of military power, Cimosco's harquebus, which, in line with Renaissance legends regarding the invention of gunpowder, is viewed as the magical work of the devil.[24] After seizing the harquebus, Orlando finally hurls the evil firearm into the sea and cries out with an apostrophe often taken to be a filtered expression of the poet's own sentiments:

O maledetto, o abominoso ordigno,
che fabricato nel tartareo fondo
fosti per man di Belzebù maligno
che ruinar per te disegnò il mondo,
all'inferno, onde uscisti, ti rasigno.—
Così dicendo, lo gittò in profondo.

(9.91)

["O loathed, O cursed piece of enginery,
Cast in Tartarean bottom, by the hand
Of Beelzebub, whose foul malignity
The ruin of this world through thee has planned!
To hell from whence thou came, I render thee."
So said, he cast away the weapon.]

Along with vainly seeking to spare the world the power of such an "abominoso ordigno," Orlando's motivation in discarding Cimosco's harquebus rests on his conviction that a knight should never distort the power of his personal strength through artificial means. Such a distortion either hides true worth or, what is worse, deceptively masks a lack of worth: "che sempre atto stimò d'animo molle / gir con vantaggio in qualsivoglia impresa" [for he still held it an ungenerous care / To go with vantage on whatever quest] (9.89). An "impresa" won by virtue of a "machina infernal" [infernal tool] (11.23) like the harquebus is fraudulent. Human value, as well as heroic human endeavors, are counterfeited. There is no true battle, no true glory, no true virtue. There is only, to broaden and extend such a vision into the future, Ariosto's Renaissance:

Per te la militar gloria è distrutta,
per te il mestier de l'arme è senza onore;
per te è il valore e la virtù ridutta,
che spesso par del buono il rio migliore:

---

24. On the various legends, see J. R. Hale, "Gunpowder and the Renaissance: An Essay in the History of Ideas," in *From the Renaissance to the Counter-Reformation: Essays in Honour of Garret Mattingly,* ed. Charles H. Carter (London: Jonathan Cape, 1966), 113–44.

non più la gagliardia, non più l'ardire
per te può in campo al paragon venire.

(11.26)

[Through thee is martial glory lost, through thee
The trade of arms become a worthless art:
And at such ebb are worth and chivalry,
That the base often plays the better part.
Through thee no more shall gallantry, no more
Shall valour prove their prowess as of yore.]

Orlando's motivation in throwing the harquebus into the sea closely mirrors Ruggiero's decision to throw Atlante's shield into the well.[25] For Ruggiero to adopt the shield in a joust is "frodo" [fraud] (6.67), a shameful counterfeiting of individual valor through the power of a blinding shield; Orlando rids himself, and humankind, of the harquebus because it distorts both moral and physical weakness into a terrifying explosive power, an "abominoso ordigno." The parallel between these two events once more reinforces the links between Ruggiero and Orlando throughout the poem. But the parallel further points to a connection of singular importance. Marvels, as a source of extraordinary concentrated power, have also been envisioned here as romance inversions of explosive Renaissance artillery.

The connection between marvels and firearms is indeed present in Renaissance culture itself in the form of the names attributed to weapons. The act of dubbing a cannon after the imaginary African serpent that burned up vegetation and whose lethal glance, according to Pliny, destroyed anyone it espied invested a manufactured weapon as the contemporary occidental analogue to a pagan marvel.[26] There may have been a dearth of fire-breathing dragons in Renaissance Europe, but bronze-

25. As Pio Rajna, *Le fonti,* 363, long ago observed: "Evidentemente s'era ispirato a sentimenti analoghi anche Orlando, quando aveva sepolto in mare l'archibugio (ix, 90)." Santoro has discussed these parallels, though in terms that overemphasize the differences, in "O scelerata e brutta invenzion," in *Ariosto e il Rinascimento,* 311–16.

26. Pliny the Elder, *Natural History,* ed. and trans. H. Rackham (Cambridge: Harvard University Press, 1956), writes that the basilisk serpent, "basiliscus," is like the "catublebas" that "alias internicio humani generis, omnibus qui oculos eius videre confestim expirantibus" (8.32.77); and that the basilisk itself "necat frutices non contactos modo verum et adflatos, exurit herbas, rumpit saxa. aliis vis malo est" (8.33.78–79). On the basilisk, see Malcolm South, ed., *Mythical and Fabulous Creatures* (New York: Greenwood, 1987).

casted basilisks existed, and they emitted flames and sparks and smoke all the same. By contrast, in Ariosto's poem, within which there are no contemporary basilisks but instead a harquebus—found and then lost for future generations to retrieve through black magic—the connection between marvels and firearms is particularly evident with regard to Ariosto's treatment of Astolfo's horn. Like the musket, to which it is in fact compared, Astolfo's magical horn "fires" [scocca], scattering people as innocent doves ("colombi") before a "horrible blast" [suono orrendo] (22.21). Moreover, just as Cimosco's harquebus has a "paventoso suono" [fearful sound] before which "trieman le mura, e sotto i piè il terreno" [the ground / Shakes under foot and city wall] (9.75) when it likewise "fires" [scocca] (9.74), so too Astolfo's horn, with its very own "spaventoso suono" (20.89), makes "la terra e tutto 'l mondo trieme" [the earth and the whole world tremble] (20.88). The narrator asserts that the sound of the horn is indeed "spaventoso," "orribile," and "orrendo" (20.89, 20.88, 22.21). There is, in truth, a moment when we may take the narrator at his word. This horn is a weapon, and one with an extraordinary explosive power. Like the harquebus, it is capable of producing "alta ruina" [mighty ruin] and "fracasso" [destruction] (20.91).

In canto 33, Astolfo uses the power of his horn to chase the filthy Harpies back into the Inferno. At the beginning of canto 34 the narrator draws on this event to offer an impassioned proem in which he compares the Harpies to the invaders who have descended into Italy and polluted its "bel vivere" [beautiful way of life] (34.2). Ever since foreign nations have invaded Italy, this land has become an impure world according to the narrator. In terms of Mary Douglas's conception of the symbolic social function of filth, Italy is a world that lacks order.[27] With Italy's confines blurred and its borders trespassed, the symbolic presence of filth indicates that a unified cultural system has begun to break down. It is not so much "quiete" [calm] (34.2) that Italy lacks, but a sense of its own totality. To reconstitute that sense of totality—the "beautiful way of life" of a once harmonious, bounded world—the narrator declares that Italy needs a liberator like Astolfo with a marvel like the fabulous horn (34.3). Yet by the logic of such a desire and such a need, the poet of the *Furioso* has become entangled in something of a double bind. There is a need for marvels to maintain order and a sense of totality. But in sixteenth-century Italy there are no such horns. There are only "abominosi ordigni."

---

27. Douglas, *Purity and Danger.*

Though the poet largely deprecates the use of marvels and the use of Renaissance artillery in his poem, both marvels and "abominosi ordigni" are nonetheless necessary to maintain a sense of totality. They provide a balance of power in a world that is never so harmoniously balanced as the complements of the moon and the earth would ideally make it out to be.[28] Both marvels and Renaissance artillery can, in this sense, serve as great civilizing forces. Without marvels in the *Furioso,* Orlando remains insane, the battle lost, the tide of the war never turned, Charlemagne's monarchy crushed (34.55–56). Without cannons, such as Duke Ercole's "Gran diavol" [great devil] (25.14) mentioned in the *Furioso,*[29] the Ferrarese dynasty ostensibly risks losing its hold in a battle or a siege.[30] Renaissance artillery, in a Burkhardtian scheme of things, had a great shaping force in constructing the state as a work of art.[31] And it was a force that Ariosto's patron, Duke Alfonso I d'Este, acknowledged and deployed,[32] even to the point of having himself portrayed by Titian in civilian dress with his hand—"a fine and beautiful courtly hand," as Edgar Wind notes[33]— lightly poised on a cannon set indoors. Titian's painting is a dispassionate reminder to foes and friends alike that this civil modern prince was capable of lethal activity to preserve his state. It all depended, as Ariosto's motto for Alfonso's heroic emblem of the threefold bursting bomb declared, on the place and time: *loco et tempore.*[34] But therein lay the prob-

---

28. The most full-scale treatment of this frustrated harmony is Ascoli, *Ariosto's Bitter Harmony.* Michael Murrin, *History and Warfare in Renaissance Epic* (Chicago: University of Chicago Press, 1994), 123–31, discusses Ariosto's attitude toward firearms as primarily negative.

29. "non quel de lo 'nferno, / ma quel del mio signor, che va col fuoco / ch'a cielo e a terra e a mar si fa dar loco" (*Fur.* 25.14)

30. See also Elizabeth A. Chesney, *The Countervoyage of Rabelais and Ariosto: A Comparative Reading of Two Renaissance Mock Epics* (Durham: Duke University Press, 1982), 42.

31. On the importance of artillery in the formation of states and territorial boundaries, see J. R. Hale, *War and Society in Renaissance Europe, 1450–1620* (Leicester: Leicester University Press, 1985), 46–51; and M. E. Mallett and J. R. Hale, *The Military Organization of a Renaissance State: Venice c. 1400 to 1617* (Cambridge: Cambridge University Press, 1984), 81–87, 394–405. Emblematic is the proclamation of the Venetian Council of Ten that "there can be no doubt whatsoever that one of the chief factors in the protection of lands and of armies is the artillery" (cited in Hale, *War and Society,* 47).

32. See, for example, Paolo Giovio's *La vita di Alfonso da Este Duca di Ferrara, scritta da il vescovo Iovio,* trans. Giovambattista Gelli Fiorentino into Tuscan (Florence: Torrentino, 1553), 18–19 and 46.

33. Edgar Wind, *Pagan Mysteries of the Renaissance* (New Haven: Yale University Press, 1958), 97.

34. Michele Catalano in his biography attributes this motto to Ariosto, *Vita di L. Ariosto ricostruita su nuovi documenti* (Geneva: Olschki, 1931), 470.

lem. As destructive falsifying powers, explosive Renaissance weapons inevitably remain "abominosi ordigni," and though they have at times served to preserve frontiers, they have also, the brooding poet laments, often destroyed that which they have meant to preserve.

Pro bono malum. There is no guarantee in Ariosto's *Furioso* that marvels, any more than explosive Renaissance weapons, will be placed at the service of good or evil. Marvels may just as easily become transformed from their use *in bono* to their abuse *in malo* as "abominosi ordigni." In this respect, the overall happy use of marvels in shaping a totality throughout the *Furioso* represents an optimistic wager for the forces of good over the forces of evil. It is a wager that nevertheless harbors no illusions that the power of marvels, like the power of Renaissance weaponry, is always open-ended, forever at the service of man's highly unpredictable capacity to act with reason and faith for the construction of society *in bono* or with folly and vengeance for the destruction of mankind *in malo.* From this perspective, the use of marvels in shaping a totality throughout the *Furioso* seems almost arbitrary, a matter of mood. It is a matter of how the poet finally chooses to shape and close his poem in relation to the inevitable ascent and descent of Fortune's revolving wheel:

> Si vede per gli essempii di che piene
> sono l'antiche e le moderne istorie,
> che 'l ben va dietro al male, e 'l male al bene,
> e fin son l'un de l'altro e biasmi e glorie;
> e che fidarsi a l'uom non si conviene
> in suo tesor, suo regno e sue vittorie,
> né disperarsi per Fortuna avversa,
> che sempre la sua ruota in giro versa.

(45.4)

> ['Tis plain to sight, through instances that fill
> The page of ancient and of modern story,
> That ill succeeds to good, and good to ill;
> That glory ends in shame, and shame in glory;
> And that man should not trust, deluded still,
> In riches, realm, or field of battle, gory
> With hostile blood, nor yet despair, for spurns
> Of Fortune; since her wheel for ever turns.]

In the overall corpus of Ariosto's works, the inevitable descent of Fortune's wheel occurs not in the *Furioso* but in the *Cinque canti,* though the additions of 1532 already seem to announce the alternative to the *Furioso.*[35] "The poet's inspiration had become, more than just tired, but turbid," Cesare Segre notes in a synthetic reading of the poet's change of mood in the *Cinque canti.*[36] The variegated but still balanced, modulating moods of the *Furioso* have grown univocally cheerless in tone, "austere and wintry," to the point where Pio Fontana can speak of a complete "conversion of the marvelous into the demonic,"[37] and Eduardo Saccone of "a general conspiracy of dark, mysterious, ultrahuman forces that coalesce with aims of completely destroying the empire, civilization—all, in truth, that is human and natural."[38]

In the fourth canto of the *Cinque canti,* a gigantic whale swallows Ruggiero. Doubtlessly this is the same two-mile whale that once bore Astolfo away to Alcina's island. But now, as Ruggiero and Astolfo once more meet, the circumstances have drastically changed. This is a "ventre cieco" [blind stomach] (4.45), much like the "carcere cieco" [dark prison] of Dante's hell (*Purg.* 22.103; *Inf.* 10.58–59). And rather than pining away for Alcina, Astolfo sits on a vacant bed in an empty room beside a makeshift temple patterned after a mosque. Shamefaced, with his head lowered, Astolfo is weeping ("piangendo," 4.52). He is crying because, as the narrator of the *Furioso* earlier predicted would happen, Astolfo has completely lost his wits and sinned:

Così 'l peccato mio brutto e nefando,
degno di questa e di più pena molta,
m'ha chiuso qui, onde di come e quando
io n'abbia a uscir, ogni speranza è tolta;
quella protezïon tutta levando,
che san Giovanni avea già di me tolta.

(4.74)

---

35. See Eduardo Saccone, *Il soggetto,* 144; Walter Moretti, "L'ideale ariostesco di un'europa pacificata e unita e la sua crisi nel terzo *Furioso,*" in *The Renaissance in Ferrara and Its European Horizons,* ed. J. Salmons and Walter Moretti (Cardiff: University of Wales Press, 1984); and Moretti, *L'ultimo Ariosto* (Bologna: Pàtron, 1977).

36. Segre, in his opening remarks to the *Cinque canti* in Ariosto, *Opere minori,* ed. Segre, 581; my translation.

37. Pio Fontana, *I "Cinque canti" e la storia della poetica del "Furioso"* (Milan: Vita e Pensiero, 1962), 37; my translation.

38. Saccone, *Il soggetto,* 125; my translation.

[Thus my ugly and evil sin, worthy of this and much more penance, imprisoned me here. For this reason, all hope of my ever leaving is gone, taking away that protection under which St. John had placed me entirely.]

"Cosa umana è a peccar" [It is human to sin], Ruggiero responds in an effort to comfort the despairing Astolfo (4.76). He then cites Scripture (4.76–77) and further reminds Astolfo that once before they had been in dire straits but nonetheless escaped (4.77). So there is hope, Ruggiero consoles. There is hope that God will liberate them, just as His goodness will conquer the evil darkly stirring about the world (4.79).

Ruggiero's faith, soon echoed by Astolfo, who quotes Scripture (4.81–82), suddenly provokes a bizarre shift of behavior in these two heroes. Astolfo and Ruggiero resolve to convert the pagans with whom they live, and as they set out to accomplish their task, they kneel down to pray:

Così dicean; poi salmi, inni e vangeli,
orazïon che a mente avean tenute,
incominciar i cavallier devoti,
e a porr'in opra i prieghi e i pianti e i voti.

(4.84)

[Thus they spoke; then the devoted knights began psalms, hymns, and gospels, sermons which they had kept in mind, and put their prayers, laments and vows into deeds.]

Outside the whale's belly, illumined from within by a lanternlike flicker of faith, darkness largely looms.[39] The power of marvels no longer belongs to

---

39. I have here followed upon the intuition of Saccone (*Il soggetto*, 146) in identifying the light from the lantern as a glimmer of "faith" amid the darkness. On the centrality of "faith" in the *Furioso* as the fundamental construct of human relations in forming a society—the humanist "pact," the worldly reasoned contract on which hinges both the *bonum* and the *malum* of Ariosto's romance and of the contemporary, cinquecento Renaissance—see also Saccone, "Cloridano e Medoro," in *Il soggetto*. The "faith" of the *Cinque canti* remains a "pact"; the context, however, has shifted, or better yet enlarged, from the purely secular binding relations of human to human in order to incorporate as well humankind's pact with God. "Non manchi in noi contrizïone e fede," are now the words of Astolfo in 4.81, who then cites Scripture. Such a shift already marks a movement in Ariosto's *Cinque canti* toward the problematics of Tasso's *Liberata*.

knights, such as Astolfo, who once yearned to travel about the entire world or hear a siren's sweet song. The power of marvels now belongs to sardonic fays, who have gathered together in a great diabolic council, and who unilaterally scheme for the total destruction of the civilized world now deeply at odds within itself. Amid this cheerless world—a world not unlike the one described in Tasso's *Liberata,* with its infernal assembly and fragmented band of wandering warriors—Astolfo's and Ruggiero's act of prayer indeed seems about the most that these two heroes can be expected to do. In any event, for Tasso, far more than prayer will be required to transform faith into action and unify the world. What will be required, in the absence of the spontaneous conversion of every heathen to Christianity, is a divinely inspired epic crusade.

Chapter 5

Individuals, Communities, and the Kinds of Marvels Told

Human life in common is only made possible when a majority comes together which is stronger than any separate individual and which remains united against all separate individuals. The power of this community is then set up as "right" in opposition to the power of the individual, which is condemned as "brute force." This replacement of the power of the individual by the power of a community constitutes the decisive step of civilization. The essence of it lies in the fact that the members of the community restrict themselves in their possibilities of satisfaction, whereas the individual knew no such restrictions.

—Sigmund Freud

Not far from the campsite of the crusading Christians in Tasso's *Liberata,* and not far from Jerusalem itself, there rises amid solitary valleys a forest where the sun barely manages to penetrate through the umbrage of ancient trees (13.2). None of the inhabitants from the surrounding region has ever dared to enter the woods and strip it of timber, for it is believed to be the nocturnal meeting place for witches and warlocks. The crusaders in Tasso's *Gerusalemme liberata* have early in their military campaign nevertheless cut down trees from this forest to build their war machines (3.74–76). In canto 13 they must return again. Clorinda and Argante have just reduced to ashes "l'immensa / machina espugnatrice de le mura" [the huge machine, the assailant of their walls] (13.1), and Goffredo refuses to attack Jerusalem once more unless this particular battle machine is repaired.[1] The forest, however, is enchanted through the black magic of the infidel Ismeno. So when the carpenters arrive at dawn the next day,

---

1. The epigraph that opens this chapter is from Sigmund Freud, *Civilization and Its Discontents,* in *The Standard Edition of the Complete Psychological Works of Sigmund Freud,* vol. 21, trans. J. Strachey (London: Hogarth, 1955), 95. Citations from the *Liberata* are from Torquato Tasso, *Gerusalemme liberata,* ed. Lanfranco Caretti, 2 vols. (Bari: Laterza, 1967); all translations are from Tasso, *Jerusalem Delivered,* ed. and trans. Ralph Nash (Detroit: Wayne State University Press, 1987).

they are incapable of passing beyond, struck by a fear that makes them halt. A squadron of select warriors are then sent by Goffredo. They too are routed by fear, as is Alcasto, who retreats after the entire woods erupts into a flaming fortress likened by the poet to an infernal Dantean Dis. For three days the most famous of the crusaders tries to move beyond the wall of fire. All turn away in fear.

At last the lot falls on Tancredi. Though he has been mourning the buried Clorinda, whom he killed four nights before, he finally advances for the good of the community toward the "rischio ignoto" [unknown risk] (13.33). Before the flames he draws back, reflects at length, and then plunges through, only to find himself in the midst of a dark storm, which soon subsides. Tancredi then advances into the heart of the forest until he approaches a huge cypress tree on which he finds inscribed various mysterious signs similar to hieroglyphics. In a language intelligible to Tancredi, there is a brief warning not to disturb the secret place into which he has come, the implication being that the spirits of the dead now inhabit the trees of the forest. Suddenly a confused "non so che" [I don't know what] (13.40) of pity, fear, and pain fills Tancredi's heart, as the sound of the wind rustling through the animated trees brings to mind the moaning of human sighs and sobs. Drawing his sword, Tancredi then strikes the tall tree. The pierced bark spews out blood and the surrounding ground turns vermillion. In anticipation of this event, the narrator exclaims: "Oh meraviglia!" [Oh marvelous!] (13.41).

Marvels, such as the marvels of the woods and the marvel of the bleeding branch—Tasso indicates in his early *Discorsi dell'arte poetica*—occupy the status of a flavor ("sapore") judiciously added to poems to attract the taste ("gusto") of his readers to the overall metaphorical dish of poetry:

> quasi di sapori, deve giudizioso scrittore condire il suo poema, perché con esse [meraviglie] invita e alletta il gusto de gli uomini vulgari, non solo senza fastidio, ma con sodisfazione ancora de' più intendenti. (*DAP*, 6)[2]

---

2. Luigi Poma, in his "nota filologica" in Tasso, *Discorsi dell'arte poetica e del poema eroico*, ed. Poma (Bari: Laterza, 1964), has set the date of the *Discorsi*, published in 1587, at circa 1562, the time when Tasso had just finished his *Rinaldo* and planned to return to the early, abandoned draft of his *Gierusalemme*. Tasso retrospectively claimed many years later that the early *Discorsi* were written for his own self-edification as he planned the poem he would write; see "Delle differenze poetiche," in Tasso, *Prose diverse*, ed. Cesare Guasti (Florence: Le Monnier, 1875), 431. On the *Discorsi*, see Guido Baldassarri, "Introduzione ai *Dis-*

[the judicious writer should season his poem as with spices because he thereby prompts and entices the appetite of the common people not only without the annoyance but with the pleasure, as well, of the most discerning.]

In terms of the proem to the *Liberata,* where the poet, adopting the Lucretian simile, likens himself to a doctor who tricks an ill child to swallow "bitter medicine" [succhi amari] by sprinkling the rim of a vase with "sweet liquids" [soavi licor] (1.3), the food imagery of the *Discorsi* is hardly irrelevant.[3] The judicious flavoring of the poem with marvels—"parlo di quelli anelli, di quelli scudi incantati, di que' corsieri volanti, di quelle navi converse in ninfe, di quelle larve che fra' combattenti si tramettono, e d'altre cose sì fatte" [I am speaking of those enchanted rings and shields, those flying steeds, those ships turned into nymphs, those phantoms that intervene between combatants, and other such things] (*DAP,* 6)—equates such "irrational" events from Ariosto to Virgil with the act of curing through deception. If marvels, then, by being "pleasurable" [dilettevole] (*DAP,* 6),[4] occupy the status of the "soavi licor" sweetening the rim of the vase of poetry, traditionally the moral truth of allegory represented the bitter sub-

---

corsi dell'arte poetica del Tasso," *Studi tassiani* 26 (1977): 5–38; and Lawrence F. Rhu, *The Genesis of Tasso's Narrative Theory* (Detroit: Wayne State University Press, 1993). Like Rhu, Guido Baldassarri has also made use of the *Discorsi* as the theoretical program for Tasso's *Liberata,* in Baldassarri, *"Inferno" e "cielo": Tipologia e funzione del "meraviglioso" nella "Liberata"* (Rome: Bulzoni, 1977). For general discussions of the marvelous in Renaissance poetics, see Hathaway, *Marvels and Commonplaces;* and Weinberg, *A History of Literary Criticism,* s.v. "marvelous" in the index. For other discussions of the marvelous in Tasso, see, in addition to the works by Baldassarri cited in this note, Eugenio Donadoni, *Torquato Tasso: Saggio critico* (Florence: La Nuova Italia, 1952), 130–51; Ettore Mazzali, *Cultura e poesia nell'opera di Torquato Tasso* (Rocca San Casciano: Cappelli, 1957), 111–22; Bortolo Tommaso Sozzi, "Il magismo nel Tasso," in *Studi sul Tasso* (Pisa: Nistri-Lischi, 1954); Charles P. Brand, *Torquato Tasso: A Study of the Poet and of His Contribution to English Literature* (Cambridge: Cambridge University Press, 1965), 99–101; Sergio Zatti, *L'uniforme cristiano e il multiforme pagano: Saggio sulla "Gerusalemme liberata"* (Milan: Il Saggiatore, 1983), 122–25; and Elizabeth J. Bellamy, *Translations of Power: Narcissism and the Unconscious in Epic History* (Ithaca: Cornell University Press, 1992), 145–51 in particular. Of Urlich Leo's study *Studien zur Vorgeschichte des Secentismo,* I have consulted his summary, "Torquato Tasso alle soglie del secentismo," *Studi tassiani* 4 (1954): 3–17. All citations from the *Discorsi dell'arte poetica* and *Discorsi del poema eroico* are abbreviated in my text as *DAP* and *DPE.* I draw the original text from Tasso, *Discorsi dell'arte poetica e del poema eroico,* and the translations from Rhu, *The Genesis of Tasso's Narrative Theory.*

3. Cf. Lucretius, *De. Re. Nat.* 1.936–42.

4. The passage reads, "poco dilettevole è veramente quel poema che non ha seco quelle maraviglie che tanto movono non solo l'animo de gli ignoranti, ma de' giudiziosi ancora."

stance, the "succhi amari," that the poet qua medic would have his readers inadvertently swallow to move them toward a deeper understanding of vice and virtue.[5]

In the episode of the enchanted woods, Tasso makes it clear that he intends his marvels to be read allegorically. As Tancredi approaches the cypress tree, he perceives the signs of "ancient mystic Egypt" [l'antico . . . misterioso Egitto] (13.38) inscribed on the bark. Tancredi cannot read these hieroglyphics, nor is he expected to. Like the narrator's simile of the cypress to a lofty pyramid ("nel suo mezzo altero sorge, / quasi eccelsa piramide, un cipresso" [in its center a cypress towers high, like a lofty pyramid] [13.38]), the hieroglyphic script is meant for the reader alone. Only the privileged reader, indoctrinated into "pagan mysteries," can fully grasp the composite image as an "emblem," and hence as an indication that we are supposed to read this episode, just as emblems throughout the Renaissance were so often read, allegorically.[6]

Though Tasso clearly intended his marvels to be read allegorically for the purposes of moral persuasion, he nevertheless avoided mentioning allegory by way of justifying their presence in his *Discorsi*.[7] Tasso instead

---

5. See on this Robert L. Montgomery, Jr., "Allegory and the Incredible Fable: The Italian View from Dante to Tasso," *Publications of the Modern Language Association* 81 (1966): 45–55. See also Zatti, *L'uniforme cristiano*, on the blurring of distinctions between container and contained.

6. As such, through the reference to the "once ancient mysterious Egypt," Tasso connects the script on the tomb to hermeticism, though not so much to the learned body of Neoplatonic philosophy first investigated in the latter half of the quattrocento by Florentine humanists but, more generally, to the popular hermeticism made fashionable through the discovery of Horapollo's *Hieroglyphics*. On hieroglyphics and emblem reading in the Renaissance see Eric Iverson, *The Myth of Egypt and Its Hieroglyphics in European Tradition* (Copenhagen: Gad, 1961); George Boas, introduction to *The Hieroglyphics of Horapollo*, ed. and trans. Boas (New York: Pantheon Books, 1950); Jean Seznec, *The Survival of the Pagan Gods: The Mythological Tradition and Its Place in Renaissance Humanism and Art*, trans. Barbara F. Sessions (New York: Pantheon Books, 1953); Wind, *Pagan Mysteries;* Francis A. Yates, *Giordano Bruno and the Hermetic Tradition* (Chicago: University of Chicago Press, 1964).

7. He perhaps did so because he was still largely under the sway of Aristotle's implicit rejection of allegory by virtue of its conspicuous absence from the *Poetics*. On Tasso's later defense of his marvels, see in particular letters 30, 42, 43, 45–48, 60, 63, and 75 in the so-called *lettere poetiche*, vol. 1 of Tasso, *Le lettere di Torquato Tasso*, ed. Cesare Guasti (Florence: Le Monnier, 1875). In his *Risposta del S. Torquato Tasso al discorso del Sig. Oratio Lombardelli intorno a i contrasti, che si fanno sopra la Gierusalemme liberata* (Ferrara: G. Vasalini, 1586), 14–24, Tasso again continued to defend the marvels of his poem on the grounds that they were verisimilar or historical; however, in his *Del Giudizio sovra la sua Gierusalemme da lui medesimo riformata*, which is admittedly the defense of a very different poem, Tasso primarily rationalized his marvels through allegory, which he declares "non si lascia alcun luogo al vacuo" (see Tasso, *Prose diverse*, 454). In "Tasso's Religion, Tasso's Platonism: The Design

formulated the concept of the "verisimilar marvelous," a very different version of Aristotle's "probable impossibility" (*Poetics* 1461b), and claimed to have been the first to do so:

> Diversissime sono, signor Scipione, queste due nature, il meraviglioso e 'l verisimile, ed in guisa diverse che sono quasi contrarie fra loro: nondimeno l'una e l'altra nel poema è necessaria, ma fa mestieri che arte di eccellente poeta sia quella che insieme le accoppi; il che, se ben è stato sin ora fatto da molti, nissuno è (ch'io mi sappia) il quale insegni come si faccia; anzi alcuni uomini di somma dottrina, veggendo la ripugnanza di queste due nature, hanno guidicato quella parte ch'è verisimile ne' poemi non essere meravigliosa, né quella ch'è meravigliosa verisimile, ma che nondimeno, essendo ambedue necessarie, si debba or seguire il verisimile, ora il meraviglioso, di maniera che l'una all'altra non ceda, ma l'una dall'altra sia temperata.[8] Io per me questa opinione non approvo, che parte alcuna debba nel poema ritrovarsi che verisimile non sia; e la ragione che mi move a così credere è tale. (*DAP*, 6–7)

[These two qualities, the wondrous and the verisimilar, are exceedingly different, Signor Scipione. Indeed, they are so different that they are nearly contrary to each other. Still, both one and the other are necessary in the epic poem. It requires, however, the skill of an excellent poet to join them together; and, though many have done so thus far, no one, to my knowledge, has taught how it is done. In fact, some men of the highest learning, seeing the tension between these two qualities, have decided that the verisimilar parts of poems are not wondrous and the wondrous parts not verisimilar but that since both are still necessary, one must advance the verisimilar at one time and the wondrous at

---

of *Gerusalemme liberata*" (paper presented at the Charles S. Singleton Center of Italian Studies, Villa Spelman, Florence, July, 1989), Walter Stephens, in light of post-Tridentine reforms, offers cogent political and theological reasons why Tasso resisted revealing his allegory when he defended his poem in 1575, the year in which he placed his poem under such fierce censorial scrutiny in preparation for its publication. On allegory in the *Liberata*, see Michael Murrin, *The Allegorical Epic: Essays in Its Rise and Decline* (Chicago: University of Chicago Press, 1980), chap. 4; Luigi Derla, "Sull'allegoria della *Gerusalemme liberata*," *Italianistica* 7 (1978): 473–88; and William Kennedy, "The Problem of Allegory."

8. Tasso would seem to have in mind Giovambattista Giraldi Cinthio, *Discorsi intorno al comporre dei romanzi, delle commedie e delle tragedie* (Venice: Gabriel Giolito De Ferrari, 1554), 55–58; and M. Giovan Battista Pigna, *I romanzi* (Venice: Vincenzo Valgrisi, 1554), especially 17: "Io crederei che temperando l'una con l'altra [il verisimile con il meraviglioso] . . . che molto bene l'una & l'altra si possa havere."

another, in such a way that one does not succumb to the other but, rather, modulates it. For myself, I hold the opinion that no part should be found in a poem that is not verisimilar; and the reason that compels me to such a belief is as follows.]

The undoubted nature of poetry is imitation, Tasso argues along Aristotelian lines, and imitation is dependent on the verisimilar. The verisimilar cannot therefore just be a condition fulfilled from time to time because "è propria e intrinseca dell'essenza sua, e in ogni sua parte sovra ogn'altra cosa necessaria" [it is proper to its essence, intrinsic, and more necessary than any other thing in any other part of it] (*DAP*, 7). Since the marvelous introduced into a poem must be verisimilar, this can be accomplished, Tasso claims, by attributing the presence of marvels to a supernatural power capable of producing such effects according to the shared beliefs—in essence the collective opinion—of a presumably unified readerly community. What at one level appears as a marvel unto itself in nature consequently seems verisimilar when considered from the vantage point of its ultimate transcendent source, as long as that source remains integral to a set of beliefs upheld by the entire religious community:

Attribuisca il poeta alcune operazioni, che di gran lunga eccedono il poter de gli uomini, a Dio, a gli angioli suoi, a' demoni o a coloro a' quali da Dio o da' demoni è concessa questa podestà, quali sono i santi, i maghi e le fate. Queste opere, se per se stesse saranno considerate, maravigliose parranno, anzi miracoli sono chiamati nel commune uso di parlare. Queste medesime, se si avrà riguardo alla virtù e alla potenza di chi l'ha operate, verisimili saranno giudicate; perchè, avendo gli uomini nostri bevuta nelle fasce insieme co 'l latte questa opinione, ed essendo poi in loro confermata da i maestri della nostra santa fede (cioè che Dio e i suoi ministri e i demoni e i maghi, permettendolo Lui, possino far cose sovra le forze della natura meravigliose), e leggendo e sentendo ogni dì ricordarne novi essempi, non parrà loro fuori del verisimile quello che credono non solo esser possibile, ma stimano spesse fiate esser avvenuto e poter di novo molte volte avvenire. [. . .] Può esser dunque una medesma azione e meravigliosa e verisimile: meravigliosa riguardandola in se stessa e circonscritta dentro a i termini naturali, verisimile considerandola divisa da questi termini, nella sua cagione, la quale è una virtù sopranaturale, potente e avezza ad operar simili meraviglie. (*DAP*, 7–8)

[Some works that greatly exceed the power of men the poet attributes to God, to His angels, to demons, or to those granted such power by God or by demons, like saints and wizards and fairies. If considered by themselves, these works seem wondrous; in fact, common usage calls them miracles. These same works, if attention is given to the virtue and the power that have wrought them, are deemed verisimilar. Since our people have imbibed this opinion in the cradle, along with their milk, and since it was confirmed in them by the masters of our blessed Faith (that is, that God and his ministers and demons and magicians, with his permission, can do things wondrous beyond the forces of nature) and, finally, since everyday they read and hear new examples related, therefore it does not appear to them beyond verisimilitude. [. . .] In sum, one and the same action can be both wondrous and verisimilar: it is wondrous considered in itself and circumscribed by natural limits; it is verisimilar considered free from these limits, in its cause, which is supernatural, powerful, and wont to work similar wonders.]

Tasso's theoretical formulation of the "verisimilar marvelous" may easily be applied to his representation of the marvel of the bleeding tree in the *Liberata*. Magicians, as Tasso claims, are by common belief capable of producing marvels, and the infidel magician Ismeno has enchanted the woods.[9] Moreover, Ismeno's capacity to enchant the woods through black magic recognizably derives from his overall pact with the devil. His actions thus represent the performative side to the wider ideological struggle underpinning the text from the first canto, between Satan's hell and God's heaven ("in van l'Inferno vi s'oppose. . . . Il Ciel gli diè favore" [vainly Hell opposed herself to it . . . . Heaven granted him favor] (1.1).[10] Ismeno may be a pagan, but he is a magician in a context that is thoroughly Christian, whether he knows it or not. Furthermore, that Ismeno was a Christian who converted to the religion of Islam only confirms that he is in truth a

---

9. On magic in the *Liberata* see Sozzi, "Il magismo nel Tasso," keeping in mind the observations of Ezio Raimondi, "Tra grammatica e magia," in *Rinascimento inquieto* (Palermo: Manfredi, 1965). On Renaissance magic in general, the studies are too wide and varied to be discussed here, but along with the previously mentioned works see, for a background study of Tasso in particular, Stuart Clark, "Tasso and the Literature of Witchcraft," in *The Renaissance in Ferrara and Its European Horizons,* eds. J. Salmons and Walter Moretti (Cardiff: University of Wales Press, 1984).

10. I have not elaborated on this point, since it has already been sufficiently discussed and developed by Guido Baldassarri throughout his *"Inferno" e "cielo."* For a discussion of the pagans as heretics, see Zatti, *L'uniforme cristiano,* 12.

heretic, a Christian who has succumbed to evil ("or Macone adora, e fu cristiano" [He now adores Mahoun, and he was a Christian] [2.2]). Accordingly, a Christian, astute or simpleminded, learned or not, while reading about the bleeding tree should, according to Tasso's poetics, be able to respond to it as a marvel (trees generally do not bleed when cut) or as a likelihood (satanic forces may be credibly channeled through an infidel's black magic). By the logic of Tasso's theoretical system, the marvel of the bleeding branch may be deemed verisimilar since it is framed and rationalized by a network of beliefs that are ostensibly shared by all Christians, a network that in turn admits no other beliefs except through negation. But then again, if this is the case, so too may we deem Dante's version of the same marvel verisimilar, if we acknowledge the contemporary opinion of Iacopo Mazzoni, for example, that God, precisely as Tasso asserts, can achieve all things in His absolute power.[11]

Tasso never actually participated in the debate over the *Commedia*. He found himself instead involved in a debate over his own poem shortly after an author, operating under the pseudonym of Castravilla, condemned the *Commedia* for lacking, among other things, verisimilitude.[12] But in his *Apologia*, written in response to his critics, Tasso gives some indication as to how he might have treated the problem of verisimilitude in the *Commedia* when he relies on the distinctions between the icastic and the fantastic as set forth in Plato's *Sophist*. In doing so, Tasso claims that, unlike Ariosto, who produced phantasms like the hippogriff, Dante imitated things as they truly are, thereby creating proper models of icastic representations.[13] Tasso's statement is, however, something of a red herring. For when he later returned to the distinction between icastic and fantastic representations in his *Discorsi del poema eroico*, he grouped Dante with such philosophical poets as Lucretius and Boethius, who demonstrate truths, and not with Homer and Virgil, who rely on the verisimilar. This being the case, the subject of the *Commedia*, as Tasso declares at the begin-

---

11. Mazzoni, *Discorso di Iacopo Mazzoni*, 83, 85–86. Here, in the fifth Particella, the emphasis is on what a reader is willing to accept as credible purely by faith.

12. Castravilla [pseud.], *Discorsi di M. Ridolfo Castravilla*, 25–26: "non essendo nessuno che pensi che uno, vestito di membra, possa discendere all'inferno et, uscitone, possa passare per il purgatorio, e quindi ascendere al paradiso, trascendendo con le membra graui i corpi celesti, e far tanti altri miracoli, o piú tosto prodigii e monstruosità."

13. All citations from the *Apologia* in my text are from Tasso, *Prose*, ed. Ettore Mazzali (Milan: Ricciardi, 1959); translations are mine. Tasso, *Prose*, 433. On the distinctions between the icastic and the fantastic as developed by Tasso in his *Apologia*, see Tasso, *Prose*, 430–33, and *DPE*, 86–91.

ning of his *Discorsi,* can be nothing other than contemplation (*DPE,* 64). Hence, if Tasso praises Dante in his early *Discorsi* for his "energia" (*DAP,* 47)—his extraordinary capacity to render images vividly real—the entire vexing issue of verisimilitude in the debate over the *Commedia*—above all, whether or not the wayfarer could or could not have taken a voyage according to a given set of beliefs—has been quietly dropped as a matter of no great concern. Dante, as a philosophical poet, is simply proving a point like a dialectician, "alcune volte dimostrando co' filosofi e usando il filosofema" [sometimes demonstrating as philosophers do through syllogism] (*DPE,* 88). Within the same framework, we may assume that Dante is proving a point with his bleeding branch as well.

Yet there is another reason why Tasso never bothered to argue the case of verisimilitude in the *Commedia*—be it regarding the voyage or, for that matter, an individual episode, such as Dante's revision of the Virgilian bleeding branch. In his *Discorsi dell'arte poetica,* Tasso begins with the assumption that the verisimilar is the essence of epic poetry. For this reason an epic poet should draw material from history because "non è verisimile ch'una azione illustre, quali sono quelle del poema eroico, non sia stata scritta e passata alla memoria de' posteri con l'aiuto d'alcuna istoria" [it is not verisimilar that an illustrious action, such as those in an heroic poem, would not have been written down and passed on to the memory of posterity with the help of history] (*DAP,* 4). As a source of verifiable truth, the authority of history derives not from the specific word of the historian but—and this is all-important in Tasso—from the community, whose collective memory the written account of the historian merely helps ("con l'aiuto di") [with the help of] refresh over time. A historian is only a historian insofar as he or she is the spokesperson for true events shared by others. Dante's poem, though it repeatedly makes historical claims, can never rely on a prior historically valid text that has been passed down through the collective memory of the ages and on which the poet may confidently build his poem. As Bellisario Bulgarini understood in the debate over the *Commedia* in the Renaissance, Dante can at best assert that what the reader has in hand is the authoritative account of a voyage that actually took place. The *Commedia* fabricates its own history, and it does so autobiographically in the first person singular, much like a medieval travelogue. The wayfarer may be taken allegorically as Everyman, but in the end his voyage remains a singular voyage, his history a personal history, his authority the only authority, his memory the only memory. From the perspective of Tasso's theoretical system as expounded in the *Discorsi,* Dante's history is no history at all. Eyewitness chronicles have no authority unto themselves unless they have been thoroughly accepted by the community. By contrast, the underlying foundation to Tasso's *Gerusalemme liberata* is, or so Tasso claims, a true historical account—not a feigned marvelous voyage, but a recorded pilgrimage-crusade.

As a result, only Tasso's marvel may legitimately arouse the desired passion of "meraviglia," because only verisimilar marvels for Tasso produce this effect on the reader:[14]

> *Forestiero:* E la meraviglia nasce da le cose credute o da le non credute?
> *Segretario:* Niun si meraviglia di quelli effetti ch'egli non crede veri, o possibili almeno.
> *Forestiero:* Dunque, delle cose o degli effetti creduti solo ci meravigliamo; e la meraviglia dell'altre cose non solo è minore, ma non è pur meraviglia.
>
> (*Apologia,* 448)

> [*Foreigner:* And the marvelous is created from things believed or disbelieved?
> *Secretary:* No one marvels over those effects that he or she does not believe to be true, or at least possible.
> *Foreigner:* In that case, we marvel only at things or effects that are believable, and our marveling over other things not only is less but, in point of fact, is not even marveling at all.]

Yet even so, after Virgil's Polydorus episode and the bleeding twig of Dante's Pier della Vigna, we can hardly imagine that the poet of the *Li-*

---

14. Virgil's and Boccaccio's versions cannot claim the privilege of being verisimilar, since they originate in pagan gods; and Ariosto's version necessarily remains for Tasso the product of "sophistic poetry." Tasso's concept that only things that are verisimilar produce "meraviglia" is widespread throughout the late Italian Renaissance. Determining what Renaissance theorists considered to be a "meraviglia" is, however, a far more difficult problem to solve. Hathaway has addressed some of these issues in his *Marvels and Commonplaces,* and much may be gleaned from Weinberg's *A History of Literary Criticism,* s.v. "admiratio" in the index. Suffice it to say, the range is extraordinarily wide and rich, from Francesco Patrizi's Aristotelian concept of "meraviglia" as the source of all philosophical inquiry, to Giraldi's concept of "meraviglia" as occupying the status of an aesthetic response that merely engages the reader's or the spectator's attention in the work of art as it is read or performed, to the widely accepted concept of "meraviglia" as a synonym for pleasure, the concept supported by, for example, Castelvetro and Minturno.

berata expects his readers to be surprised, much less shocked, in their "meraviglia" before this verisimilar marvel. We have been deliberately led through scattered literary allusions as Tancredi penetrates the nocturnal woods to finally arrive at a marvel fully authorized by tradition.[15] The exclamation "Oh meraviglia!" (13.41), voiced by the poet just after Tancredi strikes the tree and just before the cypress bleeds, is not so much a rhetorical prompt commanding surprise. It is, rather, a diacritical sign, indicating, beyond the suspense it may or may not create, that the marvel of the *Liberata* still derives from Virgil and Dante. Mutatis mutandis, we have seen this all twice, if not vaguely four times, before.

The voice that cries out with the Dantean expression "Oh meraviglia!" exclaims above all with the authority of literary tradition.[16] If we are supposed to be surprised in this instance, it is not by the verisimilar presence of this familiar marvel. It is instead by the way Tasso has calculatingly made this marvel operate in his poem according to the expectations codified by literary conventions. What matters, in other words, is how this marvel figures not into a community's theological beliefs but into the kinds of stories we, as a community, tell and are told over time.[17] How, then, do Tasso's marvels rhetorically operate in his poem, not just in terms of his own theory, but as part of a culture's inherited and changing representational practices? How do they figure into the normative structure of a community's shared literary strategies? To what extent are marvels constitutive of literary strategies and genres? Finally, what is at stake for a poet who already anticipates, by way of the defense mechanisms Margaret Ferguson locates in the *Gerusalemme liberata*,[18] a community of censorial readers who would rob him of the marvels in his poem?

We may begin by addressing the last question first. The complaint con-

---

15. The text alludes to, for example, Lucretius (13.18), Lucan (13.21), Dante (13.27), and Horace (13.21).

16. Dante uses the expression "oh maraviglia!" in *Purgatorio* 1.134, on the significance of which, in relation to the Virgilian formulas, see chap. 2.

17. When Tasso has Ismeno tell Solimano that he will speak of marvels ("Maraviglie dirò," 10.16), the reader may rest assured that those same marvels derive from a canonical source, in this particular instance from the mist shrouding Aeneas as he approaches Carthage. This is virtually true with each of Tasso's marvels. What is important for Tasso, however, is not the "materia," the *argumentum,* but the *inventio,* even above the *elocutio* (*DAP,* 4). An alternative, of course, lies in the *secentismo* of Marino and his followers, where no claim to verisimilitude is being made, or in such a poem as *Il mondo creato,* where all the marvels originate directly in God.

18. Margaret Ferguson, *Trials of Desire: Renaissance Defenses of Poetry* (New Haven: Yale University Press, 1983).

sistently registered against the *Liberata* after its unauthorized publication was that there were simply too many marvels in the poem. This was a complaint against which Tasso could finally marshal no sure defense. Allegory (letter 48), verisimilitude (letter 46), history (letters 47 and 60), and literary tradition (letters 42, 45, and 60) could all be alternatively called on to provide an explanation. But in the end Tasso could only eclectically validate the presence of marvels, not their quantity. By including too many, Tasso had, in the end, overstepped the bounds of decorum, the judgment of the epic poet, which, to return to the metaphor of the early *Discorsi,* judiciously flavors the poem for a community of readers. This indecorous overstepping of bounds is the true cause of the "nausea" Tasso in one instance fears his marvels will arouse in his readers by virtue of their overabundance in the enchanted forest ("moveranno quasi nausea i miracoli del bosco" [the miracles of the forest will make [people] nauseous] [letter 47]). Tastes change; tastes differ. Silvio Antoniano, acting as the spokesperson for a post-Tridentine community, wants few marvels; others—indeed, those who had already begun to canonize the *Furioso*[19]—want many. And no matter how much Tasso rationalized the presence of marvels in his poem, there always remained the inevitable element of the superfluous, those marvels that could not even be accounted for by allegory.[20] Some marvels are just there, Tasso seems to acquiesce, like excess dead weight, signifying nothing yet providing the sweetness, in a Horatian context, for the deeper lesson to be learned—*dulce et utile.*

What, then, does Tasso obstinately here defend when he seeks to justify the presence of marvels in his poem? I suggest that Tasso here defends, among other things, a presumed right to include in his poem what he takes to be his alone but what nevertheless belongs all along to the community as public property. For epic, in Tasso's conception of it, is a work constructed for a community and in large measure by a community. The epic poet in essence represents the voice of a shared heroic past authorized by collective memory inscribed into history (in this case, William of Tyre's *Historia della guerra sacra di Gierusalemme*) and by a religious community's deep abiding beliefs transferred from age to age (first through the nursing mother and then through the patriarchy of the Church; *DAP,* 7–8). As a result, when Tasso writes, he aims to fashion a voice that is ide-

---

19. See on this Daniel Javitch, *Proclaiming a Classic: The Canonization of "Orlando furioso"* (Princeton: Princeton University Press, 1991).

20. "Se dunque vi fosse alcuna particella vota d'allegoria, non credo d'aver errato" (letter 48), *Le lettere,* 119.

ally the voice not of many communities but of a single unified community.[21] Yet to perform this function in and through epic means in truth that nothing in the poem is ever purely Tasso's, least of all the presence of marvels. In a very real sense, it means the absence of privacy, as Tasso goes about composing his epic, gravely cognizant of the greater corporate task.

Along these lines, I argue, the marvelous throughout the *Liberata* may best be understood within the context of Renaissance notions of privacy rather than verisimilitude. Privacy is here taken as the desire to withdraw to a secluded space that nevertheless remains all along within the public sphere or purview, whether it be the privacy of the Petrarchan retreat in Vaucluse, Montaigne's "a back shop all our own," More's "secret solitary place in his own house," or St. Teresa's "interior castle."[22] The inherent difficulties of determining and negotiating between what belongs to the individual and what belongs to the community, what is private and what is public, are central issues in Tasso's treatment of the marvelous throughout the *Gerusalemme liberata,* just as they are crucial elements underlying Tasso's defense of the marvelous in his poem. For when Tasso's heroic warriors act, they too act in their most private moments beneath a public gaze. And nowhere is this more conspicuously the case, we shall see, as when Tasso's crusaders come into contact with the marvelous.

With this in mind, let us begin by turning to a marvel that is patently *not*

---

21. On the rhetorical norms of Tasso's epic voice, see Durling, *The Figure of the Poet,* in particular 198–99, who also earlier notes in terms congenial to my discussion of Tasso's defense of the marvels, "What is at stake for Tasso, in his struggle with the problem of poetry, is ultimately the claims of the individual poet's subjectivity against the massive institutionalization and formulation of doctrine that was then taking place in Italy" (195).

22. Giovanni Getto—in his "Struttura e poesia nella *Gerusalemme liberata,*" in *Interpretazione del Tasso* (Naples: Edizioni Scientifiche Italiane, 1951), 379–417; and throughout his *Nel Mondo della "Gerusalemme"* (Florence: Valecchi, 1968)—has discussed in great detail the concept of "solitude" in Tasso; he has done so, however, in terms that make the concept operate as a near synonym for uniqueness. Stephen Greenblatt has discussed issues of privacy in his *Renaissance Self-Fashioning: From More to Shakespeare* (Chicago: University of Chicago Press, 1980), 45–46. For privacy in the Renaissance, there is much material in the essays collected in Philippe Ariés and Georges Duby, eds., *Histoire de la vie privée III: De la Renaissance aux Lumiéres* (Paris: Editions du Seuil, 1986); and on solitude and the humanist initiative outside the academy, beginning with Petrarch, see Nancy Struever, *Theory as Practice: Ethical Inquiry in the Renaissance* (Chicago: University of Chicago Press, 1992). On the private and the public in Tasso as conflicting codes, see above all Zatti, *L'uniforme cristiano;* and Timothy Hampton, *Writing From History: The Rhetoric of Exemplarity in Renaissance Literature* (Ithaca: Cornell University Press, 1990). The notion of privacy does not in Tasso, any more than in Petrarch, simply denote the activity of *vita contemplativa;* rather it denotes a host of conflicting desires that Tasso aims to explore and finally channel in an ideologically acceptable way toward God and the reinstitution of God's kingdom on earth.

verisimilar according to Tasso's own theory, and thus one that Tasso should have readily rejected from his poem. In canto 7, Argante has returned to battle Tancredi after an imposed six-day truce. As Goffredo looks about, he suddenly realizes that he lacks his bravest warriors (7.58). The honor of the Christians is at stake, Goffredo cries out, "l'onor di nostra gente!" [the honor of our people] (7.60), yet no one is willing or present to fight for the community. Seeing this, Goffredo calls for his own arms. But Raimondo steps forward and insists that Goffredo cannot battle, for his death would represent a public, rather than a private, loss, the destruction of the entire community: "publico fòra e non privato il lutto" [the mourning would be public, and not private] (7.62). Goffredo cannot battle, so Raimondo offers himself instead. His bravery stirs the other soldiers, they all draw lots, and as chance would have it—a chance governed by God (7.70)—Raimondo wins. There is a round of applause, and the old warrior sets out to battle Argante, after having accepted the sword offered him by Goffredo.

At this point, the poet interrupts his narrative to describe the wonders of a horse called Aquilino:

Questo su 'l Tago nacque, ove talora
l'avida madre del guerriero armento,
quando l'alma stagion che n'innamora
nel cor le instiga il natural talento,
volta l'aperta bocca incontra l'òra,
raccoglie i semi del fecondo vento,
e de' tepidi fiati (oh meraviglia!)
cupidamente ella concipe e figlia.

E ben questo Aquilin nato diresti
di quale aura del ciel più lieve spiri,
o se veloce sì ch'orma non resti
stendere il corso per l'arena il miri,
o se 'l vedi addoppiar leggieri e presti
a destra ed a sinistra angusti giri.

(7.76–77)

[This steed was born on the Tagus, where sometimes the avid matron of the martial herd (when the fertile season that inspires love arouses in her heart her natural bent), her open mouth being turned against the breeze, gathers in the seed of the fructifying wind; and from warm breezes (oh marvelous!) full of desire she conceives and bears a foal. And indeed you would say that this Aquiline was born of whatever breeze most lightly breathes from heaven, whether you watch him running his course across the sand so swift that not a print remains, or see him doubling his tight curvets, agile and quick.]

No attempt has been made to render this marvel verisimilar. There is no black magic or natural magic called on to explain its existence, no saints or fays or divine messengers involved. No such horse is mentioned in William of Tyre's history either. Aquilino, as the poet's apostrophe makes plain, is emphatically a marvel ("oh meraviglia!"), and it is a marvel that remains, even according to Tasso's own poetics, stubbornly unnatural. Like the marvels that Tasso often singled out for criticism in Ariosto's poem, it is in truth a fantastic representation.[23]

In such romances as the *Innamorato* or the *Furioso,* when a knight first sits on a horse of this kind, especially toward the very beginning of a poem, he tends to gravitate toward a labyrinthine forest. He plays truant and wanders. He engages in one-on-one combats for the sake of personal honor, saddling up for an adventure that will test his individual prowess and valor. He gives himself up to Fortune to prove himself and himself alone. By and large, a romance hero's initial impulse is not to ride out into the middle of an epic battlefield to sacrifice his own life for the honor of all. Yet that is precisely what Raimondo does. While Tancredi and all the bravest knights have deserted the battle field and the community for the sake of their own individual desire or honor, Raimondo mounts a horse that codifies the desire to wander in romance, where the individual will is tantamount and heroes characteristically pursue Fortune through a maze of adventures. In doing so, Tasso has already begun to place a romance marvel at the service of the community in an epic poem.[24]

---

23. On marvelous horses see Rajna, *Le fonti,* 116–20; Lanfranco Caretti—in his commentary in Tasso, *Gerusalemme liberata,* ed. Caretti (Bari: Laterza, 1976), 1:227—considers as the most likely sources both Pliny (*Natural History* 8.42) and Bernardo Tasso's *Amadigi* (29.17.1–6).

24. Studies that discuss Tasso's treatment of romance in his epic include Kristen Olson Murtaugh, "Erminia Delivered: Notes on Tasso and Romance," *Quaderni d'italianistica* 3 (1982): 12–25; Andrew Fichter, "Tasso's Epic of Deliverance," *Publications of the Modern Language Association* 93 (1978): 265–74; Judith A. Kates, *Tasso and Milton: The Problem of Christian Epic* (Lewisburg, Pa.: Bucknell University Press, 1983); Zatti, *L'uniforme cristiano;* and Hampton, *Writing from History,* who discusses this episode in the light of the contesting

Nevertheless, even the "fantastic" marvels of romance are not sufficient to preserve the integrity of the community in Tasso's *Liberata*. As Raimondo sits on his horse, he looks up to the heavens and prays to God that he may defeat Argante, just as on a similar plain David once conquered the giant Goliath. "And the example," Raimondo begs, "will be parallel" [e fia pari l'essempio] (7.78). To signal a shift away from the marvels of romance, Tasso makes use of typology.[25] Called on by God, Raimondo's guardian angel bypasses an assortment of wondrous arms—the lance that struck the Edenic serpent, the lightning that afflicts humankind, the trident that upturns the earth (7.81). At last the angel grasps a shield so big that it may cover whole countries and people between Asia and Africa. The shield of heaven, employed to cover whole races and vast territories, has been seized to protect a single individual; inversely, the horse of romance, used so often by knights in search of Fortune, has been harnessed and placed at the service of the entire community. Both the horse and the shield serve to protect, but it is clear by comparison which form of protection is more powerful and enduring.

The shield diminishes by contrast the marvel of Aquilino, though Raimondo's horse serves him well at first (7.89). Yet in the end Aquilino can never completely protect Raimondo. One sword-thrust is bound to hit home (7.92), and at that very moment God's angel stands waiting (7.92). Against this shield, weapons of terrestrial matter cannot endure. The lance shatters like glass and falls on the sand in the smallest pieces. Argante can hardly believe his eyes (7.93), thinking his sword has been broken on an ordinary shield. Raimondo, oblivious of the celestial aid, is of the same mind (7.94), even though he had prayed for divine assistance before.

Raimondo's ignorance of the true underlying causes of his victory demonstrates that God protects the weak and deserving, now as with David before Goliath. But Raimondo's ignorance has a purpose that fur-

---

codes of behavior of early humanism and Counter-Reformation Europe (100–108), though I here stress the resolution of that contest, as do Zatti (*L'uniforme cristiano,* 18–19) and Quint (*Epic and Empire,* chaps. 5 and 6).

25. On typology in the *Liberata,* see Thomas P. Roche, Jr., "Tasso's Enchanted Woods," in *Literary Uses of Typology from Late Middle Ages to Present,* ed. Earl Miner (Princeton: Princeton University Press, 1977), 49–78. Hampton, *Writing from History,* argues that typology is not a feature of Renaissance exemplarity because of its reliance on pagan models, though I argue that it is a reliance that is nevertheless corrected in Tasso through just such examples as David and Goliath; the alternative between pagan and sacred exempla, and thus between secularly open or typologically closed readings, is foregrounded earlier as Argante stands "qual Encelado in Flegra, o qual mostrosse / ne l'ima valle il filisteo gigante" (6.23).

ther transcends the exemplum of typology. For Raimondo to know of the celestial shield would only render him certain of his duty. For him to remain ignorant instead plunges him directly into the contingencies of worldly human affairs and values. His ignorance leaves him open to the codes of romance that his fabulous horse exemplifies. He sees before him shattered pieces of metal, and believing his own shield to have been the cause, Raimondo momentarily considers allowing the defenseless Argante to seize another sword: "Prendi—volea già dirgli—un'altra spada" [He was about to say "Take another sword"] (7.95). Sitting on the horse of romance, Raimondo instinctively obeys the law of the chivalric romance subject, who will gradually strip himself of weaponry to remain on equal terms. Without parity the individual in a romance is never adequately tested. But the test of the individual in Tasso's epic can only be valued as a performance of a duty and sacrifice to the community. A new thought therefore arises: it is not his own honor that is at stake, Raimondo realizes, but the honor of all that he defends, a matter of public, rather than private, concern:

> novo pensier nacque nel core,
> ch'alto scorno è de' suoi dove egli cada,
> che di publica causa è difensore.
> Così né indegna a lui vittoria aggrada,
> né in dubbio vuol porre il comune onore.
>
> (7.95)

[a new thought sprang up in his heart, that it is a deep dishonor for his people if he falls who is defender of the public cause. So an undeserved victory brings him no pleasure, but neither does he want to hazard the general honor.]

Though Raimondo returns to battle only after he has been wounded in his moment of hesitation, the fabulous horse—which in romance would have surely led a knight to wander through a labyrinth of adventures in search of Fortune—is finally placed at the service of the community.

As with the marvel of Aquilino, the marvels throughout the *Liberata* may be best understood not as a problem of verisimilitude but as a problem of the individual's relation to the community and his or her need for privacy. This is manifestly true regarding the marvels of the enchanted forest, the episode with which we began and to which we may now briefly return.[26] The episode in fact begins with a plural reaction of the carpenters to the marvels of the woods and gradually narrows down to the efforts of warriors who one by one step forward to test their courage. In this respect, the movement toward the forest reflects a channeled movement toward a greater degree of individuality. As each group or individual moves closer to the forest, new and more powerful marvels arise to instill even greater fear. Yet these marvels, while directed to halt the approach of the crusaders, also become part of a shared subjective experience that in truth binds the community together.

Tancredi's approach to the woods dramatizes this point in particular. He stands apart from the outset, "in sé ristretto" [concentered in himself] (13.33). Yet in approaching the woods, he also passes on ("trapassa," 13.33), and in doing so he ritually passes through the previous experiences of those who approached the enchanted forest before him. First he encounters the "fero aspetto" [forbidding aspect] (13.33) of the forest that initially troubled the carpenters (13.18–19); then he confronts " 'l gran romor del tuono e del tremoto" [the great noise of thunder and of quake] (13.33) that had caused the squadron sent by Goffredo to afterward return in fear (13.19–21). Finally, by the time Tancredi has reached the wall of flames, he has shared the prior experiences of the community. At last he decides to put down his own life, to sacrifice the individual, for the common good:

> Non mai la vita, ove cagione onesta
> del comun pro la chieda, altri risparmi.

> (13.34)

> [One never should be saving of his life where a valid reason of the common good demands it.]

Once beyond the wall of flames, there are no more experiences to share in common, only those that the enchanted woods provides specifically for Tancredi. The cypress tree, the sobs, the warnings like an epitaph on the

---

26. On Tancredi's reencounter with Clorinda in the enchanted woods, which remains a locus classicus of Tasso studies, see in recent years, above all, Murrin, *The Allegorical Epic,* chap. 4; Ferguson, *Trials of Desire,* 126–36; Kennedy,"The Problem of Allegory," 35–40; Bellamy, *Translations of Power,* 174–76; and Juliana Schiesari, *The Gendering of Melancholia: Feminism, Psychoanalysis, and the Symbolics of Loss in Renaissance Literature* (Ithaca: Cornell University Press, 1992), 204–5.

tomb of a pyramid, the blood, the guilt-invoked cry from the false spirit of Clorinda—all these experiences sway Tancredi from his aim. Though Tancredi is motivated to pass beyond the wall of flames for the sake of the community, his ability to transcend the marvels circumscribing the woods marks him as a superior individual. Hence, the enchanted forest can only respond to such an exceptional individual by drawing on Tancredi's past and producing plaintive, "personalized" marvels made just for him. For this reason, whereas Tancredi earlier stood in mourning seeking forgiveness from Clorinda by the tall pine tree that marked her tomb, the enchanted woods now offers up a funereal cypress as the graveyard of Tancredi's own past. In this way, the forest finally provides the knight with both the place and the privacy to undertake, in Freudian terms, "the work of mourning," a work earlier denied to Tancredi (12.77).[27]

Nevertheless, even as Tancredi duplicates the loss of Clorinda and his own guilt in slaying her by night, he stands alone within an amphitheatric space: "Al fine un largo spazio in forma scorge / d'anfiteatro" [At length he discovers a broad clearing in the shape of an amphitheater] (13.38).[28] No one sits on the seats here. The invisible, imaginary theater is empty. Yet Tancredi's actions are implicitly rendered a performance all the same, as though the eyes of the community were somehow surreptitiously watching. However much the passage into the enchanted woods may indicate a movement toward a greater degree of individuality, Tancredi is thus never permitted, in Greenblatt's memorable phrase, "moments of pure, unfettered subjectivity."[29] There is no private psychological space where a knight can simply experience his own pain and sorrow upon hearing the accusing voice of the woman he has loved and slain. Tancredi's failure is always the community's failure, his quest the community's quest. He strikes the tree for the community. But the efficacy of the marvel in then

---

27. Peter the Hermit's earlier injunction is for Tancredi to suppress such passionate mourning ("frena / quel dolor" [bridle that sorrow] [12.88]). For an interpretation of Tasso's episode of the bleeding tree that draws on the parallels between Ariosto and Tasso's version in an intricate psychoanalytic rereading of Freud's reading of the episode in *Beyond the Pleasure Principle,* see Margaret F. Ferguson, *Trials of Desire,* 126–36. See also Bellamy, *Translations of Power,* 174–76; and Schiesari, *The Gendering of Melancholia,* 204–5.

28. For discussions of the theater in Tasso see Mario Costanzo, *Il "Gran theatro del mondo"* (Milan: Vanni Scheiwiller, 1964); Ezio Raimondi, "Il Dramma nel racconto," in *Poesia come retorica* (Florence: Olschki, 1980); and Riccardo Scrivano, "Tasso e il teatro," in *La norma e lo scarto: Proposte per il cinquecento letterario italiano* (Rome: Bonacci, 1980). Donadoni, *Torquato Tasso,* has a negative reading of theatricality in Tasso as "melodramma" (180–81).

29. Greenblatt, *Renaissance Self-Fashioning,* 256.

deflecting Tancredi from his overall communal purpose in turn reveals how profoundly Tancredi needs some sort of private sheltered retreat.

The marvel of love in Tasso's poem would at first glance seem to hold out just such a promise for a space where the individual can retreat and live in a state of pure private subjectivity. In this respect, the miracle of love represents a threat to the unity of the crusaders as a community, precisely because it offers the possibility of privacy. "Oh meraviglia!" the narrator exclaims when Tancredi falls in love with Clorinda in a pastoral setting (1.47). Yet when a troop of soldiers then abruptly invades this shaded world, the marvel of love may be said to have only disclosed a longing within Tancredi, without ever locating a physical space wherein that love may endlessly triumph.

Armida's great charm in the *Liberata* lies in her capacity to locate just such a space for the crusaders by enticing men to imagine penetrating beneath the half-open folds of her garments and beholding within her body "tante meraviglie" [many marvels] (4.32). Like Tancredi's sword-thrust into the bleeding tree, the penetrating, phallic glances of the male crusaders are seeking "hidden secrets" [occulti secreti] (4.31), where their imagination "can move inside" [s'interna] (4.31) and "stretch out in space" [ivi si spazia] (4.32). And the effect of Armida's forbidden "marvels" on the community is both apparent and calculatingly negative.[30] Seducing the best of the warriors from the camp, Armida challenges Goffredo's authority to rule and control his male crusaders as a unified collective body. Yet the luring erotic power of Armida's "meraviglie" also preys on a collective need for the community to somehow respond to the individual's exigencies for an interiorized space, a space where human frailty and emotions and sexual desires are not only permitted but prized.

Nowhere is this more evident than with the marvels that Armida employs to imprison and woo Rinaldo. From the outset, Rinaldo stands apart from the entire corps of crusaders by virtue of his valor and his ire; he is the Achilles hero without whom Goffredo cannot win his war. Alone, traveling toward Antioch in exile along the river Oronte, he comes on a message that beckons him to take a small skiff moored nearby and then pass beyond to a little island, for there he will witness "the greatest marvels" [meraviglie maggior] beneath the sun (14.58). Rinaldo passes beyond, and in doing so he succumbs to the alluring romance attraction of

---

30. For the large-scale gendering of romance and epic, see Quint, *Epic and Empire,* chap. 1.

the marvelous. But at first glance, the marvel of this little island would seem to be nothing more than its peaceful isolation:

Come è là giunto, cupido e vagante
volge intorno lo sguardo, e nulla vede
fuor ch'antri ed acque e fiori ed erbe e piante,
onde quasi schernito esser si crede.

(14.59)

[When he is arrived there, footloose and eager he casts his gaze around, and sees nothing, other than caverns and waters and flowers and bushes and trees, so that he thinks himself in a manner mocked.]

There is, to Rinaldo's dismay, nothing wondrous to see here. The *otium* of privacy is about the most this island seems to offer. Nevertheless, such privacy, in what is literally deemed a *locus amoenus* ("loco . . . lieto") is not readily shunned (14.59), and as Rinaldo relaxes along the shore, a naked siren emerges from the waves:

Il fiume gorgogliar fra tanto udio
con novo suono, e là con gli occhi corse,
e mover vide un'onda in mezzo al rio
che in se stessa si volse e si ritorse;
e quinci alquanto d'un crin biondo uscio,
e quinci di donzella un volto sorse,
e quinci il petto e le mammelle, e de la
sua forma infin dove vergogna cela.

(14.60)

[Meanwhile he heard the stream murmur with a new sound, and ran over it with his eyes, and saw rising in the river's midst a wave that turned and returned upon itself; and then came forth a quantity of blonde hair, and then rose up a damsel's face, and then her bosom and her breasts, and her whole shape, to where modesty makes concealment.]

This is a marvel made for Rinaldo—the exact image of Armida lurking in ambush—and Rinaldo is completely alone to enjoy his "magical phantom" [magica larva] (14.61). He is without squires, whom he has just left by the riverside "perché mal capace era la barca" [because the skiff had lit-tle room] (14.58). He is also without commanders and fellow crusaders, whom he has abandoned in his self-imposed exile. But in truth, as subse-quent verses indicate, Rinaldo is not alone at all. The entire episode of seduction begins in what appears to be an isolated place—a small island in the middle of a river in Africa—and then gradually develops into the sym-bolic space of a theatrical performance:

> Così dal palco di notturna scena
> o ninfa o dea, tarda sorgendo, appare.
>
> (14.61)

[So from the flooring of a stage at night a nymph or goddess, rising slowly, comes into view.]

Rinaldo is being observed; and in the most disconcerting of ways, he is being watched by the community. For the narrator of this scene of seduc-tion is not an omniscient epic author overseeing the tale. Rather, Rinaldo's scene of seduction is being narrated by the Magus of Ascalona to two righteous knights. His "private matter" unfolds from the outset as public knowledge.

Rinaldo, of course, is all along being observed by Armida too. She stages this drama as she hovers nearby, hatching her plan of vengeance. Armida, however, also falls in love with the peacefulness of the sleeping Rinaldo. She thus falls prey to the seductive attraction of her own private world. She becomes, in essence, an integral performer in her own pastoral play, taking on the role of the substitute siren as she entwines Rinaldo's neck, arms, and legs with a garland of flowers (14.66–68). Flying across the sky, Armida then seeks out an island in the immense ocean, a "solitary place" [solinga . . . stanza] (14.69), quite literally a "room" of privacy where she and her lover can completely retreat from the gaze of the world. The marvel of love both offers and needs peaceful privacy, and a little island in the middle of the river is evidently not isolated enough for Armida. In the Petrarchan phrase, Armida wants a realm "beyond all our shores" [fuor tutti i nostri lidi] (14.69; *Canz.* 125.76), to ensure the absolute protection of her privacy.

To this effect, Armida flies as far as the Canary Islands and there con-structs an enchanted bower in an already fabulous realm where naked nymphs lure knights to drink from the lethal fountain of laughter. Yet even in this golden-age world, still for the moment unexposed to Western civilization or the Word of God,[31] neither Armida nor Rinaldo are ever lost from the view of the community in the privacy of the bower. The first time Rinaldo and Armida are presented together in an amorous embrace, they are envisioned through the eyes of two snooping knights:

> Ecco tra fronde e fronde il guardo inante
> penetra e vede, o pargli di vedere,
> vede pur certo il vago e la diletta,
> ch'egli è in grembo a la donna, essa a l'erbetta.

> (16.17)

[Now lo, their vision pierces ahead among the leaves, and sees, or seems to see; it sees for certain the lover and his beloved, how he is in his lady's lap, she on the lawn.]

Though the outside world has no significance for these lovers, the community is still somehow always there, peering in through a dense coverage of sheltering fronds: "Ascosi / mirano i duo guerrier gli atti amorosi" [Hidden away the two warriors watch the amorous interplay] (16.19).

Awakened from his trance of love and reminded of his public duty, Rinaldo at last returns to the community so that he may conquer the enchanted forest. This is Rinaldo's "alta impresa" [lofty enterprise], and in preparation for his feat he passes the day and night withdrawn in penitent thought (18.11). The next morning, as he sets out for Mount Olivet following Peter the Hermit's orders, he remains alone: "tutto solo e tacito e pedone / lascia i compagni e lascia il padiglione" [And all alone and silent and on foot he leaves his companions and leaves his tent] (18.11). In solitude Rinaldo climbs the mountain, contemplating the dawn and the stars, the sun and the moon, the Lucretian "causes of things," which Rinaldo makes no effort at understanding. Rinaldo then bends down on his knees on the highest peak and fixes his eyes toward the east beyond the most sublime part of heaven. He prays and is transfigured by the grace of dew from penitent ashen gray to a sanctified shimmering candor.[32]

---

31. Quint has discussed the subordination of romance to epic, connecting the islet and its marvels to Armida's bower, in *Epic and Empire*, 248–53.

32. On this scene, the particular significance of the dew, and the work of demonic parody throughout the enchanted forest, see Quint, *Origin and Originality*, chap. 4, 112–14.

Thus rewarded, Rinaldo descends to the forest, admiring his own trans-formation: "il bel candor de la mutata vesta / egli medesmo riguardando ammira" [Viewing himself he marvels at the lovely whiteness of his trans-formed surcout] (18.17). He does not perceive what the other knights saw as he approaches the woods. The forest, rather than greeting Rinaldo with the horrid sound of beasts or even the fearful wall of flames, appears as a shady bower (18.17). Marvels after marvels then appear, tempting Rinaldo toward the center of the forest. A bridge arches over a stream, "ecco un ponte mirabile" [behold a marvelous bridge] (18.21), but no sooner has Rinaldo crossed to the other side than the stream turns into a torrent and washes the collapsed bridge away. Separated from the com-munity by a river, Rinaldo is drawn by the marvels further inside, deep into privacy, into what Tasso calls "savage solitudes":

> Ma pur desio di novitade il tira
> a spiar tra le piante antiche e folte,
> e 'n quelle solitudini selvagge
> sempre a sé nova meraviglia il tragge.
>
> (18.22)

[But still desire of novelty draws him on to explore among the thick and ancient trees; and in those savage solitudes always some new marvel draws him to it.]

"Oh meraviglia!" the narrator parenthetically exclaims as an oak tree opens and gives birth to a nymph from its womb (18.26). A hundred other nymphs, emerging from trees in the very same way, then dance about Rinaldo in a circle. Finally, the false image of Armida steps forth from a myrtle:

> Già ne l'aprir d'un rustico sileno
> meraviglie vedea l'antica etade,
> ma quel gran mirto da l'aperto seno
> imagini mostrò più belle e rade:
> donna mostrò ch'assomigliava a pieno
> nel falso aspetto angelica beltade.
>
> (18.30)

[Long since in the opening of a rustic Silenus the ancient age saw mar-velous things; but that immense myrtle from its open bosom showed forth images more lovely and rare: it showed a lady who fully simulated in her false countenance angelic beauty.]

From the interior to the exterior, Armida and her nymphs offer Rinaldo the treasured marvels of the silenus figure, the very image of Christ and Socratic concealment for Erasmus.[33] In a parody of Neoplatonic and Christian disclosure of Truth and Beauty, the marvelous, originating from within, discloses itself painlessly through wounds, and it is made, as the chorus of nymphs informs, just for Rinaldo. It is the exteriorization of a private world, permissible only because Rinaldo is presumably alone.

But just as Rinaldo was never entirely alone when he lay in solitude on the little island by the shore or embraced Armida in the bower beyond the straits of Hercules, so too, even in the seclusion of this enchanted forest in "solitary valleys" [solitarie valli] (13.2), Rinaldo is not entirely alone again. He stands, much as Tancredi earlier stood, in a "great square" [gran piazza] (18.25, 26). And in this wide, public space, a pastoral drama is being enacted:

Quai le mostra la scena o quai dipinte
tal volta rimiriam dèe boscareccie,
nude le braccia e l'abito succinte,
con bei coturni e con disciolte treccie,
tali in sembianza si vedean le finte
figlie de le selvatiche corteccie;
se non che in vede d'arco o di faretra,
chi tien leuto, e chi viola o cetra.

(18.27)

[As the stage displays, or as we see sometimes painted the woodland goddesses, their arms bare and their gowns girt up, with buskins fine and tresses disarrayed, in such manner appeared the fictive daughters of the rude tree trunks, except that in place of bow and quiver one holds a lute, another viola or lyre.]

---

33. As Ascoli, *Ariosto's Bitter Harmony,* 343, notes, "the *locus classicus* for this figure is Alcibiades' comparison of Socrates to the *sileni* in the *Symposium* (215a–b). . . . The *sileni* are ludicrous little statues, named for the comical Silenus of the dionysian entourage, which, when opened, reveal unexpected treasures, just as the unprepossessing outer appearance of Socrates conceals staggering intellectual riches. Erasmus picked upon the figure, focusing on it in one of the most famous of the *Adagia* (III.iii.I) as emblem of Christ's comic concealment of deity within a human frame. . . . he also uses it in the *Encomium* to suggest that human things are always double, the appearance of one thing always covering its opposite."

Though Rinaldo is being drawn by the nymphs and the marvels of the woods to act out an individual fantasy in the privacy of "forestal solitudes" [solitudini selvagge] (18.22), the square symbolically places Rinaldo within the context of a wider communal view. Like Tancredi, who stood before him in an amphitheatric space (13.38), Rinaldo is a performer on a stage in this wide piazza, and his ability to act correctly in this instance can only be judged in terms of his capacity to recognize the theater here for what it is: a web of illusions that he must destroy to win the collective applause of the public outside (18.40).

Rinaldo's ability to pierce through the illusions of the enchanted forest and unflinchingly chop down the myrtle tree reveals a willingness to suppress the marvel of love in the privacy of the bower for the greater pressing demands and needs of the community engaged in a holy war. He has performed a play like this before, on the shore near Antioch and on the Canary Islands. So, perhaps not surprisingly, Rinaldo does not shirk his responsibilities and find himself trapped once again in the very same drama from which he earlier escaped. But far more importantly, Rinaldo has also ascended Mount Olivet, and there, like Christ before him, he has been transfigured. Touched by the grace of dew, in the one moment of the epic, according to David Quint, when Tasso portrays "a divine presence working *through* the processes of nature," Rinaldo may now distinguish "the demonic counterfeit from the Christian original."[34] As a result, Rinaldo can recognize once and for all the value of one performance over another, and he can thus value the public mission to liberate Jerusalem over his private quest for an Armidian bower.

With the destruction of the enchantments of the forest, the marvelous no longer exists in the *Liberata* as an expression of the desire for individuality, solitude, subjectivity, privacy, love, and interiority. As Rinaldo emerges from the woods, Tasso has moved his crusaders beyond the dark enchanted forest and its plenitude of marvels to an epic battlefield where two opposing communities meet in combat and fiercely struggle in daylight for victory. Now Rinaldo himself becomes a "marvelous sight" as he openly performs in battle for the community of crusaders:

> Mirabil vista! a un grande e fermo stuolo
> resister può, sospeso in aria, un solo.

(18.77)

---

34. Quint, *Origin and Originality*, 112 and 116, respectively. See also Andrew Fichter, "Tasso's Epic of Deliverance," 272.

[Marvelous sight! one man alone, suspended in the air, has strength to resist a large and determined crowd.]

From this moment on, Rinaldo's performance wins the unabashed admiration of the epic narrator, because, in broad public view, he has completely subordinated his personal desires for the goal of the corporate crusade and thus gloriously begun to transform through heroic actions all of Jerusalem into Solimano's tragic theater of war ("mirò, quasi in teatro od in agone, / l'aspra tragedia de lo stato umano" [he watched, as if in a theater or a stadium, the bitter tragedy of the human condition] [20.73]). Were this not the case, the dominant emotions elicited at the very end of the epic would not be "meraviglia," the passion proper to the heroic poem according to Tasso,[35] but fear and pity, as Solimano looks down from the tower's top at the victorious rival crusaders.

With Rinaldo's return to battle, we have finally come full circle in the *Liberata* to the concept of the marvelous as it was first subtly introduced into the poem. In canto 1, Goffredo gathers his companions together after having received in a dream God's assurance that he is to deliver Jerusalem. He speaks of their past victories as marvels.[36] Yet these wondrous victories are gifts of God, and they serve to bind the community together. They remind the crusaders that they are a select group with a mission and that their worldly achievements could never have been accomplished without God:

Turchi, Persi, Antiochia (illustre suono
e di nome magnifico e di cose)
opre nostre non già, ma del Ciel dono
furo, e vittorie fur meravigliose.

(1.26)

---

35. Tasso maintains: "il poema epico . . . ha per fine la meraviglia, la quale nasce solo da le cose sublimi e magnifiche" (*DAP,* 40). This point is sustained with even greater vigor in a letter of 16 September 1575: "avendo l'epico per proprio fine il mirabile, che non è proprio fine del drammatico, cerca più il mirabile per tutte le strade." *Le lettere,* 110. See also *DPE,* 74, where the moral rhetorical aim is more clearly outlined: "Diremo dunque che 'l poema eroico sia imitazione d'azione illustre, grande e perfetta, fatta narrando con altissimo verso, affine di muovere gli animi con la maraviglia e di giovare in questa guisa." Francesco Tateo, *"Retorica" e "poetica" fra medioevo e rinascimento* (Bari: Adriatica, 1961), attributes Tasso's statement from the *DAP* to Pontano (244). Durling has written on Tasso's concept of "meraviglia" as Ciceronian *admiratio,* in his *The Figure of the Poet,* 184–92. See also Brand, *Torquato Tasso,* 90–101.

36. See also Rhu, *The Genesis of Tasso's Narrative Theory,* 38–39.

[The Turks, the Persians, Antioch (a noble list, redoubtable both for the names and for the deeds)—they were not at all our doing, but Heaven's gift, and marvelous victories they were.]

Inversely, in canto 2, when the same issue of the marvelous in history is raised again, the crusaders have gathered together for the second time. This time, however, the pagan Alete speaks to the crusaders of their communal marvels—now represented as Goffredo's marvels alone—as simply impressive victories told in entertaining stories:

la fama d'Egitto in ogni parte
del tuo valor chiare novelle ha sparte.

Né v'è fra tanti alcun che non le ascolte
come egli suol le meraviglie estreme,
ma dal mio re con istupore accolte
sono non sol, ma con diletto insieme;
e s'appaga in narrarle anco a le volte,
amando in te ciò ch'altri invidia e teme:
ama il valore, e volontario elegge
teco unirsi d'amor, se non di legge.

(2.62–63)

[And Fame has sown in every region of Egypt fresh tidings of your valor. Among so many there is not one who does not hear them as he is wont to hear the greatest marvels. But by my king they have been received not with astonishment alone, but with pleasure too; and he himself takes pleasure in recounting them at times, loving in you that which another envies or fears. He loves valor and willingly chooses to unite himself with you—in love, if not in law.]

The Christian victories, he claims, are widely known. They constitute the tales the Egyptian king often listens to with great admiration, stupor, and delight, so much so that he repeats them over and over again. They evoke admiration, but they are not signs of success. Quite the contrary, whereas the marvelous victories for Goffredo distinguish the Christians from the pagans and set them apart as a chosen community with a guiding commitment, the Egyptian king is said to respond to the "extreme marvels" of the crusaders as a sign of equality, a mark of sameness rather than difference.

Nothing, moreover, could be more alien to the pagan conception of these victories than to take them as the work of providence. Goffredo reads his "vittorie meravigliose" religiously, as heavenly gifts; the pagans read them more as the delightful, awe-inspiring marvels of romance, tales of extreme wonders, feats achieved by human valor alone. The marvelous victories for the Christians are a sign of Fate, for the pagans a sign of Fortune. In a short, the marvels for the Christians are "miracles," God's providence writ large in human history, deeds guaranteeing the success of a community.

Though the pagans deny that the marvels of the Christian victories are miracles, they do not fail to acknowledge that the miraculous exists as a real force and that it is a force to which they may appeal for justification of their own vision of history or their own system of beliefs. In canto 3, the magician Ismeno informs Aladino that the crusaders will never enter Jerusalem if the effigy of the Virgin Mary, secretly held in a subterranean altar of a temple, is stolen and transported into a mosque (2.6). The next day the effigy has disappeared. As a result, Aladino is determined to destroy the Christian community at large. In the words of the narrator (who prefers to remain ambiguous on the subject [2.9]), Aladino is convinced that the disappearance of the effigy is due to "arte humana" [human handiwork] (2.9). Sofronia, in sacrificing herself for the good of the community, is only too willing to support this belief. But Clorinda, who soon arrives, reasons that the disappearance of the effigy is not the work of human art but the result of divine intervention. Mohammed performed the miracle of removing the effigy, she claims, because he could not suffer to have idols in his temple. The disappearance of the effigy is thus conceived as an act of purification, a sign to all the pagans that their religion is the true religion and that their community of believers must be set apart by the ritual of its worship. Miracles, as in David Hume's conception, have here become foundational, the determining sites anchoring a system of beliefs. "Every miracle," Hume writes,

pretended to have been wrought in any of these religions (and all of them abound in miracles), as its direct scope is to establish the particular system to which it is attributed, so has it the same force, though more indirectly, to overthrow every other system. In destroying a rival system, it likewise destroys the credit of those miracles on which that system was established, so that all the prodigies of different religions are to be regarded as contrary facts, and the evidences of these prodigies, whether weak or strong, as opposite to each other. According to this method of reasoning, when we believe any miracle of Mahomet or his successors, we have for our warrant the testimony of a few barbarous Arabians. And, on the other hand, we are to regard the authority of Titus Livius, Plutarch, Tacitus, and, in short, of all the authors and witnesses Grecian, Chinese, and Roman Catholic, who have related any miracle in their particular religion—I say we are to regard their testimony in the same light as if they had mentioned the Mahometan miracle and had in express terms contradicted it with the same certainty as they have for the miracle they relate. This argument may appear oversubtle and refined, but is not in reality different from the reasoning of a judge who supposes that the credit of two witnesses maintaining a crime against anyone is destroyed by the testimony of two others who affirm to have been two hundred leagues distant at the same instant when the crime is said to have been committed.[37]

To the extent that the Christian God rules the universe in Tasso's poem, we may safely take it as a foregone conclusion that Clorinda's reading of the miracle is profoundly wrong. But as long as we are willing to allow for an autonomous set of rival beliefs, Clorinda's reading is also impeccably argued. From this perspective, the difficulty and risk in interpreting miracles, as early reformers were quick to recognize, is that they may always be made to accommodate and confirm the validity of any given set of beliefs and, in Hume's terms, the legitimacy of a given community of believers.[38] What determines the validity of the Christian interpretation over any other possible reading in Tasso's poem is not just the reigning presence of the Christian God but, in essence, the historical outcome of the events related and the poet's ability to shape these events as purposeful within the overarching, mastering structure of epic. When Goffredo refers to the "vittorie meravigliose" of the crusaders as a sign of Providence, he does so with a prior retrospective glance over the expanse of terrain conquered, over Asia in flames and kingdoms in ruins:

---

37. Hume, "Of Miracles," in *An Inquiry concerning Human Understanding,* 129–30.

38. See on this, Carlos M. N. Eire, *War Against the Idols: The Reformation of Worship from Erasmus to Calvin* (Cambridge: Cambridge University Press, 1986); and Bernard Vogler, "La réforme et le concept de miracle au XVIme sieclè," *Revue d'histoire de la spiritualité: Revue d'ascétique et de mystique* 48 (1972): 145–49. For differentiating marvels from miracles in the Renaissance, see also Lorraine Daston, "Marvelous Facts and Miraculous Evidence in Early Modern Europe," *Critical Inquiry* 18 (1991): 93–124.

Che gioverà l'aver d'Europa accolto
sì grande sforzo, e posto in Asia il foco,
quando sia poi di sì gran moti il fine
non fabriche di regni, ma ruine?

(1.24)

[What profit will it be to have gathered from Europe so great a force, and spread the fire through Asia, if the end of such great movements is after all not the building of kingdoms but only their undoing?]

Marvelous victories are the miracles of providential signs as long as they may be connected to the unifying purpose of liberating Jerusalem. Otherwise the vision of Goffredo's aimless epic war finds its perfect mirror image in Solimano's tragic theater of endless, worldly conflict.

The poet's historical consciousness has therefore seen to it that the crusaders achieve their destined goal, fashioning the small world of his epic poem in the pattern of God's "mirabile magisterio" [marvelous domain] (*DAP,* 35). In doing so, the poet of the *Liberata* has made certain that the marvels of his religious epic fit into a teleological plan that is ultimately God's providential plan of history. But history, of course, had it differently. Though liberated in the first crusade, Jerusalem was soon lost. So the goal, the poet announces at the outset (1.5), needs to be achieved yet again in Counter-Reformation Europe, once more in a period of intense local and national rivalries. Tasso's communities of readers may therefore be urged at the outset to unite beneath the banner of a glorious Tridentine crusade. But they have not been moved to do so without a deeper understanding of the price that has to be paid both in history and in ourselves. For if Solimano's final descent from the tower and decision to engage in heroic battle marks the success of epic over tragedy, along with the success of epic's attendant linear vision of history over the circular vision of decline and decay, the final two books of the *Liberata* cannot celebrate this triumph of epic unequivocally, not, at least, without a haunting sense of loss.

"Homo homini lupus," Freud writes in his *Civilization and Its Discontents* before asking a question that we would do well to recall in conclusion,

Who, in the face of all his experience of life and of history, will have the courage to dispute this assertion? As a rule this cruel aggressiveness waits for some provocation or puts itself at the service of some other purpose, whose goal might also have been reached by milder measures. In circumstances that are favorable to it, when the mental counter-forces which ordinarily inhibit are out of action, it also manifests itself spontaneously and reveals man as a savage beast to whom considera-tion toward his own kind is something alien. Anyone who calls to mind the atrocities committed during the racial migrations or the invasions of the Huns, or by the people known as Mongols under Jenghiz Khan and Tamerlane, or at the capture of Jerusalem by the pious Crusaders, or even, indeed, the horrors of the recent World War—anyone who calls these thing to mind will have to bow humbly before the truth of this view.[39]

We might humbly agree with Freud, but Tasso would surely have disputed such a singularly negative reading of the savage massacres at the end of the *Liberata*. For as Goffredo reminds us, history's epic goals are necessarily made of ruins and flames.[40] And to achieve such worthy civilized and civ-ilizing goals, Tasso reveals through his marvels how individuals must con-tinually sacrifice some measure of themselves for the sake of the commu-nity, or else, in perfectly Dellacasian terms, we may all just as well return to the happy or horrid woods whence we all once came. For Tasso, as for the colonizing Spenser, who was likewise committed to European con-quest and the ideal of the city, there was always a path beyond the private and public darkness of our woods.

---

39. Freud, *Standard Edition*, 21:111–12.

40. Nowhere is this point made so evident as in the words spoken by the archangel Michael to Goffredo, as the latter successfully storms Jerusalem and witnesses above and around him a heavenly militia (18.94). Not surprisingly, Zatti, who relates ruins with "deside-rio pagano" (*L'uniforme cristiano*, chap. 4), does not discuss this use of the term *ruina*.

Chapter 6

A Spenserian Conclusion: Purity and Danger

All margins are dangerous. If they are pulled this way or that the shape of fundamental experience is altered. Any structure of ideas is vulnerable at its margins. We should expect the orifices of the body to symbolize its specially vulnerable points. Matter issuing from them is marginal stuff of the most obvious kind. Spittle, blood, milk, urine, faeces or tears by simply issuing forth have traversed the boundary of the body. So also have bodily parings, skin, nail, hair clippings and sweat. The mistake is to treat bodily margins in isolation from all other margins.

—Mary Douglas

In the second canto of book 1 of Spenser's *Faerie Queene,* Redcrosse and Duessa alight beneath two trees and rest on "vnlucky ground," in a pastoral place, the narrator informs, where "the fearefull Shepheard often there aghast / Vnder them neuer sat" (1.2.28).[1] In the calm shadow cast strangely enough by trembling leaves, Redcrosse bends his "gentle wit" to "expresse" his "falsed fancy" (1.2.30), taking his new lady to be the most beautiful creature that ever lived. He woos and is wooed. And as "faire seemely pleasaunce each to other makes" (1.2.30), he plucks a bough to prepare a pastoral garland, just "like the one Flora had earlier placed on the false Una's head," when Redcrosse had dreamed in Archimago's hermitage "of loues and lustfull play / That nigh his manly hart did melt away, / Bathed in wanton blis and wicked ioy" (1.1.47).[2] Yet unlike the previous dream vision, the broken branch here bleeds in broad daylight before a fully awakened, as well as sexually aroused, knight:

---

1. The epigraph heading this chapter is from Douglas, *Purity and Danger,* 121. The commentary on *The Faerie Queene* consulted and cited is in Spenser, *The Faerie Queene,* ed. A. C. Hamilton (London and New York: Longman, 1977). All citations from Spenser's poetry are drawn from Edmund Spenser, *Poetical Works,* ed. J. C. Smith and E. de Selincourt (Oxford: Oxford University Press, 1985).

2. Donald Cheney, *Spenser's Image of Nature: Wild Man and Shepherd in "The Faerie Queene"* (New Haven: Yale University Press, 1966), 38.

> He pluckt a bough; out of whose rift there came
> Small drops of gory bloud, that trickled downe the same.

(1.2.30)

The branch cries out in pain, and Redcrosse, no longer in an amorous mood but speechless, jumps up in "suddein horror." His hair stands on end, and his body is so frozen in fear that he "could no member moue" (1.2.31).

This is a "straunge occasion" for Redcrosse, and in his "dreadfull passion" before the marvel, he fails to speak until his "manhood" has first been awakened (1.2.32). We may interpret this awakening, and thus momentary loss, of manhood in a variety of ways.[3] But in specifically Freudian terms the "dreadfull passion" depriving Redcrosse of his strength has all the qualities of a castration anxiety, with the branch the displacement of the male member torn from the vaginal wound. It is, moreover, an anxiety manifested in Fradubio, Redcrosse's unmistakable double in the allegory of the poem, who describes how he had earlier sexually "toucht" Duessa. "I chaunst to see her in her proper hew," Fradubio tells the knight,

> Bathing her selfe in origane and thyme:
> A filthy foule old woman I did vew,
> That euer to haue toucht her, I did deadly rew.
>
> Her neather partes misshapen, monstrous,
> Were hidd in water, that I could not see,
> But they did seeme more foule and hideous,
> Then womans shape man would beleeue to bee.

(1.2.40–41)

---

3. For different readings of this episode, see above all Cheney, *Spenser's Image of Nature,* 19–43; Quilligan, *The Language of Allegory,* 109–13; James Nohrnberg, *The Analogy of "The Faerie Queene"* (Princeton: Princeton University Press, 1976), 159–66 and 787; Kennedy, "Rhetoric, Allegory, and Dramatic Modality"; and Scott, "From Polydorus to Fradubio." C. S. Lewis reminds us of what he calls a "paradox" in allegorical structures, namely, that "to the characters participating in an allegory, nothing is allegorical. They live in a world compact of wonders, beauties, and terrors, which are mostly quite unintelligible to them" (*Spenser's Images of Life,* ed. A. Fowler [Cambridge: Cambridge University Press, 1967], 29). Lewis's is an observation of some importance, since not every marvel constitutes a "straunge occasion" for Redcrosse.

The anxiety of Redcrosse's double, emblematic of the classic dreaded anxiety of male dismemberment before the Medusa-head, permeates *The Faerie Queene,* not only in the multiple representations based on such traditional iconographies of Mars in the lap of Venus (earlier evoked in 1 proem 3), but, as Patricia Parker has shown, representations "of a whole series of subject males and dominating female figures, from Hercules and Omphale to Samson reclining in the lap of the Delilah who deprives him of his strength, a figure of the man dedicated to higher things who cannot, however, ultimately escape the power of women."[4] Though Redcrosse has not yet succumbed to the power of Duessa, his sudden loss of manhood anticipates the moment when, in canto 7, he will give himself over to the charms of Duessa in a near identical landscape and there "pour[/] out in loosnesse on the grassy grownd" (1.7.7).[5] The marvel of the bleeding branch foreshadows the moment when Redcrosse, stripped of his protective armor, will lose, as he only momentarily loses here, his "manhood." The vulnerable male subject, like the paradigmatic pair of Acrasia and Vernant in the bower of Bliss, will then become completely subjected to the powers of a "witch" (1.7.3) and a "whore" (1.8.29).

Midway into the first book of *The Faerie Queene,* then, Redcrosse is in truth less like his double Fradubio and more, as Isabel MacCaffrey

---

4. Patricia Parker, "Suspended Instruments: Lyric and Power in the Bower of Bliss," in *Literary Fat Ladies: Rhetoric, Gender, Property* (London: Methuen, 1987), 55; see also the "Medusa-Head," in Freud, *Standard Edition* (Parker draws on Freud's discussion of the problems of sexual remastery); and Neil Hertz, "Medusa's Head: Male Hysteria under Political Pressure," *Representations* 4 (1983): 30–31. On emasculation in Spenser, see Greenblatt, *Renaissance Self-Fashioning,* chap. 3. Studies of gender in Spenser are now numerous. I have benefited from the synthetic study of Parker cited in this note and from Louis Montrose, "The Elizabethan Subject and the Spenserian Text," in *Literary Theory/Renaissance Texts,* ed. P. Parker and D. Quint (Baltimore: Johns Hopkins University Press, 1986); Maureen Quilligan, *Milton's Spenser: The Politics of Reading* (Ithaca: Cornell University Press, 1983); Jonathan Goldberg, *Endlesse Worke: Spenser and the Structures of Discourse* (Baltimore: Johns Hopkins University Press, 1981); Lauren Silberman, "Singing Unsung Heroines: Androgynous Discourse in Book 3 of *The Faerie Queene,*" and the magisterially succinct pages in Peter Stallybrass, "The Patriarchal Territories: The Body Enclosed," both in *Rewriting the Renaissance: The Discourses of Sexual Difference in Early Modern Europe,* ed. M. Ferguson, M. Quilligan, and N. Vickers (Chicago: University of Chicago Press, 1986), 130–34; Theresa Krier, *Gazing on Secret Sights: Spenser, Classical Imitation, and the Decorums of Vision* (Ithaca: Cornell University Press, 1990); and David Miller, *The Poem's Two Bodies: The Poetics of the 1590 "Faerie Queene"* (Princeton: Princeton University Press, 1988).

5. The connection between the episode is drawn by many, but see in particular Cheney, *Spenser's Image of Nature,* 32, who early on drew the parallel with Adonis. For an extended discussion of this episode see Kennedy, "Rhetoric, Allegory, and Dramatic Modality." For erotic imagery underpinning the episode, see John W. Schroeder, "Spenser's Erotic Drama: The Orgoglio Episode," *English Literary History* 29 (1962): 140–59.

observed,[6] like Fradubio's feminine counterpart and complement, Fraelissa:

> Eftsoones his manly forces gan to faile,
> And mightie strong was turnd to feeble fraile.

$$(1.7.6)$$

From male to female, the earlier, momentary loss of manhood in canto 2 has become a matter of more pressing concern as the knight now lies "so faint in euery ioynt and vaine, / Through that fraile fountaine, which him feeble made, / That scarsely could he weeld his bootlesse single blade" (1.7.11). The knight's identification with Fraelissa marks the anticipated fulfillment of a loss, of which his weapon, soon abandoned, is the consequent, vestigial phallic sign in a process of emasculation already subtly initiated in Redcrosse's loss of virility in canto 2. For, if Donald Cheney is correct in linking the transformation of Amoret and Scudamour into "two senceles stockes" (1.12.45, 1590 *Faerie Queene*) with the earlier metamorphosis of Fradubio and Fraelissa into "two goodly trees" (1.2.28), then the figure of the hermaphrodite underpins the "straunge occasion" of the bleeding branch long before Redcrosse has become—as Spenser's fable of the fountain inevitably recalls through the presence of Ovid's myth—a "semi-*vir*," a "half-man."[7]

Redcrosse's loss of "manhood" in the face of the marvel of the bleeding branch constitutes, both within and beyond the context of this dreaded loss of male potency, a loss in his sense of being complete, of having an integral, secure, bounded self, of being not the knight of "wholeness" tied to Una but the knight of "holeness."[8] Redcrosse breaks the twig to woo

---

6. Isabel MacCaffrey, *Spenser's Allegory: The Anatomy of Imagination* (Princeton: Princeton University Press, 1976), 167.

7. Donald Cheney, "Spenser's Hermaphrodite and the 1590 *Faerie Queene*," *Publications of the Modern Language Association* 87 (1972): 198. For a discussion connecting and differentiating the hermaphrodite concluding book 3 along with its underpinning in book 1, both in terms of gender and in terms of Spenser's poetics, see Lauren Silberman, "The Hermaphrodite and the Metamorphosis of Spenserian Allegory," *English Literary Renaissance* 17 (1987): 207–23. While it is true that Spenser's etiological fable concerning the enervating power of the fountain is vitiated of sexual desire, the obvious contrasting presence of the Ovidian myth on which Spenser models his tale, along with the very setting and realization of Redcrosse's lust, brings back into play issues of sexual desire.

8. Goldberg, *Endlesse Worke*, has persuasively argued that Redcrosse is a knight founded on lack and loss in an overall poetics of inescapable and irretrievable, "endlesse" lack and loss.

Duessa in an act that proleptically marks, long before it happens, the moment when his identity, or sense of identity, is most threatened because the self vulnerably risks dissolution, as in the Ovidian myth of Hermaphroditus, through the act of pouring out. Redcrosse, to borrow from and adapt the narrator's description, is in this respect a knight "left to losse" (1.7.10).

Yet it is not only the knight who is potentially left open to loss in this text. "The laureate," Richard Helgerson has written, "is both contemplative shepherd and questing knight. In this he resembles Redcrosse, the 'clownishe younge man,' raised as a ploughman."[9] Along these lines, we may understand Redcrosse's loss of manhood as a re-presentation of the poet's own fear of speechlessness. In *The Faerie Queene* the male poet divests himself of "lowly Shepheards weeds" (1 proem 1) and subjects his aspiring "gentle wit" to the sexual politics of a ruling queen often represented as a virgin maid but nevertheless sometimes slandered as "an arrant whore."[10] Within the context of what Louis Montrose has called the "pastoral of power" of the Elizabethan court and patronage system,[11] the configuration of Duessa as an evil "quaenly" double of Elizabeth[12]— indeed, as a demonized parody of Spenser's own "fayre *Eliza,* Queene of shepheardes all," "Yclad in Scarlot" and resting alike on "grassie greene" (*Aprill,* 34, 55, 57)—renders this episode by analogy a "straunge occasion" for the poet as well. Through the representation of Redcrosse's/Fradubio's anxiety before the threat of Duessa, Spenser indirectly reconstructs his own prior pastoral identity in relation to an ideological counterpart of the poem's radiating center of feminine solar power:

> O Goddesse heauenly bright,
> Mirrour of grace and Maiestie diuine,

---

9. Richard Helgerson, *Self-Crowned Laureates: Spenser, Jonson, Milton, and the Literary System* (Berkeley: University of California Press, 1983), 98. See also Hamilton's very first note to book 1 in Spenser, *The Faerie Queene;* Cheney, *Spenser's Image of Nature,* 358; and Kennedy, "Rhetoric, Allegory, and Dramatic Modality," 19.

10. The quote is taken from Stallybrass, "The Patriarchal Territories," 132; but see in particular Montrose, "The Elizabethan Subject and the Spenserian Text," 111. All these qualities, of course, are "officially" attributed not to Queen Elizabeth but to her royal rival, Mary Queen of Scots, with whom Duessa is linked from the first allegorizers of the poem.

11. Montrose, "'Eliza, Queene of shepheardes,' and the Pastoral of Power," *English Literary Renaissance* 10 (1980): 153–82.

12. See, for example, Stallybrass, "The Patriarchal Territories"; and John N. King, *Spenser's Poetry and the Reformation Tradition* (Princeton: Princeton University Press, 1990), 114–16.

Great Lady of the greatest Isle, whose light
Like *Phoebus* lampe throughout the world doth shine,
Shed thy faire beames into my feeble eyne,
And raise my thoughts too humble and too vile,
To thinke of that true glorious type of thine,
The argument of mine afflicted stile:
The which to heare, vouchsafe, O dearest dred a-while.

(1 proem 4)

Beginning with Redcrosse, who is denied his attempt to "bend his gen-tle wit" in order to woo his lady, this episode, I argue, is as much about the desire for expression as it is about its active suppression in the process of identity formation. And it is not just about Redcrosse's difficulty in finding expression but also about Spenser's as he employs for the first time a full-blown Virgilian episode, previously revised by a number of authors, in his epic poem. The opening proem's poet, who speaks of being "enforst" to take up a "far vnfitter taske," has here held out the possibility of pas-toral retreat, rest, and shade only to deny it to the Redcrosse knight and to himself (1 proem 4.1).[13] Through a self-imposed act of suppression, the pastoral poet of the *Shepheardes Calender* fashions himself in the ideal development as the new English Virgil as he simultaneously fashions the rustic Redcrosse into a new type of epic Christian hero with a distinct national identity. In having Redcrosse break the branch and respond to the marvel almost exactly as Aeneas did—Virgil's "obstipui steteruntque comae" (*Aen.* 3.48) perfectly matches Spenser's "Astond he stood, and vp his haire did houe" (*FQ* 1.2.31)—England's "new Poete" at once seeks to sever himself from his own literary past as the man disguised in "Shep-heards weeds" and to become the poet of empire, the "poet historicall" of Elizabeth "Qveene of England Fravnce and Ireland and of Virginia."

The knight being fashioned into the perfection of national heroism and sainthood in the first book of *The Faerie Queene* wins early victories over the filthy beast of Errour and the proud Sansfoy. These are momentary victories, however—the result of brute force, not demonstrated intelli-

---

13. On the significance of the Virgilian project in Spenser see Helgerson, *Self-Crowned Laureates;* Michael O'Connell, *Mirror and Veil: The Historical Dimension of Spenser's "Faerie Queene"* (Chapel Hill: University of North Carolina Press, 1977); and Jeffrey Knapp, *An Empire Nowhere: England, America, and Literature from "Utopia" to the "Tempest"* (Berkeley: University of California Press, 1992). See also Merritt Hughes, *Virgil and Spenser* (Berkeley: University of California Press, 1929), 2:263–418, especially 368–69 on this episode.

gence. By canto 2, Redcrosse has instead come up against Duessa, and as Spenser's equivocal syntax makes clear, she is just like Redcrosse, "too simple and too trew" (1.2.45). Redcrosse's simpleness and trueness, however, are not the calculated Machiavellian effect of a disguise but the defect of excessive ignorance and innocence. Like the poet of the opening proem, Redcrosse is a man of excess, always too this or too that—too proud, too true, too simple, too solemn. Yet unlike the self-styled, inadequate narrator of the proem (who is "too meane," "too humble," and "too vile" [1 proem 1 and 4]), Redcrosse is rarely too intelligent. In this instance, Redcrosse cannot recognize a *monstrum* as a portentous warning, and so he refuses to heed Fradubio's counsel to flee long after he has been urged to go (1.2.31).[14] He mistakenly decides that the blood defiles him, but in truth it anticipates the excremental impurity of Duessa, who contaminates the knight as he embraces and repeatedly kisses her on the lips. Finally, Redcrosse does not realize, as Fradubio infers, that his hands are already guilty, stained with original sin: "O spare with guilty hands to teare / My tender sides" (1.2.31). As Shirley Clay Scott writes:

Polydorus . . . had warned Aeneas not to defile his pious hands, and Spenser's exacting change [from pious to already guilty] indicates that the voice here is not that of one victim of history but that of every son of Adam who comes to know his fallen condition and his own complicity in it. There was, as William Nelson and others have shown, an exegetical tradition that Spenser could rely upon to support the association of Fradubio and Fraelissa with Adam and Eve. The phrase in the Vulgate that described the fallen Adam and Eve hiding "*in medio ligne paradisi*" was sometimes taken to mean that Adam and Eve hid *inside* a tree or within the shade of a tree rather than *among* the trees. And as Nelson shows, the idea had enough currency in Elizabethan England to be a figure in biblical commentary by Bishop Pilkington, in Raleigh's *History of the World,* and in an entertainment produced at Woodstock in 1575 for Queen Elizabeth. And as D. W. Robertson has shown, there was a medieval allegory of trees that associated man's fallen condition with the umbragiousness of trees. By a typological extension also supported by medieval tradition, Spenser's figure alludes as well to the second Adam whose "tender sides" were torn when he ascended the tree of death to restore man to life. James Nohrnberg cites as one precedent for

---

14. For a synopsis of *monstra* as warnings, see Friedman, *The Monstrous Races,* chap. 6; and Céard, *La nature et les prodiges.*

this figure these lines from *Piers Plowman:* "And as Adam and all thorw a tre deyden, / Adam and all thorwe a tree shall torne ageine to lyve."[15]

Redcrosse's fallen condition, universalized through typology, at once enacts a convention of epic literature from Homer on that the hero must encounter and pass through the impure to acquire a higher consciousness of himself and the world in which he is destined to live and play a leading role.[16] The path to knowledge of the causes of things always lies through a full engagement with the filth of this and/or the other world. Christian Neoplatonic thought, so powerfully shaped for the Middle Ages and the Renaissance in St. Augustine's *Confessions,* maintains that we are born pure and innocent in a prediscursive state but then gradually lose the memory of our prior privileged existence in the Good through contact with, and attachment to, the world of baser sensual desires. Within the structure of divine origins that privileges speech over writing, the aim of the true Christian is to rid himself or herself of such desires in and through language and make every effort to remember whence he or she came within the context of larger communal and spiritual goals.

So it must be for the hero of book 1 of *The Faerie Queene.* He confronts a highly textualized form of uncleanliness through Errour and her inky brood (1.1.22), only to be cleansed ("the filthy blots of sinne to wash away," 1.10.27) in the House of Holinesse, where he may "taste" Fidelia's speech (1.10.18). This speech, moreover, is drawn now not from a multiplicity of written sources, as was Errour, but from a single unreadable book composed of blood rather than ink: "And that her sacred Booke, with bloud ywrit, / That none could read . . . That wonder was to heare her goodly speach: / For she was able, with her words to kill, / And raise againe to life the hart, that she did thrill" (1.10.19). As a just reward for undergoing this edifying ritual of purification, Redcrosse then acquires in the clarifying moment of anagnorisis on Mount Contemplation a "name and nation" (1.10.67).[17]

But if the blood from the branch anticipates the impurity of Redcrosse's contact with Duessa and his necessary fall into sinfulness, the

---

15. Scott, "From Polydorus to Fradubio," 49–50.

16. The scholar who has most extensively placed Spenser within the epic tradition is Nohrnberg, *The Analogy.*

17. For discussions of such moments of clarity in Spenser, see A. Bartlett Giamatti, "Spenser: From Magic to Miracle," in *Exile and Change in Renaissance Literature* (New Haven: Yale University Press, 1984).

blood also immediately suggests why the shepherds, long before Redcrosse's arrival, shunned the "vnlucky ground" despite its alluring protection. By all appearances, this is a perfect green cabinet fit for pastoral singing contests in which love's virtues and torments are sung. The trembling leaves, the soft moss, the handsome two trees, the placid wide shadow—all these images work to fix an ideal picture of fertility, which in primitive, "soft" pastoral often works to enforce the conjunction of the fertility of a creative mind and the capacious reproductive capacity of nature, the labor of the shepherd who sounds his "mery oaten pipe" (1.2.28) and the birthing labor of nature that provides not merely the substance for the shepherd's instrument but the fruitful idyllic setting within which it is all sung. Yet here one plucks a bough to find all the sexual energies of the land, which the shepherds struggle to harness in their performances, suddenly transformed into what Fradubio calls a "desert waste"—the wasteland, Jessie Weston would have surely reminded us, of romance.

We do not have a pastoral singer in this landscape. We do, however, have a "clownishe" knight who suddenly reveals in his wanton mood a powerful need to "expresse" his "fancy"; it is, however, a "false" and therefore deceptive representation of the world before him. He aims to woo Duessa, and in the process "bend his gentle wit," perhaps with the conventional intent of extemporizing on her hair and eyes, much as Sacripante did in the *Orlando furioso* (*Fur.* 2.41–44), or as Sansloy will later attempt to do when he forestalls his initial decision to rape Una and deploy the art of amorous persuasion instead:

With fawning wordes he courted her a while,
And looking louely, and oft sighing sore,
Her constant hart did tempt with diuerse guile.

(*FQ* 1.6.4)

But having Redcrosse reveal his "gentle wit" in a pastoral setting is about the last thing the poet of *The Faerie Queene* is prepared to permit. The shock of the marvel therefore silences the knight, forcing him out of the role of a Petrarchan lover. This knight steps too boldly out of character when he attempts to become, as Castiglione's model urbane courtier who can accomplish just about any feat, a poet as well. Redcrosse must remain a knight on a journey to become a patron saint. Though he seeks glory, he must be taught the way to the simplicity and trueness of theological "grace," not the complicated artful "grazia" of an Elizabethan courtly poet.

For Redcrosse, to be sure, is out to conquer and liberate from sin a foreign empire in book 1. And in the process, he encounters marvels of extraordinary fertility like those that Pliny described existing in the Near East and that Renaissance discoverers in turn inherited and claimed to have witnessed in an even far surpassing degree close to where Columbus located Eden.[18] Through the catalog of trees in canto 1, the narrator unfolds a richness and copiousness that spills out into verbal *copia,* where the sexual fertility of the land mirrors the textual fertility of the poet's mind and the various traditions within which he is working. Exemplified in Redcrosse's and Una's praise, all this productivity is admirable, pleasant, and praiseworthy in large measure because nature has reached, in its extraordinary reproductive variety and abundance, a stage of purposive orderly completion. Yet where the labyrinthine forest then proves the most dense ("amid the thickest woods," 1.1.11), we soon discover not more praiseworthy useful fertility but a "monster vile" (1.1.13) iconographically linked to the Edenic serpent whose vomit contains, along with undigested books and putrid papers, unfinished shapes of grotesque creatures, each of which is likened to those that breed in the mud of the retreating Nile:

> Therewith she spewd out of her filthy maw
> A floud of poyson horrible and blacke,
> Full of great lumpes of flesh and gobbets raw,
> Which stunck so vildly, that it forst him slacke
> His grasping hold, and from her turne him backe:
> Her vomit full of bookes and papers was,
> With loathly frogs and toades, which eyes did lacke,
> And creeping sought way in the weedy gras:
> Her filthy parbreake all the place defiled has.

> As when old father *Nilus* gins to swell
> With timely pride aboue the *Aegyptian* vale,
> His fattie waues do fertile slime outwell,
> And ouerflow each plaine and lowly dale:
> But when his later spring gins to auale,

---

18. On the marvels of the Orient and the new world, see in particular Wittkower, "Marvels of the East"; and Greenblatt, *Marvelous Possessions.* For connections between Redcrosse and the Renaissance explorers, see Knapp, *An Empire Nowhere.*

Huge heapes of mudd he leaues, wherein there breed
Ten thousand kinds of creatures, partly male
And partly female of his fruitfull seed;
Such vgly monstrous shapes elswhere may no man reed.

(1.1.20–21)

The egress into this forest, operating under ideologically normative stable gender categories, provides us first with the productive gifts of the flourishing fertile exchange between the active "angry" male agent of Jove's rain and the earth as the recipient "lap" of the passive, feminine lover (1.1.6). The heart of this forest has instead gone madly askew, and we are given a description of an active, male-dominated generative process (these are "*his* fattie waues" and "*his* fruitful seed"), which indicates by similitude how a female monster "all the place defiled has" with the outwelling of "*her* vomit," "*her* parbreake," and "*her* fruitful cursed spawne" (1.1.22). As David Miller writes:

Not only is the vomit itself a strange brew, the act of vomiting passes by way of similitude into a peculiarly unsavory image of generation. In stanza 22 [book 1, canto 1] this image will metamorphose yet again into a parturition that (as Hamilton notes) resembles defecation: "She poured forth out of her hellish sinke / Her fruitful cursed spawned of serpents small" (lines 5–6). Meanwhile, Mother Errour has modulated into Father Nile and back; the "frogs and toads" she coughs up are themselves of mixed (amphibious) nature; and the simile of stanza 21 has compared them to Nile's "vgly monstrous" brood, "partly male / And partly female"—an image, as the repeated word suggests, not of perfected form but of incomplete formation and dreadful mixed anatomy.[19]

In the opening cantos, Faerie Land moves back and forth from being truly a productive place of protection and useful fertility, of nature admired at the apex of its fulfillment and perfection, to suddenly a place of "monstrous female creation," impurity, revulsion, sexual perversion, and gender confusion.[20] The "vnlucky ground," the filthy, blood-bespattered

19. Miller, *The Poem's Two Bodies,* 247; but see the entire section "The Nausea of Fertility" in the chapter entitled "The Wide Womb of the World."

20. Quilligan, *Milton's Spenser,* 82; see the following pages in Quilligan for a discussion of this episode. For discussions of Faerie Land, see Murrin in *The Allegorical Epic,* especially 133–44; Greenblatt, *Renaissance Self-Fashioning,* 190–92; Isabel Rathborne, *The Meaning of Spenser's Fairyland* (New York: Columbia University Press, 1937); and Bellamy, *Translations of Power.*

caves, and the wood of Errour therefore remind us that Faerie Land is only benign in appearance. As one moves into the depths of the forest or pierces beneath the bark of a handsome tree, Faerie Land turns out to be dangerously impure—a place of arrested, stunted growth; a fallen, Edenic landscape redefined, in the words of Fradubio, as a "desert waste" (1.2.42). But even amid the "desert darknesse" (1.1.16) embodied in Errour's monstrous womblike cave, Faerie Land is *not,* it is important to point out, a land that is barren. Rather this is a land of such excess fecundity that it constantly produces creatures that transgress normal boundaries: generative fluid issues forth from a mouth imaged simultaneously as an anus and a vagina; fruitful seed and fruitful slime overflow the channeled embankments.

The marvel of Errour, perhaps more than any other marvel in *The Faerie Queene,* conspicuously breaks boundaries, and therein lies for Spenser not its great, replenishing dynamic character within the realm of the Bakhtinian carnivalesque[21] but its great ideological threat as a *monstrum* of female sexuality and reproduction. For what consistently comes through in Renaissance discourses on monsters and marvels as drawn from classical antiquity is the destabilizing transgression of boundaries so tenuously defined from the moment of conception in the womb.[22] In this context it is a marvel not so much that there are abnormalities—strange births, prodigies, and monsters—but that there are not so many more. Were it merely a matter of excess seed, of copulating with a woman during her menstrual flow, or of women having bad dreams while pregnant, we should always be on our guard against the impure moment and contact,

---

21. Bakhtin, *Rabelais and His World;* I draw as well from the discussion of Stallybrass, "The Patriarchal Territories"; and Stallybrass and White, *The Politics and Poetics of Transgression.*

22. See in particular for Spenser, Miller, *The Poem's Two Bodies,* 250. On the marvelous and the wonder of monstrous births in Renaissance medicine, see Céard, *La nature et les prodiges;* the concise pages of Greenblatt, "Fiction and Friction," in *Shakespearean Negotiations: The Circulation of Social Energy in Renaissance England* (Berkeley: University of California Press, 1988), 78–86; and Lorraine Daston and Katherine Park, "Unnatural Conceptions: The Study of Monsters in Sixteenth- and Seventeenth-Century France and England," *Past and Present* 92 (1981): 20–54, who note the following: "Although God was of course still ultimately responsible for all monstrous births, the emphasis shifted from final causes (God's will) to proximate ones (physical explanations and the natural order)" to the point where "prodigies have been denuded of their supernatural aura and presented as intrinsically interesting facts to surprise and entertain the reader, rather than to acquaint him with immanent apocalypse and judgement" (35 and 36); the apocalyptic strain is still clearly present in Spenser.

lest we produce something as grotesque and monstrous as maternal Errour's brood. The effect of reading such a text as Ambroise Paré's *On Monsters and Marvels,* for example, which seeks along Aristotelian lines primarily a biological cause in all deformities, is to normalize even the slightest aberrations, thereby rendering the reader only more keenly aware of the tender malleability of the human body. If Pico della Mirandola claimed in his "Oration on the Dignity of Man" that humankind was in spirit metaphorically a chameleon, for the soul and intelligence of humans could move them up to angelic heights or down to the unplumbed depths of insensate matter, Paré instead reminds us that men and women, as helpless products in a delicate biological process, can physically turn into something as strange as chameleons themselves. Hypothetically, a woman who dreams of a tree while pregnant effectively leaves the child within the womb at risk of being born with bark for skin. The marvelous, and the wonder that accompanies it, freely traverses normative boundaries in Renaissance medical conceptualizations of the body. It therefore stands as a reminder of the risk we all confront in losing identities that are highly vulnerable constructs from the moment we are conceived.

In the face of this risk before the *monstrum* of the bleeding branch, Redcrosse's reaction is not one of aggression or revulsion but one of instinctive wonder ("astond he stood," 1.2.31), then fear and curiosity, and finally terrified distancing. Indeed, unlike any other hero in all previous versions of the Polydorus episode, Redcrosse reveals, if only at the very end of the episode, a need to rid himself forcefully of the contaminating contact of the blood. He does not merely drop the branch but plunges it into the soil as soon as it has ceased to speak:

> But the good knight
> Full of sad feare and ghastly dreriment,
> When all this speech the liuing tree had spent,
> The bleeding bough did thrust into the ground,
> That from the bloud he might be innocent.

> (1.2.44)

The branch is "thrust into" the ground, as if Redcrosse were attempting to ensure that the opened end completely disappeared and spoke no more. This is a significant gesture, and it is followed by an equally unprecedented one. After having disposed of the branch, Redcrosse then turns to seal the other wound, shutting off the aperture ("And with fresh clay did close the wooden wound," 1.1.44). We may, of course, read this final gesture as one more diacritical act in this episode of the suppression of expression. But in light of the evident literary precedents to which Spenser's version seeks to constitute a conclusion, the key verb *close* is emblematic of not just literary but corporeal closure.

In an earlier version of this episode, Dante has Pier della Vigna describe his wounds as windows, "al dolor fenestra" [windows to pain] (*Inf.* 13.102) and thus, by virtue of the relation of body to spirit in the *Commedia*, windows to souls. But the wayfarer, though his pity may be construed as an act of identification, does not exhibit any fear or need to close off those openings. Nor do we find this in any other prior version. In the Fradubio episode, however, wounds must be closed, for in a characteristically Spenserian fashion, they hold out the possibility of contaminating exchange. What pours out from the inside may mix with what is outside; what is external may become internalized. Like Vernant vulnerably lying in the lap of Acrasia, who sucks up his "spright," Redcrosse may indeed lose his autonomy by blending with what is most "straunge." In this respect, surfaces supremely matter in Spenser:[23] they represent the boundaries where selves, in all their vulnerability, may visibly "blend" to the point of becoming the marvel of the hermaphrodite, or, in terms more directly relevant to the Fradubio episode, the completely dissolute, deliquescent male bewitched by a sorceress and a whore: "O horrible enchantment, that him so did blend" (2.12.80). Redcrosse's belated desire for an "innocence" that he has already lost may thus best be understood as the desire for a perfectly chaste self. Loss of identity, and a specifically male identity, is what Redcrosse instinctively fears most at the end of the Fradubio episode. And it is for this reason that he closes off openings in acts that are fundamentally gestures of symbolic bodily closure.

With this in mind, let me conclude by turning not to the two Spenserian paradigms that I have suggested underpin the Fradubio episode (Vernant in the lap of Acrasia and the hermaphrodite of the 1590 ending) but to the poet's description of the immaculate conception of Belphoebe, the moon goddess shadowing forth Elizabeth's private virtue.[24] In canto 6 of book 3, the book of "chastitie," Spenser writes:

---

23. On the vulnerability of the body in Spenser, see now Krier, *Gazing on Secret Sights.*

24. The theological underpinnings are discussed by Thomas P. Roche, Jr., *The Kindly Flame: A Study of the Third and Fourth Books of Spenser's "Faerie Queene"* (Princeton: Princeton University Press, 1964), 105–6. My reading of this episode in the concluding pages follows Miller, *The Poem's Two Bodies,* rather than Krier, *Gazing on Secret Sights.*

In that same shadie couert, whereas lay
Faire *Crysogone* in slombry traunce whilere:
Who in her sleepe (a wondrous thing to say)
Vnwares had borne two babes, as faire as springing day.

Vnwares she them conceiu'd, vnwares she bore:
She bore withouten paine, that she conceiued
Withouten pleasure: ne her need implore
Lucinaes aide:

(3.6.26–27)

Clearly the "thing" that is so "wondrous" here and that renders the nymphs speechless in their awe is Crysogone's spontaneous generation of beings without the knowledge of ever having done so, just as Spenser's "golden one" had no knowledge on her part of ever having been impregnated in what the narrator earlier deemed "a straunge ensample" (3.6.8). Yet the voice that cries out with the familiar formula of wonder (*mirabile dictu*) belongs to the poet. At the same time, the "thing" that is wondrous is partly the process of saying, the poet's act of representing, of having, indeed, something "to say." In this context we may invoke David Miller's argument that "the story of Crysogone entails a genealogy of allegorical poesis," the male poet's metanarrative of his mind giving birth like a womb to a wondrous conceit.[25] Yet, as the poet likens his process of creation to the immaculate conception of Crysogone's process of reproduction, the marvel does not shock the poet into the silent recognition of the otherness of the body that gives birth to perfected creatures, such as Belphoebe and Amoret. The poet's wonder elicits only more speech and reflexive admiration at the recognition of the subject in the object. The poet gives birth to a theologically inspired conceit that objectifies the poet's process of conception and expression as perfect, pure, and complete. He then proceeds to acknowledge the need to protect and preserve the product of this process. We have gradually moved, then, from the reaction of the male poet, for whom this is parenthetically such "a wondrous thing to say," to the reaction of the dumbstruck female viewers, who quietly take possession of the wonder they have witnessed and leave Crysogone behind:

---

25. For a discussion of this, see Miller, *The Poem's Two Bodies;* the quote is from 240. On the familiarity of the conceit, see Jay L. Halio, "The Metaphor of Conception and Elizabethan Theories of the Imagination," *Neophilologus* 50 (1966): 454–61.

> when they both perceiued,
> They were through wonder nigh of sense bereaued,
> And gazing each on other, nought bespake:
> At last they both agreed, her seeming grieued
> Out of her heauy swowne not to awake,
> But from her louing side the tender babes to take.
>
> (3.6.27)

Manhood is neither threatened, reawakened, nor momentarily lost with this "straunge ensample"; and the marvelous need not be distanced or buried, because, far from being estranged, the male subject has taken over the body of the feminine as a figure of Platonic plenitude through and in the representation of the poetic process. Now the sun, "Great father he of generation" (3.6.9), pierces beneath the shade as it was never able to do in the dark labyrinthine forest and, "bright upon her body playd" (3.1.7), quickens life to perfection in an extended textual revision of Errour's generative vomiting:

> Miraculous may seeme to him, that reades
> So straunge ensample of conception;
> But reason teacheth that the fruitfull seades
> Of all things liuing, through impression
> Of the sunbeames in moyst complexion,
> Doe life conceiue and quickned are by kynd:
> So after the *Nilus* invndation,
> Infinite shapes of creatures men do fynd,
> Informed in the mud, on which the Sunne hath shynd.
>
> (3.6.8)

Epic forest, once cataloged, explored, and tainted by blood, gives way to purified pastoral, where naked nymphs freely roam from the gaze of mortal men. And the poet, though still perhaps "for fear through want of words her excellence to marre" (3 proem 2), reveals the significance of the male subject's role in constructing an ideal image of his queen, who may here behold in "mirrours more then one her selfe to see" another spotless vision of "her rare chastitee" (3 proem 5). Nothing, in this moment of apparent plenitude and perfection in representing the marvelous, is lost—nothing, that is, except for the actual body of the marvel. The fruitful Crysogone has disappeared from the scene, never to return. And in the meantime Crysogone has felt nothing and experienced nothing as she was impregnated and gave birth to the re-presentation in *The Faerie Queene* of "*Eliza,* Queene of shepheardes all" (*Aprill,* 34) as the pure unblemished Belphoebe, the epic's inviolable virgin maid (3.6.3; sc. *Aprill,* 50, 54).

By patterning his own process of poetic representation as a "straunge ensample" of undefiled textual pathogenesis motivated and controlled by male sexuality, the poet of *The Faerie Queene* indirectly ingratiates himself as the perfect courtly poet-subject in the very moment that he refashions his queen into the impregnable figure of absolute bodily closure. Through this "straunge ensample," the poet thus expresses the remastered "fancy" of an unsuppressed "gentle wit," humbling the queen into a pastoral product of the epic poet, while uplifting male sexuality into the opening proem's image of the powerful solar queen. As a Spenserian conclusion to the subjects of the marvelous, then, queen and poet, object of adoration and wooing courtly subject, have become one, bound through the presence of a mutual loss and gendered lack, somewhat like the hermaphrodite when viewed from a distanced vantage point at the very end of the 1590 *Faerie Queene,* all ablur "so seemed those two, as growne together quite" (3.12.46; first edition).

Epilogue

What became of the marvelous in epic after Spenser, and what gradually eclipsed it as a matter of greater interest? In an effort to hint at its eventual transmission and dispersal beyond the baroque period and toward the romantic period, I close briefly with the last, great epic achievement of the period under discussion, *Paradise Lost,* and Milton's deliberate use of the Homeric formula of wonder at the end of book I:

Behold a wonder! they but now who seemed
In bigness to surpass Earth's giant sons
Now less than smallest dwarfs, in narrow room
Throng numberless, like that Pygmean race
Beyond the Indian mount, or fairy elves,
Whose midnight revels, by a forest side
Or fountain some belated peasant sees,
Or dreams he sees, while overhead the moon
Sits arbitress, and nearer to the earth
Wheels her pale course: they on their mirth and dance
Intent, with jocund music charm his ear;
At once with joy and fear his heart rebounds.
Thus incorporeal Spirits to the smallest forms
Reduced their shapes immense, and were at large,
Though without number still amidst the hall
Of that infernal court.[1]

(777–92)

---

1. John Milton, *Complete Poems and Major Prose,* ed. Merritt Y. Hughes (New York: Odyssey, 1957).

Much can be said about this passage in the context of the marvelous. Stephen Greenblatt has alerted us to some of its more salient features as "for a moment epic is confounded with comedy, as are giant with dwarf, torment with mirth, demonic with harmless, what lies outside the mind with what lies within."[2] Yet what I find most remarkable about this passage is not just the familiar transgressive blurring of boundaries, the superfluousness of the marvelous as I would have emphasized in the introduction. Neither do I find most striking Milton's deliberate return to the Homeric formula, now consciously revised to place greater emphasis on the reader's, as opposed to the author's, role in reflexively making meaning of and through the poem. What is so astonishing, I believe, is the radical perspectival shift of focus effected through the juxtaposition of incomprehensibly big things with small things.

This poetic technique of contrasting the huge with the puny is familiar to baroque aesthetics of wonder, but Milton has now pushed it to unparalleled novel extremes. The marvelous, in Milton's word, has been drastically "reduced" before our very eyes, rendered so distant and unreal as to seem not ugly and terrifying but joyful and beautiful. The marvelous, momentarily placed in a dreamy pastoral landscape, has become an "idyll" in the sense of "a little picture" (*eidyllion*). Yet the transgressive power of the marvelous has not so much been diminished and forever rendered beautiful through this process. Rather, it has been subtly absorbed and subsumed into what eighteenth-century scholars would later begin to identify as the poetics of the sublime.

"Beautiful objects," Edmund Burke wrote in his *A Philosophical Enquiry,* "are comparatively small," whereas "sublime objects are of vast dimensions"—vast, we might say, like the boundless wild regions of Milton's chaos, not the small contained vision, the comparatively idyllic little picture of a broken bleeding branch.[3] The marvelous is no longer a "won-

---

2. Greenblatt, *Marvelous Possessions,* 21.

3. Edmund Burke, *A Philosophical Enquiry into the Origin of Our Ideas of the Sublime and Beautiful,* ed. James T. Boulton (Notre Dame: University of Notre Dame Press, 1968). For "Milton Sublime," see Leslie E. Moore, *Beautiful Sublime: The Making of "Paradise Lost"* (Stanford: Stanford University Press, 1990); for the period immediately following the Renaissance in Italy, see James V. Mirollo, *The Poet of the Marvelous: Giambattista Marino* (New York: Columbia University Press, 1963); for neoclassical to romantic notions of the marvelous, see Meyer H. Abrams, *The Mirror and the Lamp: Romantic Theory and the Critical Tradition* (London: Oxford University Press, 1953). My discussion of Milton, it is perhaps worth emphasizing, is meant to indicate not how the marvelous necessarily operates in *Paradise Lost* but how the marvelous is then later absorbed into the romantic aesthetic of the sublime.

der to tell" or even strictly a "wonder to behold." With his powerful injunction Milton places the burden squarely on the reader's shoulders. "Behold a wonder!"—the poet of *Paradise Lost* here forcefully commands the reader to experience primarily shock, if there is shock, at the impossibility of the collapse of all hell's near infinite throng into a small narrow room. And with this, we have moved through the marvelous in epic, far away from Aristotle's "probable impossibilities," toward the vast and dimensionless infinities of the Longinian sublime.

Bibliography

Primary Sources

Albertus Magnus. *Opera Omnia.* Ed. Augustus Borgnet. Vol. 6. Paris: Ludovicus Vives, 1890.

Alighieri, Dante. *"Il Convivio" ridotto a miglior lezione e commentato.* Ed. G. Busnelli and G. Vandelli. Vols. 4–5 of *Opere di Dante,* ed. M. Barbi, and V. Branca et al. Florence: Le Monnier, 1934 and 1954.

———. *The Divine Comedy.* Ed. and trans. Charles S. Singleton. 6 vols. Princeton: Princeton University Press, 1970–75.

———. *De monarchia.* Ed. Pier Giorgio Ricci. Vol. 5 of *Le opere di Dante Alighieri.* Verona: Mondadori, 1965.

Aquinas, Thomas. *Summa Theologiae.* 61 vols. New York: McGraw-Hill, 1964–81.

Ariosto, Ludovico. *Five Cantos.* Trans. Leslie Z. Morgan. New York and London: Garland Publishing, 1992.

———. *Opere minori.* Ed. Cesare Segre. Milan: Ricciardi, 1954.

———. *Orlando furioso.* Ed. Emilio Bigi. 2 vols. Milan: Rusconi, 1982.

———. *The "Orlando Furioso" of Ludovico Ariosto.* Ed. Stewart A. Baker and A. Bartlett Giamatti. Trans. William Stewart Rose. Indianapolis: Bobbs-Merrill, 1968.

Aristotle. *Aristotle's "Poetics": The Argument.* Ed. Gerald F. Else. Cambridge: Harvard University Press, 1957.

———. *Metaphysics.* Trans. Hugh Tredennich. 2 vols. London: Putnam's Sons, 1933.

———. *The "Poetics" of Aristotle: Translation and Commentary.* Trans. Stephen Halliwell. Chapel Hill: University of North Carolina Press, 1987.

Berlinghieri, Francesco. *Geographia.* Florence: n.p., 1482.

Boccaccio, Giovanni. *The Decameron.* Trans. G. H. McWilliam. Middlesex: Penguin, 1972.

———. *Il Decameron.* Ed. Vittore Branca. Vol. 4 of *Tutte le opere,* ed. Vittore Branca. Milan: Mondadori, 1976.

————. *Il filocolo*. Trans. Donald Cheney. With an introduction by Thomas G. Bergin. New York: Garland Publishing, 1985.

————. *Il Filocolo*. Ed. Antonio Enzo Quaglio. Vol. 1 of *Tutte le opere*, ed. Vittore Branca. Milan: Mondadori, 1967.

Boiardo, Matteo Maria. *Orlando innamorato*. Ed. Aldo Scaglione. 2 vols. Turin: Unione Tipografico-Editrice Torinese, 1951.

Bonciani, Franceso. ["Difesa di Dante"]. MS 2435. Biblioteca Riccardiana, Florence.

Bulgarini, Bellisario. *Alcune considerazioni di Bellisario Bulgarini, gentilhuomo sanese, sopra 'l discorso di M. Giacopo Mazzoni, fatto in difesa della "Comedia" di Dante*. Siena: Luca Bonetti, 1583.

————. *Repliche di Bellisario Bulgarini alle risposte del Sig. Orazio Capponi sopra le prime cinque particelle delle sue considerazioni, intorno al discorso di M. Giacopo Mazzoni, composto in difesa della "Comedia" di Dante*. Siena: Luca Bonetti, 1585.

————. *Risposte di Bellisario Bulgarini a' ragionamenti del Sig. Ieronimo Zoppio, intorno alla "Commedia" di Dante*. Siena: Luca Bonetti, 1586.

Capellanus, Andreas. *The Art of Courtly Love*. Trans. John Jay Parry. New York: Norton, 1969.

Capponi, Oratio. *Risposte del Sig. Oratio Capponi alle prime cinque particelle delle considerazioni di Bellisario Bulgarini sopra 'l discorso del Sig. Giacopo Mazzoni*. MS G.IX. Biblioteca Comunale, Siena.

Castravilla [pseud.]. *Discorso di M. Ridolfo Castravilla contro Dante*. Ed. Mario Rossi. Vols. 40–41 of *Collezione di opuscoli danteschi inediti o rari*, ed. G. L. Passerini. Città di Castello: Lapi, 1897.

Euripides. *Hecuba*. Trans. William Arrowsmith. In *Euripides*, eds. David Greene and Richard Lattimore. Vol. 3. Chicago: University of Chicago Press, 1958.

Giovio, Paolo. *La vita di Alfonso da Este Duca di Ferrara, scritta da il vescovo Iovio*. Trans. Giovanbattista Gelli Fiorentino into Tuscan. Florence: Torrentino, 1553.

Giraldi Cinthio, Giovambattista. *Discorsi intorno al comporre dei romanzi, delle commedie e delle tragedie*. Venice: Gabriel Giolito De Ferrari, 1554.

Hugh of St. Victor. *De Scriptoris*. Vol. 175 of *Patrologiae Cursus Completus: Series Latina*, ed. J. P. Migne. Paris: Garnier Fratres, 1879.

Hume, David. *An Inquiry concerning Human Understanding*. Ed. Charles W. Hendel. Indianapolis: Bobbs-Merrill, 1955.

Lucan. *The Civil War*. Cambridge: Harvard University Press, 1969.

Marretti, Lelio. "Avvertimenti del Sig. Lelio Marretti." MS H.VII.19. Biblioteca Comunale, Siena.

Mazzoni, Iacopo. *Difesa di Dante*. Cesena: Bartolomeo Rauerij, 1587.

————. *Discorso di Giacopo Mazzoni in difesa della "Commedia" del divino poeta Dante*. Ed. Mario Rossi. Vols. 51–52 of *Collezione di opuscoli danteschi inediti o rari*, ed. G. L. Passerini. Città di Castello: Lapi, 1898.

Milton, John. *Complete Poems and Major Prose*. Ed. Merritt Y. Hughes. New York: Odyssey, 1957.

Patrizi da Cherso, Francesco. *Della poetica.* Ed. Danilo Aguzzi Barbagli. 3 vols. Florence: Istituto di Studi Rinascimentali, 1970.

Pigna, M. Giovan Battista. *I romanzi.* Venice: Vincenzo Valgrisi, 1554.

Plato. *The Collected Diologues.* Ed. Edith Hamilton and Huntington Cairns. Princeton: Princeton University Press, 1961.

Pliny the Elder. *Natural History.* Ed. and trans. H. Rackham. Cambridge: Harvard University Press, 1956.

Pontano, Giovanni. *Actius Dialogus.* In *Girolamo Fracastoro "Naugerius, sive de Poetica Dialogus,"* trans. Ruth Kelso, with an introduction by M. Bundy, vol. 9. Urbana: University of Illinois Press, 1924.

[Rinuccini, Alessandro]. MS Ashburnham 562. Biblioteca Laurenziana, Florence.

Robortello, Francesco. *Francisci Robortelli Utinensis in librum Aristotelis De Arte Poetica Explicationes.* Florence: Laurentii Torrentini, 1548.

Sassetti, Filippo. *Sopra Dante di Filippo Sassetti.* Vols. 40–41 of *Collezione di opuscoli danteschi inediti o rari,* ed. G. L. Passerini. Città di Castello: Lapi, 1897.

Servius. *Commentarii in Vergilii Carmina.* Ed. G. Thilo and H. Hagen. 2 vols. Hildesheim: Georg Olms, 1961.

Spenser, Edmund. *The Faerie Queene.* Ed. A. C. Hamilton. London and New York: Longman, 1977.

———. *Poetical Works.* Ed. J. C. Smith and E. de Selincourt. Oxford: Oxford University Press, 1985.

Tasso, Torquato. *Discorsi dell'arte poetica e del poema eroico.* Ed. Luigi Poma. Bari: Laterza, 1964.

———. *Gerusalemme liberata.* Ed. Lanfranco Caretti. 2 vols. Bari: Laterza, 1967.

———. *Jerusalem Delivered.* Ed. and trans. Ralph Nash. Detroit: Wayne State University Press, 1987.

———. *Le lettere di Torquato Tasso.* Ed. Cesare Guasti. Vol. 1. Florence: Le Monnier, 1852.

———. *Il mondo creato in sette giorni.* Ed. Giorgio Petrocchi. Florence: Le Monnier, 1951.

———. *Prose.* Ed. Ettore Mazzali. Milan: Ricciardi, 1959.

———. *Prose diverse.* Ed. Cesare Guasti. Florence: Le Monnier, 1875.

———. *Risposta del S. Torquato Tasso al discorso del Sig. Oratio Lombardelli intorno a i contrasti, che si fanno sopra la "Gierusalemme liberata."* Ferrara: G. Vasalini, 1586.

Virgil. *Eclogues, Georgics, Aeneid.* Ed. and trans. H. Rushton Fairclough. 2 vols. Cambridge: Harvard University Press, 1986.

———. *L'"Eneide": Libri III–IV.* Vol. 2. Ed. Ettore Paratore. Trans. L. Canali. Verona: Mondadori, 1978.

———. *Liber tertius.* Ed. R. D. Williams. Oxford: Clarendon, 1962.

———. *Opera.* Ed. R. A. B. Mynors. Oxford: Oxford University Press, 1985.

Secondary Sources

Abrams, Meyer H. *The Mirror and the Lamp: Romantic Theory and the Critical Tradition.* London: Oxford University Press, 1953.

Aglianò, Sebastiano. "Lettura del canto XIII dell'*Inferno.*" *Studi danteschi* 33 (1955): 143–86.

Allen, A. W. "The Dullest Book of the *Aeneid.*" *Classical Journal* 47 (1952): 119–23.

Allen, D. C. *Mysteriously Meant: The Rediscovery of Pagan Symbolism and Allegorical Interpretation in the Renaissance.* Baltimore: Johns Hopkins University Press, 1970.

Almansi, Guido. "Tattica del meravilgioso ariostesco." In *Ludovico Ariosto: Lingua, stile, e tradizione. Atti del congresso organizzato dai comuni di Reggio Emilia e Ferrara (12–16 ottobre 1974).* Ed. Cesare Segre. Milan: Feltrinelli, 1976.

Ariés, Philippe, and Georges Duby, eds. *Histoire de la vie privée III: De la Renaissance aux Lumiéres.* Paris: Editions du Seuil, 1986.

Ascoli, Albert R. *Ariosto's Bitter Harmony: Crisis and Evasion in the Italian Renaissance.* Princeton: Princeton University Press, 1987.

Ashworth, William B., Jr. "Remarkable Humans and Singular Beasts." In *The Age of the Marvelous,* ed. J. Kenseth. Chicago: University of Chicago Press, 1991.

Auerbach, Erich. *Mimesis: The Representation of Reality in Western Literature.* Trans. Willard R. Trask. Princeton: Princeton University Press, 1968.

———. *Scenes from the Drama of European Literature: Six Essays.* Trans. Ralph Manheim. New York: Meridian Books, 1959.

Bacchelli, Riccardo. "Orlando fatato e l'elmo di Mambrino: Saggio di idee sul meraviglioso in Ariosto e per Cervantes." In *La congiura di Don Giulio e altri scritti Ariosteschi.* Milan: Garzanti, 1958.

Bacon, J. R. "Aeneas in Wonderland." *Classical Review* 53 (1939): 97–104.

Bailet, M. H. *L'homme de verre: Essai d'interprétation thématique.* Padua: Studio Bibliografico Antenore, 1972.

Bakhtin, Mikhail. *Rabelais and His World.* Trans. Hélène Iswolsky. Cambridge: MIT Press, 1968.

Baldassarri, Guido. *"Inferno" e "cielo": Tipologia e funzione del "meraviglioso" nella "Liberata."* Rome: Bulzoni, 1977.

———. "Introduzione ai *Discorsi dell'arte poetica* del Tasso." *Studi tassiani* 26 (1977): 5–38.

Barański, Zygmunt. "The 'Marvellous' and the 'Comic': Toward a Reading of *Inferno* XVI." *Lectura Dantis: A Forum for Dante Research and Interpretation* 7 (1990): 72–95.

Baratto, Mario. *Realtà e stile nel "Decameron."* Vicenza: Pozza, 1970.

Barbi, Michele. *Della fortuna di Dante nel secolo xvi.* Florence: Fratelli Bocca, 1890.

Barkan, Leonard. *The Gods Made Flesh: Metamorphosis and the Pursuit of Paganism.* New Haven: Yale University Press, 1986.

Barolini, Teodolinda. *Dante's Poets: Textuality and Truth in the "Comedy."* Princeton: Princeton University Press, 1984.

———. *The Undivine "Comedy": Detheologizing Dante.* Princeton: Princeton University Press, 1992.

Battaglia, Salvatore. *Giovanni Boccaccio e la riforma della narrativa.* Naples: Liguori, 1969.

Bec, Christian. *Les marchands écrivains: Affaires et humanisme à Florence, 1375–1434.* Paris: Mouton, 1967.

Bellamy, Elizabeth J. "From Virgil to Tasso: The Epic Topos as an Uncanny Return." In *Desire in the Renaissance: Psychoanalysis and Literature,* ed. Valeria Finucci and Regina Schwartz. Princeton: Princeton University Press, 1994.

———. *Translations of Power: Narcissism and the Unconscious in Epic History.* Ithaca: Cornell University Press, 1992.

Bergin, Thomas. *Boccaccio.* New York: Viking, 1981.

Bertoni, Giulio. *La biblioteca estense e la cultura ferrarese ai tempi del duca Ercole I (1471–1505).* Turin: Loescher, 1903.

Billanovich, Giuseppe. *Restauri boccacceschi.* Rome: Edizione di Storia e Letteratura, 1945.

Blasucci, Luigi. *Studi su Dante e Ariosto.* Milan: Ricciardi, 1969.

Bloch, R. Howard. *Etymologies and Genealogies: A Literary Anthropology of the French Middle Ages.* Chicago: University of Chicago Press, 1983.

Boas, George. Introduction to *The Hieroglyphics of Horapollo.* Ed. and trans. G. Boas. New York: Pantheon Books, 1950.

Bosco, Umberto. *Dante vicino.* Caltanisetta and Rome: Salvatore Sciascia, 1966.

Bowra, Cecil. *From Virgil to Milton.* London: Macmillan, 1945.

Boyde, Patrick. *Dante Philomythes and Philosopher: Man in the Cosmos.* Cambridge: Cambridge University Press, 1981.

Branca, Vittore. *Boccaccio medievale e nuovi studi sul "Decameron."* 5th ed. Florence: Sansoni, 1981.

———. *Boccaccio: The Man and His Works.* Trans. Richard Monges. New York: New York University Press, 1976.

Brand, Charles P. *Torquato Tasso: A Study of the Poet and of His Contribution to English Literature.* Cambridge: Cambridge University Press, 1965.

Brooks, Robert. "*Discolor Aura:* Reflections of a Golden Bough." *American Journal of Philology* 74 (1953): 260–80.

Brownlee, Kevin. "Phaeton's Fall and Dante's Ascent." *Dante Studies* 102 (1984): 135–44.

Bruni, Francesco. *Boccaccio e dintorni.* Florence: Olschki, 1983.

Burke, Edmund. *A Philosophical Enquiry into the Origin of Our Ideas of the Sublime and Beautiful.* Ed. James T. Boulton. Notre Dame: University of Notre Dame Press, 1968.

Burke, Peter. *The Renaissance Sense of the Past.* London: Arnold, 1969.

Campbell, Mary B. *The Witness and the Other World.* Ithaca: Cornell University Press, 1988.

Carne-Ross, D. S. "The One and the Many: A Reading of *Orlando furioso,* Cantos I and VIII." *Arion* 5 (1966): 195–234.

Cassell, Anthony K. "Pier della Vigna's Metamorphosis: Iconography and History." In *Dante, Petrarch, Boccaccio: Studies in the Italian Trecento in Honor of Charles S. Singleton,* eds. Aldo S. Bernardo and Anthony L. Pellegrini. Binghamton: Medieval and Renaissance Texts and Studies, 1983.

Catalano, Michele. *Vita di L. Ariosto ricostruita su nuovi documenti.* Geneva: Olschki, 1931.

Céard, Jean. *La nature et les prodiges: L'insolite au 16e siècle en France.* Geneva: Droz, 1971.

Cheney, Donald. "Spenser's Hermaphrodite and the 1590 *Faerie Queene.*" *Publications of the Modern Language Association* 87 (1972): 192–200.

———. *Spenser's Image of Nature: Wild Man and Shepherd in "The Faerie Queene."* New Haven: Yale University Press, 1966.

Cherchi, Paolo. "Sulle 'quistioni d'amore' nel *Filocolo.*" In *Andrea Cappellano, trovatori e altri temi romanzi.* Rome: Bulzoni, 1979.

Chesney, Elizabeth A. *The Countervoyage of Rabelais and Ariosto: A Comparative Reading of Two Renaissance Mock Epics.* Durham: Duke University Press, 1982.

Cipolla, Carlo M. *The Monetary Policy of Fourteenth-Century Florence.* Berkeley: University of California Press, 1982.

Clark, Stuart. "Tasso and the Literature of Witchcraft." In *The Renaissance in Ferrara and Its European Horizons,* eds. J. Salmons and Walter Moretti. Cardiff: University of Wales Press, 1984.

Colish, Marcia L. *The Mirror of Language: A Study in the Medieval Theory of Knowledge.* New Haven: Yale University Press, 1968.

Conacher, D. J. *Euripidean Drama: Myth, Theme, and Structure.* Toronto: University of Toronto Press, 1967.

Conte, Gian Biagio. *The Rhetoric of Imitation: Genre and Poetic Memory in Virgil and Other Latin Poets.* Trans. C. Segal. Ithaca: Cornell University Press, 1986.

Costanzo, Mario. *Il "Gran theatro del mondo."* Milan: Vanni Scheiwiller, 1964.

Cottino-Jones, Marga. "Magic and Superstition in Boccaccio's *Decameron.* " *Italian Quarterly* 18 (1975): 5–32.

Cunningham, James V. *Woe and Wonder.* Denver: Denver University Press, 1951.

Curtius, Ernst Robert. *European Literature and the Latin Middle Ages.* Trans. Willard R. Trask. Princeton: Princeton University Press, 1953.

Daston, Lorraine. "Marvelous Facts and Miraculous Evidence in Early Modern Europe." *Critical Inquiry* 18 (1991): 93–124.

Daston, Loraine, and Katherine Park. "Unnatural Conceptions: The Study of Monsters in Sixteenth and Seventeenth-Century France and England." *Past and Present* 92 (1981): 20–54.

Derla, Luigi. "Sull'allegoria della *Gerusalemme liberata.*" *Italianistica* 7 (1978): 473–88.

De Sanctis, Francesco. *Storia della letteratura italiana.* Vol. 1. Milan: Rizzoli, 1983.

Di Cesare, Mario. *The Altar and the City: A Reading of Vergil's "Aeneid."* New York: Columbia University Press, 1974.

Donadoni, Eugenio. *Torquato Tasso: Saggio critico.* Florence: La Nuova Italia, 1952.

Donato, Eugenio. "'Per selve e boscherecci labirinti': Desire and Narrative Structure in Ariosto's *Orlando furioso.*" In *Literary Theory/Renaissance Texts,* ed. P. Parker and D. Quint. Baltimore: Johns Hopkins University Press, 1986.

Douglas, Mary. *Purity and Danger: An Analysis of Concepts of Pollution and Taboo.* New York: Praeger, 1966.

D'Ovidio, Francesco. *Nuovi studii danteschi.* Milan: Hoepli, 1907.

Durling, Robert. *The Figure of the Poet in Renaissance Epic.* Cambridge: Harvard University Press, 1965.

Eire, Carlos M. N. *War Against the Idols: The Reformation of Worship from Erasmus to Calvin.* Cambridge: Cambridge University Press, 1986.

Fantham, Elaine. "*Nymphas . . . e Navibus Esse:* Decorum and Poetic Fiction in *Aeneid* 9.77–122 and 10.215–59." *Classical Philology* 85 (1990): 102–19.

Fava, Domenico, and Carlo Montagnani, eds. *Mostra columbiana e americana della R. biblioteca estense.* Modena: Società Tipografia Modena, 1925.

Ferguson, Margaret. *Trials of Desire: Renaissance Defenses of Poetry.* New Haven: Yale University Press, 1983.

Ferrero, Giuseppe Guido. "Astolfo (Storia di un personaggio)." *Convivium* 29 (1961): 513–30.

Ferruci, Franco. "Comedìa." *Yearbook of Italian Studies* 1 (1971): 29–52.

Fichter, Andrew. "Tasso's Epic of Deliverance." *Publications of the Modern Language Association* 93 (1978): 265–74.

Fido, Franco. *Le metamorfosi del centauro: Studi e letture da Boccaccio a Pirandello.* Rome: Bulzoni, 1977.

Findlen, Paula. "Jokes of Nature and Jokes of Knowledge." *Renaissance Quarterly* 43 (1990): 292–331.

Fontana, Pio. *I "Cinque canti" e la storia della poetica del "Furioso."* Milan: Vita e Pensiero, 1962.

Frazer, Sir James George. *The Golden Bough.* Vol. 2. London: Macmillan, 1920.

Freccero, John. "Infernal Irony: The Gates of Hell." In *Dante: The Poetics of Conversion.* Ed. Rachel Jacoff. Cambridge: Harvard University Press, 1986.

———. "*Paradiso* X: The Dance of the Stars." In *Dante: Poetics of Conversion.* Ed. Rachel Jacoff. Cambridge: Harvard University Press, 1986.

Freud, Sigmund. *The Standard Edition of the Complete Psychological Works of Sigmund Freud.* Vol. 21. Trans. J. Strachey. London: Hogarth, 1955.

Friedman, John Block. *The Monstrous Races in Medieval Art and Thought.* Cambridge: Harvard University Press, 1981.

Fubini, Mario. *Studi sulla letteratura del Rinascimento.* Florence: La Nuova Italia, 1971.

Getto, Giovanni. *Interpretazione del Tasso.* Naples: Edizioni Scientifiche Italiane, 1951.

———. *Nel mondo della "Gerusalemme."* Florence: Valecchi, 1968.

———. *Vita di forme e forme di vita nel "Decameron."* Turin: Petrini, 1958.

Giamatti, A. Bartlett. *The Earthly Paradise and the Renaissance Epic.* Princeton: Princeton University Press, 1966.

———. *Exile and Change in Renaissance Literature.* New Haven: Yale University Press, 1984.

———. *Play of Double Senses: Spenser's "Faerie Queene."* Englewood Cliffs: Prentice Hall, 1975.

Gilson, Étienne. "Poésie et théologie dans la *Divine Comédie.*" In *Atti del congresso internazionale di studi danteschi.* Florence: Sansoni, 1965.

Girard, René. *Violence and the Sacred.* Trans. Patrick Gregory. Baltimore: Johns Hopkins University Press, 1977.

Goldberg, Jonathan. *Endlesse Worke: Spenser and the Structures of Discourse.* Baltimore: Johns Hopkins University Press, 1981.

Goux, Jean-Joseph. *Symbolic Economies: After Marx and Freud.* Trans. Jennifer Curtiss Gage. Ithaca: Cornell University Press, 1990.

Gransden, K. W. *Virgil's "Iliad": An Essay on Epic Narrative.* Cambridge: Cambridge University Press, 1984.

Greenblatt, Stephen. *Marvelous Possessions: The Wonder of the New World.* Chicago: University of Chicago Press, 1991.

―――. *Renaissance Self-Fashioning: From More to Shakespeare.* Chicago: University of Chicago Press, 1980.

―――. *Shakespearean Negotiations: The Circulation of Social Energy in Renaissance England.* Berkeley: University of California Press, 1988.

Greene, Thomas. *Descent from Heaven: A Study in Epic Continuity.* New Haven: Yale University Press, 1963.

―――. *The Light in Troy: Imitation and Discovery in Renaissance Poetry.* New Haven: Yale University Press, 1982.

Greppi, Claudio. "Una carta per la corte: Il viaggiatore immobile." In *The Renaissance in Ferrara and Its European Horizons,* ed. J. Salmons and Walter Moretti. Cardiff: University of Wales Press, 1984.

Grossvogel, Steven. *Ambiguity and Allusion in Boccaccio's "Filocolo."* Florence: Olschki, 1992.

Grosz, Elizabeth. *Jacques Lacan: A Feminist Introduction.* London: Routledge, 1990.

Guardiani, Francesco. "Boccaccio dal *Filocolo* al *Decameron:* Variazioni di poetica e di retorica dall'esame di due racconti." *Carte Italiane: A Journal of Italian Studies* 7 (1985–86): 28–46.

Hale, J. R. "Gunpowder and the Renaissance: An Essay in the History of Ideas." In *From the Renaissance to the Counter-Reformation: Essays in Honour of Garret Mattingly,* ed. Charles H. Carter. London: Jonathan Cape, 1966.

―――. *War and Society in Renaissance Europe, 1450–1620.* Leicester: Leicester University Press, 1985.

Halio, Jay L. "The Metaphor of Conception and Elizabethan Theories of the Imagination." *Neophilologus* 50 (1966): 454–61.

Halliwell, Stephen. *Aristotle's "Poetics."* Chapel Hill: University of North Carolina Press, 1986.

Hampton, Timothy. *Writing From History: The Rhetoric of Exemplarity in Renaissance Literature.* Ithaca: Cornell University Press, 1990.

Hardie, Philip. "Ships and Ship-names in the *Aeneid.*" In *Homo Viator: Classical Essays for John Bramble,* ed. Michael Whitby, Mary Whitby, and P. Hardie. Bristol: Bristol Classical Press, 1987.

Hathaway, Baxter. *Marvels and Commonplaces: Renaissance Literary Theory.* New York: Random House, 1968.

Helgerson, Richard. *Self-Crowned Laureates: Spenser, Jonson, Milton, and the Literary System.* Berkeley: University of California Press, 1983.

Hertz, Neil. "Medusa's Head: Male Hysteria under Political Pressure." *Representations* 4 (1983): 27–54.

Heuzé, Philippe. *L'image du corps dans l'oeuvre de Virgile.* Rome: École Française de Rome, Palais Farnèse, 1985.

Hollander, Robert. *Allegory in Dante's "Commedia."* Princeton: Princeton University Press, 1969.

———. *Studies in Dante.* Ravenna: Longo, 1980.

———. *Il Virgilio Dantesco: Tragedia nella "Commedia."* Florence: Olschki, 1983.

Hughes, Merritt. *Virgil and Spenser.* Vol. 2. Berkeley: University of California Press, 1929.

Iversen, Eric. *The Myth of Egypt and Its Hieroglyphics in European Tradition.* Copenhagen: Gad, 1961.

Jacoff, Rachel, and Jeffrey T. Schnapp, eds. *The Poetry of Allusion: Virgil and Ovid in Dante's "Commedia."* Stanford: Stanford University Press, 1991.

Javitch, Daniel. "The Imitation of Imitations in *Orlando furioso.*" *Renaissance Quarterly* 38 (1985): 215–39.

———. *Proclaiming a Classic: The Canonization of "Orlando furioso."* Princeton: Princeton University Press, 1991.

Johnson, W. R. *Darkness Visible: A Study of Vergil's "Aeneid."* Berkeley: University of California Press, 1976.

Jonard, N. "Le temps dans la 'Jérusalem delivrée.'" *Studi tassiani* 24 (1974): 7–22.

Kantorowicz, Ernst H. *The King's Two Bodies: A Study in Mediaeval Political Theology.* Princeton: Princeton University Press, 1957.

Kates, Judith A. *Tasso and Milton: The Problem of Christian Epic.* Lewisburg, Pa.: Bucknell University Press, 1983.

Kennedy, William. "Ariosto's Ironic Allegory." *Modern Language Notes* 88 (1973): 44–67.

———. "Irony, Allegoresis, and Allegory in Virgil, Ovid, and Dante." *Arcadia: Zeitschrift für vergleichnende Literaturwissenschaft* 7 (1972): 115–34.

———. "Modes of Allegory in Ariosto, Tasso, and Spenser." Ph.D. Diss., Yale University, 1969.

———. "The Problem of Allegory in Tasso's *Gerusalemme liberata.*" *Italian Quarterly* 15–16 (1972): 27–52.

———. "Rhetoric, Allegory, and Dramatic Modality in Spenser's Fradubio Episode." *English Literary Renaissance* 3 (1973): 351–68.

Kermode, Frank. *The Classic.* Cambridge: Harvard University Press, 1983.

King, John N. *Spenser's Poetry and the Reformation Tradition.* Princeton: Princeton University Press, 1990.

Kirkham, Victoria. "Reckoning with Boccaccio's *Questioni d'amore.*" *Modern Language Notes* 89 (1974): 47–59.

Kleiner, John. *Mismapping the Underworld: Daring and Error in Dante's "Comedy."* Stanford: Stanford University Press, 1994.

Knapp, Jeffrey. *An Empire Nowhere: England, America, and Literature from "Utopia" to the "Tempest."* Berkeley: University of California Press, 1992.

Krier, Theresa. *Gazing on Secret Sights: Spenser, Classical Imitation, and the Decorums of Vision.* Ithaca: Cornell University Press, 1990.

Le Goff, Jacques. *L'imaginaire médiéval.* Paris: Gallimard, 1985.

Leo, Urlich. "Torquato Tasso alle soglie del secentismo." *Studi tassiani* 4 (1954): 3–17.

Lewis, C. S. *Spenser's Images of Life.* Ed. A. Fowler. Cambridge: Cambridge University Press, 1967.

Little, Lester K. "Pride Goes before Avarice: Social Change and the Vice in Latin Christendom." *American Historical Review* 76 (1971): 16–49.

———. *Religious Poverty and the Profit Economy in Medieval Europe.* Ithaca: Cornell University Press, 1978.

Lloyd, R. B. "*Aeneid* III: A New Approach." *American Journal of Philology* 78 (1957): 131–51.

———. "*Aeneid* III and the Aeneas Legend." *American Journal of Philology* 78 (1957): 382–400.

Lukács, Georg. *The Theory of the Novel.* Trans. Anna Bostock. Cambridge: MIT Press, 1971.

Mabille, Pierre. *Le merveilleux.* With an introduction by Luc de Heusch. Paris: Pierre Jean Oswald, 1977.

———. *Le miroir du merveilleux.* With an introduction by André Breton. Paris: Minuit, 1962.

MacCaffrey, Isabel. *Spenser's Allegory: The Anatomy of Imagination.* Princeton: Princeton University Press, 1976.

Mallet, M. E., and J. R. Hale. *The Military Organization of a Renaissance State: Venice c. 1400 to 1617.* Cambridge: Cambridge University Press, 1984.

Marcus, Millicent Joy. *An Allegory of Form: Literary Self-Consciousness in the "Decameron."* Saratoga: Anma Libri, 1979.

———. "An Allegory of Two Gardens: The Tale of Madonna Dianora (*Decameron* X, 5)." *Forum Italicum* 14 (1980): 162–74.

Marinelli, Peter V. *Ariosto and Boiardo: The Origins of "Orlando furioso."* Columbia: University of Missouri Press, 1987.

Marti, Mario. *Cultura e stile nei poeti giocosi del tempo di Dante.* Pisa: Nistri-Lischi, 1953.

Martines, Lauro. *Power and Imagination: City-States in Renaissance Italy.* New York: Knopf, 1979.

Marx, Karl. *A Contribution to the Critique of Political Economy.* With an introduction by Maurice Dobb. Trans. S. W. Ryazanskaya. New York: International Publishers, 1970.

———. *The Marx-Engles Reader.* Ed. Robert C. Tucker. New York: Norton, 1972.

Massèra, Aldo Francesco, ed. *Sonetti burleschi e realistici dei primi due secoli.* Revised by Luigi Russo. Bari: Laterza, 1940.

Mazzali, Ettore. *Cultura e poesia nell'opera di Torquato Tasso.* Rocca San Casciano: Cappelli, 1957.

Mazzotta, Giuseppe. *Dante, Poet of the Desert: History and Allegory in the "Divine Comedy."* Princeton: Princeton University Press, 1979.

————. *The World at Play in Boccaccio's "Decameron."* Princeton: Princeton University Press, 1986.

McGovern, John. "The Rise of New Economic Attitudes— Economic Humanism, Economic Nationalism—during the Later Middle Ages and the Renaissance, A.D. 1200–1550." *Traditio* 26 (1970): 217–53.

McGregor, James. *The Image of Antiquity in Boccaccio's "Filocolo," "Filostrato," and "Teseida."* New York: Peter Lang, 1991.

————. *The Shades of Aeneas: The Imitation of Vergil and the History of Paganism in Boccaccio's "Filostrato," "Filocolo," and "Teseida."* Athens: University of Georgia Press, 1991.

Miller, David. *The Poem's Two Bodies: The Poetics of the 1590 "Faerie Queene."* Princeton: Princeton University Press, 1988.

Mirollo, James V. "The Aesthetics of the Marvelous." In *The Age of the Marvelous,* ed. J. Kenseth. Chicago: University of Chicago Press, 1991.

————. *The Poet of the Marvelous: Giambattista Marino.* New York: Columbia University Press, 1963.

Momigliano, Attilio. *Saggio sull'"Orlando furioso."* Bari: Laterza, 1928.

Montgomery, Robert L., Jr. "Allegory and the Incredible Fable: The Italian View from Dante to Tasso." *Publications of the Modern Language Association* 81 (1966): 45–55.

Montrose, Louis. "The Elizabethan Subject and the Spenserian Text." In *Literary Theory/Renaissance Texts,* ed. P. Parker and D. Quint. Baltimore: Johns Hopkins University Press, 1986.

————. "'Eliza, Queene of shepheardes,' and the Pastoral of Power." *English Literary Renaissance* 10 (1980): 153–82.

Moore, Leslie E. *Beautiful Sublime: The Making of "Paradise Lost."* Stanford: Stanford University Press, 1990.

Moretti, Walter. "L'ideale ariostesco di un'europa pacificata e unita e la sua crisi nel terzo *Furioso.*" In *The Renaissance in Ferrara and Its European Horizons,* ed. J. Salmons and Walter Moretti. Cardiff: University of Wales Press, 1984.

————. *L'ultimo Ariosto.* Bologna: Pàtron, 1977.

Murrin, Michael. *The Allegorical Epic: Essays in Its Rise and Decline.* Chicago: University of Chicago Press, 1980.

————. *History and Warfare in Renaissance Epic.* Chicago: University of Chicago Press, 1994.

Murtaugh, Kristen Olson. "Erminia Delivered: Notes on Tasso and Romance." *Quaderni d'italianistica* 3 (1982): 12–25.

Muscetta, Carlo. *Giovanni Boccaccio.* Bari: Laterza, 1972.

Nenci, Giuseppe. "A concezione del miracoloso nei poemi omerici." *Atto della Accademia delle Scienze di Torino* 92 (1957–58): 275–311.

Nohrnberg, James. *The Analogy of "The Faerie Queene."* Princeton: Princeton University Press, 1976.

O'Connell, Michael. *Mirror and Veil: The Historical Dimension of Spenser's "Faerie Queene."* Chapel Hill: University of North Carolina Press, 1977.

Olschki, Leonardo. *Storia della letteratura delle scoperte geografiche.* Florence: Olschki, 1937.

Otis, Brooks. *Virgil: A Study in Civilized Poetry.* Oxford: Clarendon, 1963.

Padoan, Giorgio. *Il Boccaccio, le muse, il parnaso e l'arno.* Florence: Olschki, 1978.

————. "Tradizione e fortuna del commento all''Eneide' di Bernardo Silvestre." *Italia medioevale e umanistica* 3 (1960): 227–40.

Paratore, Ettore. *Tradizione e struttura in Dante.* Florence: Sansoni, 1968.

Parker, Patricia. *Inescapable Romance: Studies in the Poetics of a Mode.* Princeton: Princeton University Press, 1979.

————. *Literary Fat Ladies: Rhetoric, Gender, Property.* London: Methuen, 1987.

Parry, Adam. "The Two Voices of Virgil's *Aeneid.*" *Arion* 2 (1963): 66–80.

Perella, Nicholas J. "The World of Boccaccio's *Filocolo.*" *Publications of the Modern Language Association* 76 (1961): 330–39.

Prier, Raymond Adolph. *Thauma Idesthai: The Phenomenology of Sight and Appearance in Archaic Greek.* Tallahassee: Florida State University Press, 1989.

Putnam, Michael C. J. *Essays on Latin Lyric, Elegy, and Epic.* Princeton: Princeton University Press, 1982.

————. *The Poetry of the "Aeneid."* Cambridge: Harvard University Press, 1965.

Quaglio, Antonio Enzo. *Scienza e mito nel Boccaccio.* Padua: Liviana, 1967.

————. "Tra fonti e testo del *Filocolo.*" Parts 1 and 2. *Giornale storico della letteratura italiana* 139 (1962): 321–69, 513–40; 160 (1963): 321–63, 489–551.

Quilligan, Maureen. *The Language of Allegory: Defining the Genre.* Ithaca: Cornell University Press, 1979.

————. *Milton's Spenser: The Politics of Reading.* Ithaca: Cornell University Press, 1983.

Quint, David. *Epic and Empire: Politics and Generic Form from Virgil to Milton.* Princeton: Princeton University Press, 1993.

————. "The Figure of Atlante: Ariosto and Boiardo's Poem." *Modern Language Notes* 94 (1979): 77–91.

————. *Origin and Originality in Renaissance Literature: Versions of the Source.* New Haven: Yale University Press, 1983.

Raimondi, Ezio. *Poesia come retorica.* Florence: Olschki, 1980.

————. *Rinascimento inquieto.* Palermo: Manfredi, 1965.

Rajna, Pio. *Le fonti del "Orlando furioso."* 2d ed. Ed. Francesco Mazzoni. Florence: Sansoni, 1975.

————. "L'episodio delle questioni d'amore nel *Filocolo* del Boccaccio." *Romania* 31 (1902): 28–81.

Rathborne, Isabel. *The Meaning of Spenser's Fairyland.* New York: Columbia University Press, 1937.

Rhu, Lawrence F. *The Genesis of Tasso's Narrative Theory.* Detroit: Wayne State University Press, 1993.

Roche, Thomas P., Jr. *The Kindly Flame: A Study of the Third and Fourth Books of Spenser's "Faerie Queene."* Princeton: Princeton University Press, 1964.

————. "Tasso's Enchanted Woods." In *Literary Uses of Typology from the Late Middle Ages to Present.* Ed. Earl Miner. Princeton: Princeton University Press, 1977.

Romero, Rosario. *Le scoperte americane nella coscienza italiana del cinquecento.* Bari: Laterza, 1989.

Russo, Luigi. *Letture critiche del "Decameron."* Bari: Laterza, 1956.

Saccone, Eduardo. *Il soggetto del "Furioso" e altri saggi tra quattro e cinquecento.* Naples: Liguori, 1974.

Santoro, Mario. *Ariosto e il Rinascimento.* Naples: Liguori, 1989.

Sarolli, Gian Roberto. *Prolegomena alla "Divina Commedia."* Florence: Olschki, 1971.

Schiesari, Juliana. *The Gendering of Melancholia: Feminism, Psychoanalysis, and the Symbolics of Loss in Renaissance Literature.* Ithaca: Cornell University Press, 1992.

Schnapp, Jeffrey T. *The Transfiguration of History at the Center of Paradise.* Princeton: Princeton University Press, 1986.

Schroeder, John W. "Spenser's Erotic Drama: The Orgoglio Episode." *English Literary History* 29 (1962): 140–59.

Scott, Shirley Clay. "From Polydorus to Fradubio: The History of a *Topos.*" *Spenser Studies* 7 (1986): 27–57.

Scrivano, Riccardo. *La norma e lo scarto: Proposte per il cinquecento letterario italiano.* Rome: Bonacci, 1980.

Segal, C. P. "*Aeternum per saecula nomen:* The Golden Bough and the Tragedy of History." Parts 1 and 2. *Arion* 4 (1965): 617–57; 5 (1966): 34–72.

Segre, Cesare. *Esperienze ariostesche.* Pisa: Nistri-Lischi, 1966.

Serra, Luciano. "Da Tolomeo alla Garfagna: La geografia dell'Ariosto." *Bollettino storico reggiano* 28 (1974): 151–84.

Seznec, Jean. *The Survival of the Pagan Gods: The Mythological Tradition and Its Place in Renaissance Humanism and Art.* Trans. Barbara F. Sessions. New York: Pantheon Books, 1953.

Shapiro, Marianne. *The Poetics of Ariosto.* Detroit: Wayne State University Press, 1988.

Shemek, Deanna. "That Elusive Object of Desire: Angelica in the *Orlando furioso.*" *Annali d'italianistica* 7 (1989): 116–41.

Silberman, Lauren. "The Hermaphrodite and the Metamorphosis of Spenserian Allegory," *English Literary Renaissance* 17 (1987): 207–23.

———. "Singing Unsung Heroines: Androgynous Discourse in Book 3 of *The Faerie Queene.*" In *Rewriting the Renaissance: The Discourses of Sexual Difference in Early Modern Europe,* ed. M. Ferguson, M. Quilligan, and N. Vickers. Chicago: University of Chicago Press, 1986.

Singleton, Charles. S. *Dante's "Commedia": Elements of Structure.* Baltimore: Johns Hopkins University Press, 1954.

———. "The Irreducible Dove." *Comparative Literature* 9 (1957): 129–35.

———. *Journey to Beatrice.* Baltimore: Johns Hopkins University Press, 1977.

Smarr, Janet Levarie. *Boccaccio and Fiammetta: The Narrator as Lover.* Urbana and Chicago: University of Illinois Press, 1986.

South, Malcolm, ed. *Mythical and Fabulous Creatures.* New York: Greenwood, 1987.

Sozzi, Bortolo Tommaso. "Il magismo nel Tasso." In *Studi sul Tasso.* Pisa: Nistri-Lischi, 1954.

Speroni, Charles. "The Motif of the Bleeding and Speaking Trees of Dante's Suicides." *Italian Quarterly* 9 (1965): 44–55.

Spitzer, Leo. "Speech and Language in *Inferno* XIII." *Italica* 19 (1942): 81–104.

Spufford, Peter. *Money and Its Use in Medieval Europe.* Cambridge: Cambridge University Press, 1988.

Stallybrass, Peter. "The Patriarchal Territories: The Body Enclosed." In *Rewriting the Renaissance: The Discourses of Sexual Difference in Early Modern Europe,* ed. M. Ferguson, M. Quilligan, and N. Vickers. Chicago: University of Chicago Press, 1986.

Stallybrass, Peter, and Alon White. *The Politics and Poetics of Transgression.* Ithaca: Cornell University Press, 1986.

Stephens, Walter. "Tasso's Religion, Tasso's Platonism: The Design of *Gerusalemme liberata.*" Paper presented at the Charles S. Singleton Center of Italian Studies, Villa Spelman, Florence, July, 1989.

Struever, Nancy. *Theory as Practice: Ethical Inquiry in the Renaissance.* Chicago: University of Chicago Press, 1992.

Tateo, Francesco. *"Retorica" e "poetica" fra medioevo e rinascimento.* Bari: Adriatica, 1961.

Vallone, Aldo. *Aspetti dell'esegesi dantesca nei secoli xvi e xvii attraverso testi inediti.* Lecce: Milella, 1966.

———. *L'interpretazione di Dante nel cinquecento: Studi e ricerche.* Florence: Olschki, 1969.

Vance, Eugene. *Mervelous Signals: Poetics and Sign Theory in the Middle Ages.* Lincoln: University of Nebraska Press, 1986.

———. "Warfare and the Structure of Thought in Virgil's *Aeneid.*" *Quaderni urbinati di cultura classica* 15 (1973): 111–62.

Vernero, Michele. *Studi critici sopra la geografia dell'"Orlando furioso."* Turin: Tipografia Palatina di Bonis e Rossi, 1913.

Vickers, Brian. "Leisure and Idleness in the Renaissance: The Ambivalence of *Otium.*" *Renaissance Studies* 1 and 2, no. 4 (1990): 1–37, 107–54.

Vogler, Bernard. "La Réforme et le concept de miracle au XVIme siècle." *Revue d'histoire de la spiritualité: Revue d'ascétique et de mystique* 48 (1972): 145–49.

Weinberg, Bernard. *A History of Literary Criticism in the Italian Renaissance.* 2 vols. Chicago: University of Chicago Press, 1961.

Wiesen, David S. "The Pessimism of the Eighth *Aeneid.*" *Latomus: Revue d'Études Latines* 32 (1973): 737–65.

Wiggens, Peter DeSa. *Figures in Ariosto's Tapestry: Character and Design in the "Orlando furioso."* Baltimore: Johns Hopkins University Press, 1986.

Williams, Gordon. *Technique and Ideas in the "Aeneid."* New Haven: Yale University Press, 1983.

Williams, R. D. "Changing Attitudes to Virgil: A Study in the History of Taste from Dryden to Tennyson." In *Virgil,* ed. D. R. Dudley. London: Routledge and Kegan Paul, 1969.

———. "The Purpose of the *Aeneid.*" *Antichthon* 1 (1967): 29–41.

———. *Virgil: Greece and Rome.* Oxford: Clarendon, 1967.

Wind, Edgar. *Pagan Mysteries of the Renaissance.* New Haven: Yale University Press, 1958.

Wise, Valerie Merriam. "Ruggiero and the Hippogriff: The Ambiguities of Vision." *Quaderni d'italianistica* 2 (1981): 39–53.

Wittkower, Rudolf. "Marvels of the East: A Study in the History of Monsters." *Journal of the Warburg and Courtauld Institutes* 5 (1942): 159–97.

Yates, Francis A. *Giordano Bruno and the Hermetic Tradition.* Chicago: University of Chicago Press, 1964.

Yunck, John A. *The Lineage of Lady Meed.* Notre Dame: University of Notre Dame Press, 1963.

Zatti, Sergio. *L'uniforme cristiano e il multiforme pagano: Saggio sulla "Gerusalemme liberata."* Milan: Il Saggiatore, 1983.

Index